A CASE FOR THE EXISTENCE OF GOD

A CASE FOR THE EXISTENCE OF GOD

Dean L. Overman

Foreword by Robert Kaita
Afterword by Armand Nicholi

ROWMAN & LITTLEFIELD PUBLISHERS, INC.
Lanham • Boulder • New York • Toronto • Plymouth, UK

ROWMAN & LITTLEFIELD PUBLISHERS, INC.

Published in the United States of America
by Rowman & Littlefield Publishers, Inc.
A wholly owned subsidiary of The Rowman & Littlefield Publishing Group, Inc.
4501 Forbes Boulevard, Suite 200, Lanham, Maryland 20706
www.rowmanlittlefield.com

Estover Road
Plymouth PL6 7PY
United Kingdom

British Library Cataloguing in Publication Information Available

Library of Congress Cataloging-in-Publication Data
Overman, Dean L.
A case for the existence of God / Dean L. Overman.
p. cm.
ISBN-13: 978-0-7425-6312-4 (cloth : alk. paper)
ISBN-10: 0-7425-6312-X (cloth : alk. paper)
eISBN-13: 978-0-7425-6553-1
eISBN-10: 0-7425-6553-X
1. Religion and science. 2. God—Proof, Cosmological. I. Title.
BL240.3.O93 2009
212'.1—dc22
2008021731

Printed in the United States of America

∞™ The paper used in this publication meets the minimum requirements of American National Standard for Information Sciences—Permanence of Paper for Printed Library Materials, ANSI/NISO Z39.48-1992.

This book is dedicated to my Family and Friends with particular gratitude to Thomas Aquinas Reynolds Jr. and Lana Couchenour, wonderful colleagues at Winston & Strawn.

ABRIDGED CONTENTS

CONTENTS

FOREWORD

"In the beginning, God created the heavens and the earth." Every culture has its creation story. It seems that people in all societies have looked about them and wondered whence everything came. None appear to be satisfied with the idea that all that surrounds them always existed. What they see had to have a cause, and the cause was some sort of supernatural being.

The process of posing the question of origins, and coming up with an answer of any sort, implies that the world is comprehensible. From the earliest of times, our forebears had plenty of empirical evidence for this. The same celestial objects that caused them to ask who was their maker also had regular patterns. They told you when to sow and when to reap, year after year. He who put the heavens and the earth in their places wanted us to understand His creation, and in doing so, could be trusted to provide for us.

For most of his history, then, *Homo sapiens*, or "wise" or "knowing" man, had an answer for the origin of the universe, and why what we observe about it is comprehensible. God created the world and as we claim in the Judeo-Christian tradition, the regularity of His creation is a demonstration of His benevolence. "As long as the earth endures," God promises, "seedtime, and harvest, cold and heat, summer and winter, day and night will never cease." Our ancestors could prove this to themselves by counting the number of days between seasons and realizing that it never varies. God's creation must then be describable "mathematically," so He could provide for us. This appreciation persists in our vernacular, where "counting" on something is an expression of confidence in it.

It is ironic that the very regularity and comprehensibility of the universe, and the success in understanding this, gave rise to doubts about the existence of the Being at its source. Could not these attributes have always existed? This is what philosophers like David Hume have argued. After all, seasons do follow seasons, so one year looks like another. If this, and everything else about the world, is what he considers to be "the eternal basic element," you do not need God to create it.

Hume's remarks were very characteristic of the Enlightenment, when determinism was also demonstrating its power. In science, this was epitomized by an encounter between Laplace and Napoleon. The great mathematician presented the First Consul of France his massive treatise, "System of the World." Napoleon supposedly asked Laplace why he did not mention God in it, to which he answered, "I have no need of that hypothesis." Historians are still not sure if Laplace actually spoke this "sound bite," but they do agree that it captures the sentiments he was known to have.

With Hume and Laplace, it looked like two critical functions of God became unnecessary. We no longer needed a Creator for a universe that existed for all eternity, and He no longer had to be "hypothesized" to account for its comprehensibility. This mindset held sway into the twentieth century. When Einstein formulated his general theory of relativity, the equations indicated that the universe should be expanding. This implies that it had an origin at a finite time in the past. If the universe was Hume's "eternal basic element," however, it could not be.

Einstein introduced something called a "cosmological constant" in his theory to counteract the expansion. This "fudge factor" restored the universe to the "steady state" it supposedly had since time immemorial. All was well and good until Hubble began doing measurements of the light from distant galaxies with a powerful new telescope atop Mount Wilson in California. He noticed that the farther they were, the faster they seem to be moving. Hubble's startling conclusion was that the galaxies must have all started from the same point at a finite time in the past.

At first, this challenge to the "steady-state" universe was greeted with derision and scorn. The idea was pejoratively referred to as the "Big Bang," as if to suggest that such an affront to "common sense" did not deserve a serious name. The evidence for an "origin" of the universe became sufficiently persuasive, however, even within Einstein's lifetime. As he admitted in the last edition of his book "The Meaning of Relativity," he would have never introduced the "cosmological constant" if Hubble's expansion had been discovered at the time of the creation of his theory.

Hume's claim about the universe as the "eternal basic element" is thus no longer persuasive. What about Laplace's assertion? We return to Einstein. His work on general relativity embodies the mathematical elegance so enamored by Laplace in what is perhaps the most widely tested and verified theory in the history of physics. In spite of this, Einstein could not explain why it "worked." As he put it, "the most incomprehensible thing about the universe is that it is comprehensible."

The irony is that the more mathematical various areas of science are becoming, the more "incomprehensible," in the Einsteinian sense, they are turning out to be. One of the truly stunning recent achievements in biology has been the sequencing of the human genome. Computational capabilities inconceivable to Laplace were needed to make this possible, and no deterministic pathway familiar to him could lead to the staggering information content the effort has revealed. Francis Collins, the leader of the Human Genome Project, is not being hyperbolic when he calls the genetic code the "language of God." If He is the Author, His comprehensibility should not be a mystery.

There are certainly alternatives to the Big Bang model for the universe that restore it as an "eternal basic element." Suppose there are an infinite number of "multiverses" that have been popping up and disappearing for all eternity. It would not be surprising, then, for creatures like ourselves to show up sooner or later in one of them. This is a solution, but not a scientific one if by definition, we cannot know anything about universes other than our own. Rather, it addresses a philosophical quandary faced by those who find it difficult to believe in God. On the other hand, if you are curious about the reasons why many of us do have such faith, the book you are about to read will help you discover them.

Dr. Robert Kaita
Principal Research Physicist
Princeton University
Plasma Physics Laboratory

PREFACE

This book is intended for people who have open minds concerning the question of God's existence. I am specifically addressing those individuals who are interested in the question from a personal perspective and are willing to think through the possibility of God's existence and the potential of humankind to engage in a transformational relationship with such a being.

For a variety of reasons, some people may not be willing to participate in such an open-minded initiative. Perhaps their presuppositions may form a worldview that precludes the recognition of any indication of a transcendent reality. I respect their freedom and their integrity of thought in interpreting evidence in a manner adverse to my perspective. I am not attempting to force my perspective on them. If one closes one's mind to the possibility of God, there is little that can be written to reverse that choice. As discussed in several sections throughout this book, the reasons for faith or nonfaith have to do with highly personal factors that either predispose people to have a theistic or naturalistic worldview. Even though we can all attempt to be purely objective, no one approaches the question of God from an impartial, neutral perspective.

Reflection about the existence of God may be the most important inquiry one can make in his or her lifetime. More consequences for thought and action flow from this reflection than from answering any other basic question. The answer one gives to the question of God's existence influences one's perception of the world, the concept of one's place in the world, and the life one leads. Every aspect of human life is affected by whether one regards human beings as the supreme beings in the universe or as beings subject to a superior being. The perception of one's own nature varies dramatically depending upon the answer one gives to the question of God's existence. The question is fundamental to an adequate contemplation of human existence and the relationships among humans.

Alvin Plantinga, a widely respected professor of philosophy at the University of Notre Dame, has become the leading proponent of a theory of knowledge that holds that a belief in the existence of God does not need supporting evidence. He argues that the existence of God is a warranted, "properly basic belief." In his argument, the term *warrant* means "a proper functioning," as when one's heart beats within a normal pulse range given one's activity level. He holds that a belief is properly basic when one's cognitive faculties properly function to arrive reliably at a truth in a certain environment. Plantinga maintains that a belief in God's existence can be properly basic where this proper cognitive functioning exists. People can hold a warranted belief in God without arguments justifying their position with evidence.

Plantinga presents a thoughtful, sophisticated argument for his theory concerning a basic belief in God. In considering Sigmund Freud's complaint about religion to be a claim that belief results from wish fulfillment, he argues that Freud offers no reasons for his claim. He notes that Freud did not (and indeed could not) establish that the cognitive functioning by which one develops belief in God is *not* aimed at truth. Instead, Freud simply assumes the truth of his belief that there is no God and then attempts to explain that a belief in God is wish fulfillment. But his explanation rests upon his unproven assumption of God's nonexistence. Like Richard Dawkins's principal argument, which I will discuss in chapter 7, Freud commits the logical fallacy of circular reasoning. Freud also failed to distinguish between mature and immature religious sentiments. Because he worked with neurotic patients, his predominant experience was with an immature religious sentiment that disintegrates one's personality. As discussed in further detail later, Gordon Allport, Harvard's famous psychologist of personality, determined that a mature religious sentiment actually integrates one's personality.

Plantinga refers to Thomas Aquinas's statement: "To know in a general and confused way that God exists is implanted in us by nature."[1] He also notes Paul's writing: "Ever since the creation of the world his invisible nature namely, his eternal power and deity, has been clearly perceived in the things that have been made,"[2] and discusses John Calvin's position that "Men of sound judgment will always be sure that a sense of divinity which can never be effaced is engraved upon men's minds . . .

which nature itself permits no one to forget, although many strive with every nerve to this end."[3]

For Plantinga, the knowledge of God or at least the capacity for such knowledge is innate. Although he notes the tendency to believe in God in his references to Aquinas, Paul, and Calvin, he does not rely on them for his concept of a warranted theistic belief. Instead he develops a highly sophisticated, rational argument for his view that such a belief can be a warranted basic belief aimed at truth without requiring further evidence. Plantinga is not dogmatic in his belief. He is open to evidence or reasons that would require him to cease believing in God, and he is receptive to evidence supporting a belief in God. His conclusion is not merely a matter of blind faith.

His position is rational and consistent with the ancient Jewish faith. The source for the belief of the God of the Jews did not arise over an examination of the evidence for a Supreme Being or from an attempt to explain the existence of the universe and its order. The ancient Israelites believed in God because they believed in God's self-revelation to Abraham, Isaac, and Jacob. Their belief in God was not the result of an investigation of the world, its origin, or its intelligibility. The main source of their religious faith came from revelation, their tradition, and then from Jewish scriptures.[4]

The question of God's existence in past and present analytic or other philosophies has its source in Greek thought, not in Hebrew thought. With a similar basis in Hellenic logic, a systematic approach to the examination of evidence becomes part of a lawyer's thought processes. Having practiced and taught law for four decades, I respect the benefits of a rational examination of evidence, even if human reason is inherently incomplete and subject to limitations.[5] Consequently, although I respect Plantinga's position and the basis for the ancient Israelite faith, I agree with Mortimer Adler, a former philosophy professor at Columbia University and the University of Chicago, who insisted that if a person has a religious faith, he or she has the duty to think about that faith, to examine evidence, and to understand the rationale for what they believe:

> I suspect that most of the individuals who have religious faith are content with blind faith. They feel no obligation to understand what they believe. They may even wish not to have their beliefs disturbed by thought. But if the God in whom they believe created them with intellectual and rational powers, that imposes upon them the duty to try to understand the creed of their religion. Not to do so is to verge on superstition.[6]

In following Adler's exhortation, in this book I set forth a cumulative case for the proposition that the existence of God is a rational, plausible belief. I discuss how the evidence indicates that although theism requires a leap of faith, it is a leap into the light, not into the dark; theism explains more than atheism, which also requires a leap of faith.

I begin by noting that everyone makes a leap of faith in accepting presuppositions that comprise a worldview, and every worldview has inevitable uncertainties. We know that this universe will end its ability to sustain life. In a search for ultimate meaning one cannot limit a theory of knowledge to only that which can be empirically verified by our senses. Reason can take us only so far. There are other ways of knowing, including credible religious knowledge by personal acquaintance. In examining the question of God's existence, one may rationally conclude that God is a personal God who can only be known in reality as a person, not as an inference. Reason and faith are both required as a basis of knowledge. They are complementary. Reason without faith experience is dead. Experience without reason can be fantasy.

Given recent discoveries in science and philosophy, it is remarkable that David Hume and Immanuel Kant still influence the question of God's existence. Kant based his theory of knowledge on a Euclidean geometry and a Newtonian view of the universe, which in today's science have been modified by Einstein's theory of relativity, non-Euclidean geometry, and quantum physics. These modifications indicate that, in excluding rational inquiry into anything beyond the senses, his theory of knowledge is too restrictive and does not include all that we can know or detect. In this book I will argue that there are several valid ways of knowing, including the empirical, the detection by theoretical constructs, the use of metaphysical reasoning, and the mystical.

Contemporary science and mathematics show that one can use reason to address basic metaphysical questions, such as the following: Why is there something rather than nothing? Why does that something have the particular members and order that it has? Why does this particular kind of universe exist? Why does the universe have an order that makes it intelligible? Einstein marveled at the intelligibility of the universe. He knew that science could not even begin if the world was not intelligible. As he noted, "Let us concede that behind any major scientific work is a conviction akin to religious belief, that the world is intelligible."[7] If one stops and thinks about it, the intelligibility of the universe is rather astonishing. After all, it could be simply a chaos and not a rational, inherently mathematical universe with substantial beauty.

Mortimer Adler's cosmological argument modified Thomas Aquinas's, Samuel Clarke's, and Gottfried Leibniz's arguments to the extent that he thought he had demonstrated the existence of God beyond a reasonable doubt (but not beyond a shadow of a doubt). His argument has been strengthened in recent decades by discoveries in philosophy and in science. I modify his argument, describe the discoveries that further invigorate the argument, and explain the misinterpretations of Hume and Kant, particularly as they relate to the term *necessary being*. I also explain why the laws of physics are not good candidates for a necessary being.

Historically, the cosmological arguments for the existence of God are a series of affiliated patterns of reasoning. I integrate these related arguments and discuss (1) a cosmological argument for a necessary cause of the continuing existence of the entire cosmos and (2) a related cosmological argument emphasizing that the Second Law of Thermodynamics requires that disorder in the universe tends toward a maximum. In the second argument I note that the universe could not be dissipating from infinity or it would have run down by now. This indicates that the universe had a beginning that had to be highly ordered. Moreover, our universe has been expanding since its initial singularity of the Big Bang. Such an expanding universe cannot have an infinite past. This is true even if our universe is only one among many multiverses. Recent work by Arvind Borde, Alan Guth, and Alexander Vilenkin indicates that even a multiverse cosmos had a beginning. Something that has a beginning requires a cause. W. L. Craig has argued convincingly that although one could hypothesize that the universe came about through a series of endless past contingent events that stretch backward through infinity, such a series may not be possible in reality.

I describe recent mathematical and scientific discoveries concerning the rationality, order, fine-tuning, and beauty in the universe. These discoveries give corroborative evidence for the inherent intelligibility of the physical world and are consistent with a rational argument for God's existence.

I also point out that the existence of God is also consistent with the underlying foundation of information as the basis for physical existence. Information is not matter or energy. Quantum physical theory challenges a strict materialistic worldview and indicates that a "knower" must exist. I will argue that mental processes appear in part to transcend the purely physical, even though our thoughts are clearly influenced by the physical brain. Many of the world's leading physicists now understand that quantum mechanics is based in information as the immaterial irreducible seed of the universe and all physical existence.

I consider the problem of evil. Our ability to recognize evil and good and distinguish between them argues for the existence of God. If God does not exist, evil is not evil and good is not good. Our human comprehension is flawed and finite; there may be reasons for suffering that are not apparent to us. Without minimizing the severe pain in the world, one must consider the totality of the evidence for the existence of God.

One may argue that the most powerful form of knowledge concerning God is not derived from empirical or theoretical constructs but from a knowledge proceeding from an encounter or personal acquaintance with the divine. Thomas Aquinas (after his mystical experience), Gabriel Marcel, and Sören Kierkegaard emphasized this form or way of knowing. God may not be knowable by only objective means because God is not an object, but a person above all categories. Consequently, the knowledge of God is ultimately a personal knowledge. According to Martin Buber, this knowledge requires commitment, action, and mission. Rudolf Otto and Emmanuel Levinas hold that God can never be reduced to an idea or a concept that one can describe by language. Language can never capture relationships between persons, let alone capture the experience of the person of God.

Although one cannot adequately describe the experience of God, some attempts are informative. I follow Marcel's advice and call nine persons of keen intellect to the witness stand to allow them to use their own words to attempt to describe their relationship with the divine. (These bright intellects belong to Augustine, Pascal, Tolstoy, Dostoevsky, Luce, Muggeridge, Weil, Mitchell, and Adler.)

After commenting on the testimony of the nine witnesses, I conclude by stating that the argument for the existence of God explains more than does the argument for atheism. The existence of God explains why there is something rather than nothing; it explains the intelligibility and order in the universe; it explains the continuing existence of the universe; it explains the beginning of the universe; it explains the inherently mathematical nature of the universe; it explains the existence of the laws of nature; it explains the beauty in the universe and the relationship between mathematical beauty and truth; it explains the existence of information; it explains the existence of free will and the ability to recognize good and evil; it explains religious experience; it explains the fine-tuning in the astrophysics of the universe that allows for conscious life; and it explains why thoughts have the capacity to produce true beliefs.

Atheism lacks an adequate, coherent explanation for any of these things. To take a leap in the direction of materialist atheism requires an enormous faith that may have more to do with one's will than we can understand. Pride and the desire to be as God (*eritus sicut dei*), to focus on one's self as equal with the divine, and to put one's own interests at the center of one's life, prior to the interests of any superior being, may have more to do with our reflections and decisions about the existence of God than may be consciously apparent to us. Many persons throughout history have claimed that, after struggling with their pride and confused desires, they finally found joy in the presence of God. I know of no valid evidence to deny their claims. The existence of God appears to be a rational, plausible belief. I have known many persons who claim to be involved in a friendship with God, a friendship that increases their capacity for love and joy. Their claims ring true because their lives demonstrate a peaceful focus on the welfare of all persons. Of course, this is not always true for all who claim to know God and no human being lives to the highest of standards, but perhaps the authenticity of one's claim may be related to the quality and character of one's love, joy, sacrifice, and mercy.

ACKNOWLEDGMENTS

This book depended upon the assistance and thoughtfulness of many people. Although I cannot name all of the people who influenced the content of this book, the following individuals were among the many remarkable friends and colleagues who contributed to my thinking: James M. Houston, a former Oxford professor and founder of Regent College, who participated in C. S. Lewis's faculty group and developed a profound understanding of religious knowledge; John Polkinghorne, Cambridge University quantum physicist and Anglican priest; Keith Ward, former head of theology at Oxford University and Canon of Christ Church Cathedral; Armand Nicholi, professor at Harvard Medical School and Harvard College; Stephen Barr, professor of physics at the University of Delaware; Hurd Baruch, brilliant Winston & Strawn partner with a broad understanding of theology, philosophy, and science; Hubert Yockey, Berkeley physicist, my coauthor in an article, and the author of the leading text on information theory and molecular biology; Willoughby Walling, gifted scholar in many fields; Robert Kaita, Princeton University physicist; Os and Jenny Guiness, thoughtful scholars in epistemological understanding; and Wes Granberg-Michaelson, Secretary General of the Reformed Church and founder of *Sojourners* and The Global Christian Forum. (None of these people are responsible for any errors that may appear in my writing; I hold complete responsibility for the words of this book.)

I am also grateful for my appointment as a Templeton scholar at Oxford University and for the many interactions with scholars in a variety of disciplines over the years. I am also grateful to the Van Raalte Institute for my appointment as a Senior Visiting Research Scholar and to my editor at

Rowman & Littlefield, Sarah Stanton, who gave wise counsel and great support to my project.

My family, including Linda, Christiana, Elisabeth, Nathan, Leif, Hayden, and Sharon, all encouraged me to write in this multidisciplined area. Each one of them contributed to my understanding in a different and significant way. I end these acknowledgments with a special thanks to my late parents who inspired me to think about the big questions of life and to examine how they related to the faith of our ancestors.

INTRODUCTION

How are we to understand our existence? How are we to understand the existence of anything at all? Why is our universe intelligible and not simply a chaos? Why are its laws mathematical? Where did these laws come from? What breathes fire into these laws that makes a physical universe? Why does our universe have its particular components?

These questions present the initial central subject matter of this book. We live on a relatively small speck of matter orbiting a star, our sun, which we now know has a finite existence. Physicists tell us with considerable certainty that our sun is exhausting its hydrogen fuel and in about five billion years will go into its death throes and expand to become a red giant. At that time this whole earth, indeed, our whole solar system, will be engulfed by the sun as it swells in its dying phase. The earth and all of the planets in our system will disintegrate. This planet and its sun will disappear completely, as will all earthly life. Not only the planets but also all of life seems to lack any permanence.

Our earth appears to be a very rare planet.[1] Even if we assume that we could find another planet hospitable to human life, we will not overcome our finitude, because all the stars in the universe will eventually follow the sun's path and extinguish their nuclear fuel and die.

We live in a relatively short niche of cosmic history. The expanding nature of our universe only allows for the possibility of conscious life after about fourteen billion years of expansion. After the fiery hot Big Bang that marked the beginning of the universe, the universe gradually cooled, allowing atoms, molecules, galaxies, stars, planets, and living matter to form. We have only a finite niche of time before all stars will exhaust their nuclear fuel and die.

John D. Barrow, professor of mathematical sciences at the University of Cambridge, has created the graph[2] on page 3 to illustrate the history of the universe and its eventual heat death.

The existence of conscious human life appears to be a finite phenomenon, whether the universe continues to expand or whether it collapses in a Big Crunch.[3] The fact that all of life will die out long before the death of the universe does not require us to conclude that there isn't any intrinsic value in existence. After all, one can enjoy a Mozart symphony and experience a value in listening to the symphony, even though the experience comes to an end.[4] Existential philosophers emphasize the importance of living in the present, and many religious persons agree. For example, French Jesuit priest, Jean-Pierre de Caussade, wrote in the eighteenth century about the sacrament of the present moment.

Viktor Frankl, a psychiatrist from Vienna who survived the death camp of Auschwitz, wrote an influential book that began a significant psychological movement in the mid-twentieth century known as "logotherapy." Frankl emphasized man's freedom to find meaning in his life even in the most horrid circumstances. Frankl developed his thought on the basis of his observations regarding the ability of persons to survive when they perceived some meaning in their lives.[5]

Although Frankl's early writings appeared to emphasize meaning even in the finite, as he continued to develop his thought, he emphasized the need for persons to find *ultimate* meaning. Many persons are familiar with Frankl's early writings but do not know that approximately forty years after writing *Man's Search for Meaning*, he wrote another book updating his perspectives, entitled *Man's Search for Ultimate Meaning.*

In his more recent book he made the argument that "a religious sense is existent and present in each and every person, albeit buried, not to say repressed, in the unconscious."[6] As one who survived the death camp and observed the psychological states of his fellow prisoners, he noted that religion did not die in Auschwitz: "The truth is that among those who actually went through the experience of Auschwitz, the number of those whose religious life was deepened—in spite, not to say because, of this experience—by far exceeds the number of those who gave up their belief."[7] As a psychiatrist, Frankl treated religion as the fulfillment of the human "*will to ultimate meaning.*"[8] He was convinced that everyone at his or her deepest core had this will to *ultimate* meaning. In other words, humans inherently have a basic desire for an ultimate meaning, not simply a meaning that transcends the self, but a permanent, ultimate meaning. For Frankl this de-

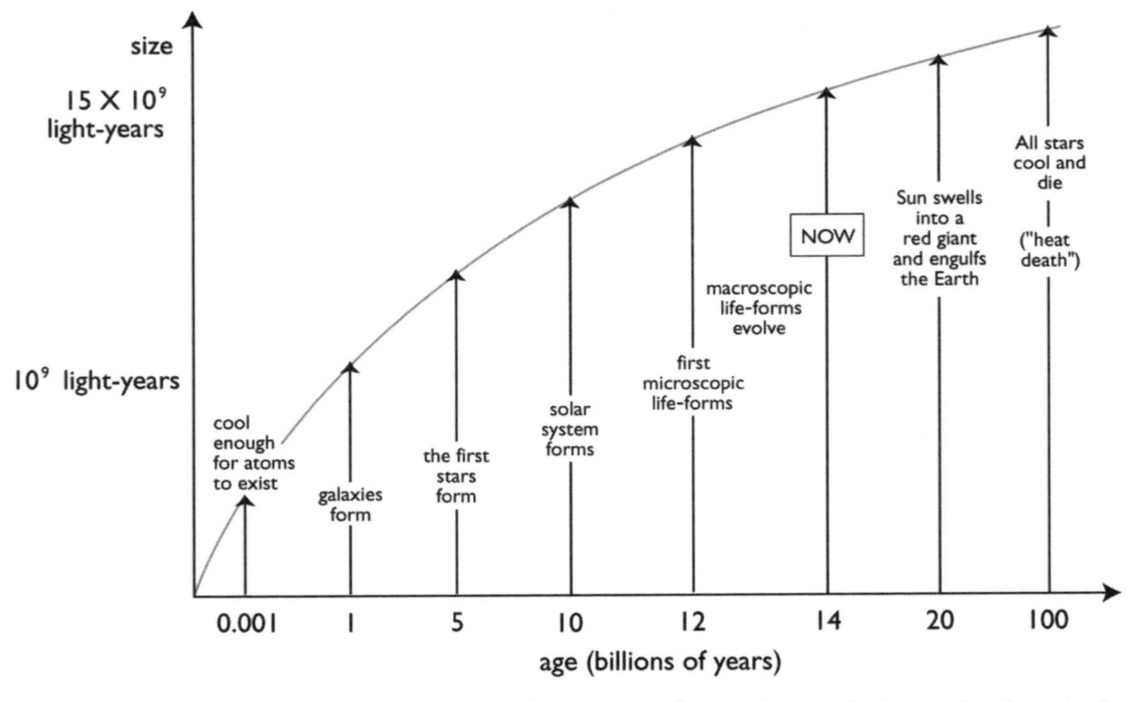

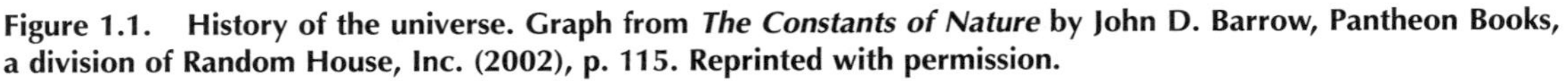

Figure 1.1. History of the universe. Graph from *The Constants of Nature* by John D. Barrow, Pantheon Books, a division of Random House, Inc. (2002), p. 115. Reprinted with permission.

sire is deeply rooted in each person's unconscious depths. In defining religion as the ubiquitous presence of a will to ultimate meaning, Frankl came to believe that every person's psyche had this will. Simply enjoying a finite symphony was not enough. The meaning had to be ultimate.

To find any ultimate meaning in our existence, perhaps something permanent, something that is not contingent or dependent on something finite, must exist. Ultimate meaning may require some infinite foundation. Some scientists who think about the finite nature of the universe fail to perceive any ultimate meaning in its existence. Realizing the bleak cosmic future described above and the eventual complete hostile nature of the universe to life, physics noble laureate Steven Weinberg remarked: "The more the universe seems comprehensible, the more it also seems pointless."[9]

Of course, we have known the finite nature of human constructs for many years. History discloses that human physical, social, and political constructs are all ephemeral. Consider nations: They rise and fall, showing little permanence in the perspective of a few thousand years. First one nation is dominant and then another. Monuments exalting once powerful leaders collapse and lie ruined in sand. This is the message in Percy Bysshe Shelley's poem *Ozymandias*:

Ozymandias

I met a traveller from an antique land
Who said: "Two vast and trunkless legs of stone
Stand in the desert. Near them, on the sand,
Half sunk, a shattered visage lies, whose frown,
And wrinkled lip, and sneer of cold command,
Tell that its sculptor well those passions read,
Which yet survive, stamped on these lifeless things,
The hand that mocked them, and the heart that fed,
And on the pedestal these words appear:
'My name is Ozymandias, King of Kings:
Look upon my works, ye Mighty, and despair!'
Nothing beside remains. Round the decay
Of that colossal wreck, boundless and bare
The lone and level sands stretch far away."[10]

Because the universe will eventually be unable to support life and be devoid of any energy, all of the knowledge, art, culture, and insights of humanity appear to be futile efforts in a ridiculous cosmic scenario. Perhaps all that humans can do is adopt a stoic attitude and move forward in a meaningless universe and face the eventual darkness and end of history. Without knowing about the modern physics of the universe and its ultimate end, Shakespeare captured this view in *Macbeth*:

> She should have died hereafter;
> There would have been a time for such a word.
> To-morrow, and to-morrow, and to-morrow,
> Creeps in this petty pace from day to day
> To the last syllable of recorded time,
> And all our yesterdays have lighted fools
> The way to dusty death. Out, out, brief candle!
> Life's but a walking shadow, a poor player
> That struts and frets his hour upon the stage
> And then is heard no more. It is a tale
> Told by an idiot, full of sound and fury,
> Signifying nothing.[11]

As Frankl observed, our innate tendency is to resist the idea that our lives, our nation, our planet, and the entire universe is valueless and without some sort of ultimate significance. After all, we spend our lives in a busy pattern of activity full of commitments based on our sense of values and meaning. Sir John Polkinghorne, Cambridge University quantum physicist and an Anglican theologian, notes that we rebel at the idea that the explosion of the sun, coupled with the ultimate collapse or heat death of the universe, will render useless the magnificent works of Mozart, Shakespeare, and St. Francis.[12] But he joins many other scientists, philosophers, and university professors who also believe in a more expansive worldview that offers some hope for meaning and a future that has continuity with history. In this book I will explore the essential basis for that hope and examine whether a concept of a new creation is a rationally plausible alternative to the despair that some persons sense in looking at the seemingly futile, inevitable end of the universe.

I write this book, not as a person with all of the answers, but as one who attempts to explore and inquire about the reality behind the visible and whose motivation derives in part from experiences that point to the presence of the divine. In making this exploration and asking questions about existence and reality, I am merely attempting to join countless others who also inquire, search, and sometimes find responses that lift a veil and reveal a glimpse of a beautiful and more perfect reality.

Most of what follows is concerned with logic, science, evidence, and history, but I want to emphasize at the outset that reason will only take us so far. Inevitably, all of us must look beyond and above reason to encounter reality. In addition to knowledge derived from reason, humans have other ways of knowing reality. Perhaps the deepest revelations of reality come to us beyond the senses in a more personal knowledge of beauty and truth. Reason should be coupled with faith in seeking an understanding of reality. For the scientist that faith will rest in the continuing reliability of the effectiveness of abstract mathematics and the laws of physics and their derivatives, such as the laws of chemistry. We cannot abandon reason or we will lose a significant source of verification.[13] But we should also be open to other ways of knowing, because we learn and experience reality as whole persons, not as Newtonian machines. The outmoded worldview of Newtonian mechanics does not address all of reality. Reason and faith are complementary ways of knowing. They need each other to understand reality more fully. Without reason, faith can become sheer fantasy, and without faith, reason can end up in contradictions and cul-de-sacs.

This book will not provide the reader with the assurance of absolute certainty about anything; however, my hope is that it will open a tiny path by which the writer and the reader can step closer to the reality that upholds the universe and sustains each and every breath of our being. For the reasons I set forth in this book, I view that reality as a Person.

THE QUESTION OF GOD'S EXISTENCE

The Radical Contingency of the Universe Points Toward a Necessary Being

EVERYONE MAKES A LEAP OF FAITH IN HOLDING PRESUPPOSITIONS THAT COMPRISE A WORLDVIEW, AND EVERY WORLDVIEW HAS INEVITABLE UNCERTAINTIES.

Everyone lives with uncertainties. We cannot be certain of anything in the sense that we cannot even prove our own existence or the existence of other minds.[1] We all lack absolute certainty in our lives and are required to live by faith in something or someone. We may have faith in many areas, such as our country's economy, our own abilities, our personal wealth, our education, our family's support, our employer, our business, our medical care providers, or any one of a vast number of persons or things. All of us live by faith.

We all hold certain presuppositions or assumptions about the world and about the areas in which we place our faith. We use these presuppositions to interpret our experiences and to make decisions and choices. We all approach reality from some framework that helps us to function in the world. Everyone interprets the world from a particular perspective, a worldview, even if one's worldview is that there are no "valid" worldviews.

The presuppositions that comprise our worldview are formed by taking a leap of faith in interpreting the nature of the world with which we interact. Our presuppositions are derived from our environment, education, family, culture, and experiences. They influence our thoughts, choices, and behavior and to a great extent determine our beliefs about life, death, the nature of humanity, and the nature of all that exists. We need to recognize that the presuppositions that make up our worldview may or may not be true, in whole or in part, and they may or may not be held consciously, consistently, or coherently. Nevertheless, these preconceived ideas that make up our worldview provide the basis by which we analyze our world and make our decisions.[2]

We should attempt to examine and evaluate the coherency of our presuppositions. They are extremely important, because they constitute the first step in the leap of faith we all must take, whether that leap is toward materialism or theism. In other words, one's thoughts and actions are dependent on faith, not certainty. For example, even science is done pursuant to a faith in the rational, intelligible structure of the universe. As physicist Paul Davies writes: ". . . science has its own faith-based belief system. All science proceeds on the assumption that nature is ordered in a rational and intelligible way. You couldn't be a scientist if you thought the universe was a meaningless jumble of odds and ends haphazardly juxtaposed. When physicists probe to a deeper level of subatomic structure, or astronomers extend the reach of their instruments, they expect to encounter additional elegant mathematical order. And so far this faith has been justified."[3] Davies makes the point that science's "claim to be free of faith is manifestly bogus." The same applies to an atheist; the belief system of an atheist is based on faith, not on knowledge. Given the visible expression of the rational intelligibility of the universe discovered in the mathematical laws of physics, I will argue that it takes a more abundant faith to be an atheist than to be a theist.

Although absolute certainty eludes us in science, that conclusion does not mean that there isn't an absolute truth underlying all of reality. The presuppositions with which we build our worldview should be as consistent as possible with what we know of reality. There is a unity in truth that requires a consistency in our presuppositions if we are to have an effective interpretation of reality and make appropriate ethical decisions. As noted by Mortimer Adler, the unity of truth requires that the presuppositions for one's worldview must be consistent with truths already known in philosophy, history, science, and other disciplines. If various worldviews claim truths that are in conflict with each other, their claims cannot all be true.

To understand further how a presupposition could influence the outcome of one's thinking, consider a presupposition stated by former Cornell University astronomer Carl Sagan that the physical universe is all there is, all there was, and all there ever will be. Sagan's statement is a leap of faith, because Sagan did not know with any certainty that his statement was true. Similarly, Nobel physicist Steven Weinberg's statement that the universe seems pointless is also a leap of faith.

Sagan's and Weinberg's statements represent leaps of faith because neither could know with any certainty whether their perspective represented a true reflection of reality.[4] But taking the leap of faith and assuming the veracity of their presuppositions, it follows that there is nothing outside of the physical aspects of the cosmos to investigate. Given this conclusion we may consider all human beings to be merely physical things that will perish and have no lasting value or meaning. Human beings may be more complex than other physical structures, but we know that the universe will eventually be unable to support any life so that complexity will not endure. Under Sagan's stated presupposition or the presuppositions implied in Weinberg's statements, it is difficult to see how human, physical, finite "objects" have any permanent, intrinsic, nonexistential value.

If one continues down the path inaugurated by their initial presuppositions in a consistent, logical manner, one can see how, in some circumstances, humans could be perceived as mere "things." Such a perspective can affect how human beings treat each other. This is one reason why Russian philosopher Nicholas Berdyaev and German theologian Paul Tillich used the term *thingification* (*Verdinglichung*) to criticize the dehumanization of persons. The Jewish philosopher Martin Buber also emphasized that human relations (for example, in the relationship between two true friends) could not be adequately expressed in an "I-It" (*Ich-Es*) analytical treatment of beings as only objects.

One's behavior is affected by complex variables so that one cannot simply assert the position that a given person's leap of faith toward theism, for example, automatically makes that person a more integrated individual with a greater capacity to love and exhibit certain characteristics that most persons consider as human virtues. We learned from Gordon Allport to distinguish between a mature religious sentiment that assists in integrating one's personality and an immature religious sentiment that assists in dis-integrating one's personality. Not all forms of theism contribute to the attributes of a mature personality.

Allport argued that most of the criticism aimed against theism is directed against an immature religious sentiment, such as one that has not progressed beyond a stage focused on impulsive self-gratification. This stage could serve only a childish wish fulfillment or an interest mainly centered around an immature self. Such an immature religious sentiment is also characterized by an unreflective attitude that does not include the ability to see one's self more objectively and does not provide a context of meaning for one's location in life. This absence of a context of meaning precludes one from finding a meaningful place in the world. A person with an immature religious sentiment cannot perceive his or her own conduct in an objective manner. Such a sentiment excludes much of reality and is disjointed and fragmented. If one's immature religious sentiment is sufficiently fanatically intensive, this sentiment will serve to dis-integrate one's personality and lessen one's capacity for love and gratitude.[5]

Allport spent his career encouraging psychologists to gauge the maturity of a religious sentiment by objective criteria. He insisted that, with respect to the wholeness, health, and integration of one's personality, the criteria of a mature religious sentiment should be more objective and that these criteria should be formed from a justifiable theory of human personality. In his insightful book, *The Individual and His Religion*, Allport set forth three attributes of a mature personality: (1) mental processes that concern ideal objects and values beyond mere infantile physical desires, (2) an ability to reflect insightfully concerning one's life and to see one's self in a cosmic perspective (with a developed sense of humor), and (3) a coherent, but not necessarily complete, unifying philosophy for one's life that serves to integrate one's personality.[6]

Allport's three criteria corroborate the importance of presuppositions in one's behavior. I want to emphasize how significant the examination of our assumptions can be in determining the outcome of logical thought processes and how these assumptions make up our worldview and affect our behavior. We will act in a manner consistent with our presuppositions. They powerfully influence how we interpret evidence and make conclusions about the nature of reality.

Recently, my classmate, Richard Smalley, who received the 1996 Nobel Prize for Chemistry, died after a six-year struggle with cancer. He was the leading academic in the area of nanotechnology. At the time of his death, his worldview was dramatically different from the worldviews expressed by Sagan and Weinberg. After receiving the Nobel Prize, he began to reflect on matters of faith and eventually made a leap of faith toward Christian theism. He wrote commenting on his worldview:

> Recently I have gone back to church regularly with a new focus to understand as best I can what it is that makes Christianity so vital and powerful

> in the lives of billions of people today, even though almost 2000 years have passed since the death and resurrection of Christ.
>
> Although I suspect I will never fully understand, I now think the answer is very simple: it's true. God did create the universe about 13.7 billion years ago, and of necessity has involved Himself with His creation ever since. The purpose of this universe is something that only God knows for sure, but it is increasingly clear to modern science that the universe was exquisitely fine-tuned to enable human life. We are somehow critically involved in His purpose. Our job is to sense that purpose as best we can, love one another, and help Him get that job done.[7]

Smalley's view is shared by many scientists, philosophers, and other academics who consider the purposeful nature of the universe in a manner diametrically opposed to the worldviews of other scientists, philosophers, and academics, such as Sagan and Weinberg. Persons from all walks of life have different presuppositions and make different leaps of faith in constructing their worldviews. How can we know which of the worldviews is more plausible or if any are plausible at all? In order to begin to consider that question, we will first have to consider valid ways of knowing.

WHAT ARE VALID WAYS OF KNOWING?

Our presuppositions also provide our basis for determining how we know anything at all. Every worldview has to confront the issue of *how* we know anything. I remember my freshman year in college attending my first philosophy class where I listened to an introductory lecture on epistemology. D. Ivan Dykstra, a profound professor with a unique ability to communicate complex philosophical ideas, began by raising the question whether it was true that one would know what one knows when one knows *how* one knows.

There are a variety of theories of knowledge or epistemologies. They are all concerned with how we can justify the statement that we know something or someone. In this book I am considering the question of God's existence. As I attempt to think about that question, I may need to understand how I will know the answer. As indicated above, this book will discuss knowledge derived from the rational and personal. It is my contention that reason and what Oxford chemist and philosopher Michael Polanyi termed "personal knowledge" are authentic ways of knowing. I am proposing that empirical verification, deduction from theoretical constructs, metaphysical reasoning, and mystical participation are all valid ways of knowing. With respect to the knowledge of God, if God is a person, perhaps such a being can only be known as a person and not merely as an inference. In the words of distinguished theologian Michael Buckley: "Whether one affirms or denies the reality of God, one does not even understand the question if it is reduced to a problem to be solved or a wrangle to be fought out rather than a mystery to be apprehended. For this great question about God also engages the depth of the human person: it shapes the fundamental interpretation of human life and human destiny."[8]

Reason can only take us so far. Dante Alighieri understood this when he wrote *The Divine Comedy*, perhaps the supreme literary masterpiece of medieval literature with its compelling portrayal of Christian love. Dante inserts himself as the principal fictional pilgrim in his symmetrical poem written in the first part of the fourteenth century. The poem begins on the eve of Good Friday, 1300, when Dante at age thirty-five finds himself in a dark forest. He does not know how he lost his way but knows that he is lost and cannot find the true path.[9]

Dante gains some footing but is confused by a Leopard (lust), then perplexed by a Lion (pride), and a She-Wolf (avarice). He turns toward a valley and meets the spirit of Virgil, who is a symbol of reason. Dante greatly admired Virgil, the Roman poet, who wrote the epic, *The Aeneid*, about the origins of Rome and the basis for political institutions and leadership. Virgil is sent by heaven to guide Dante through hell and purgatory and appeals to Dante to think more rationally on his journey. But Dante is convinced that reason can only take us so far. Hence it is Beatrice, a symbol of divine grace and love, who ultimately takes over as Dante's guide to usher him into the Empyrean, "the Heaven of pure light, a light intellectual, full of love." Here Dante beholds the Beatific Vision and participates in a marvelous feast of light, song, and dance. It is only through a personal encounter with divine love that Dante fulfills his purpose in *Paradiso*.

Dante stresses that reason is important and helpful, but to complete the journey one must also be willing to follow the revelation of divine love. As I will discuss in describing the thought and life of Mortimer Adler, reason, coupled with a revelation of divine love, produces a very profound way of knowing. I will argue that reason is important but not sufficient. Ultimately it is the realization and experience of divine love that enhances the knowledge of the reality of God's existence.

In more recent times, in his magisterial opus, *At the Origins of Modern Atheism*, Michael Buckley agreed with Dante and demonstrated how the strategies of theistic apologetics in the eighteenth century resulted in theologians relying on the new sciences for evidence of the existence of God, excluding the evidential force of religious experience. According to Buckley, by insisting on a focus on the evidence from scientific discoveries and disregarding the authenticity of religion's own foundation and the unique character of religious knowledge, the apologists inadvertently laid the groundwork for modern atheism.

In his subsequent book, *Denying and Disclosing God*, Buckley calls for a restoration of the use of the evidential force of religious experience and an acknowledgement of the credibility of religious knowledge. In this regard, although he does not rely on Kierkegaard's writings, his arguments are consistent with Kierkegaard's epistemology of knowledge by personal acquaintance (*kendskab*), which I will discuss more thoroughly later. For one with religious experience, this kind of cognition carries more knowledge than the deductive arguments that result only in an abstract inference. Although the latter also has credibility and is important, one cannot have transformational knowledge only from mere reason, no matter how compelling one might consider the inference from deductive logic. A personal God disclosed as a presence is a required foundation for the knowledge of the reality of God. If God is a person, such a being can only be known in reality as a person, not merely as an inference: "One will not long affirm a God who is fundamentally inferred from a conclusion rather than disclosed as a presence, one with whom there is no intersubjective communication. The most compelling witness to a personal God must itself be personal."[10]

As noted in the preface, in this book I will examine an argument that modifies and expands an argument for the existence of God made by Mortimer Adler, who modified the arguments of Aristotle, Aquinas, Clarke, Leibniz, and others. Adler believed that his argument produced a rational inference with certainty beyond a reasonable doubt (but not beyond a shadow of a doubt).[11] In discussions with Clare Boothe Luce at the Aspen Institute, he insisted that his argument did not create a real faith for him, even though he was convinced of its intellectual integrity. What many readers of Adler's significant writings do not know is the story of his conversion experience. Many years after the development of his argument for the existence of God, he experienced a personal God, disclosed to him as a presence in a hospital room. Adler then dramatically moved from what he called a "dead faith" to a transformational belief in the reality of God. Deeply moved by his experience of that reality, he converted to the Anglican faith and later died a Roman Catholic. I will let Adler describe his story in his own words later, but for now I only point out how his story confirms Buckley's insistence that, when concerned with the knowledge of God's existence, the rational can never be separated from the experiential. Religious experience carries its own form of cognition or way of knowledge that is beyond pure reason.

Scottish theologian Thomas Torrance corroborated this perspective emphasizing that in revelation the person of the divine brings a unique logic and method of knowing into the revelatory experience. This way of personal knowing may be a higher degree of knowledge than logical inference alone. For example, Thomas Aquinas, after a lifetime of brilliant writings, had a mystical experience that made him consider all of his writings (including *Summa Contra Gentiles* and his *Summa Theologiae*) as "mere straw" (*sicut palea*) compared to the knowledge of God that came to him in this experience. His experience is not unusual in history. It is a repeated phenomenon well attested in a vast array of excellent literature.

At the same time, one cannot rely only on mystical, religious experience. If one accepts the principle of the unity of truth, one must also use his or her mind to consider the rational merits of any proposition. Reason and faith complement each other. Saint Anselm of Canterbury described this unity of knowledge as *fides quaerens intellectum*, or "faith seeking understanding."

Many persons hold the perception that science and faith are adversaries. Not only are science and Christian belief compatible, science gives supportive evidence to many aspects of faith. In order to conduct science one must believe in the intelligibility of the laws of nature. Nature proceeds in accordance with laws that can be described by abstract mathematical principles. Abstract mathematics allows us to discover their existence. Eugene Wigner called this "the unreasonable effectiveness of mathematics," and its significance in examining the question of God's existence is difficult to overstate.

In their most successful theories, physicists do not impose their equations on nature but rather *discover* the mathematical characteristics that are *inherently present in nature*. The inherently mathematical structure of the laws of nature allows physicists to predict events in the physical world. On this basis, scientists and engineers have invented many useful and productive machines and devices. This predictable, intelligible aspect to nature is a prerequisite to science. Science could not be done if the universe was only a chaos of arbitrary events. The intelligibility of the laws that are the foundation of science is consistent with a worldview that a rational mind is behind the universe.[12]

Science, however, is not the only avenue for knowledge or evidence concerning the question of God. I am emphasizing that religious experience has its own method of knowledge and cognition. This method should not be isolated from some of the interesting work moving forward in theology and science. If science alone is embraced for evidence, one may follow a misconception of Immanuel Kant, which I will discuss more thoroughly later. The Kantian criticism of any knowledge reaching beyond the explanation of an empirical verification of our senses has been refuted by contemporary physics, mathematics, and information theory. Although the scientific method is consistent with much of the theologian's method of inquiry, religious evidence also supplies a justification with its own internal integrity, its own intellectual cogency, and its own inherent grounds for belief. One seeking understanding should hold to Adler's criteria on the unity of truth and should include all the avenues available for the knowledge of reality without ignoring the cognition that comes from personal religious acquaintance. Even the highly empirical Bertrand Russell noted that one kind of knowledge (abstract, descriptive knowledge) may come from hearing or reading about Julius Caesar, but another more basic knowledge (knowledge of acquaintance) comes from *meeting* Julius Caesar.

I want to be clear that I am not arguing against an openness to the disclosure of God implied in the scientific evidence and in the fact that there is something rather than nothing. This book contains several discussions in that area. I merely want to include the witness of concrete religious experience and note that the most compelling evidence for the reality of a personal God may be from personal experience.[13]

How we think about God to a significant extent, perhaps far more than contemporary figures may realize, is heavily influenced by the intellectual movement effected by the dynamic persuasive abilities of Immanuel Kant, the greatest philosopher of the eighteenth century. The effect of his writings strengthened and grew in influence through succeeding centuries. *Inter alia*, he influenced the development of German idealism and then logical positivism in the Vienna Circle of philosophy, the atheist English positivist position of A. J. Ayer, the mid-twentieth century theological phenomena of the "Death of God" movement, current scientific materialist reductionism, and even the presuppositions of Rudolf Bultmann's New Testament scholarship.

Because many interpreted Kant's theory of knowledge as an account that removes the philosophy of religion outside the realm of reason, Kant's theory also influenced the turn toward human subjectivity in the writings of Sören Kierkegaard, Rudolf Otto, Martin Buber, Paul Tillich, and other philosophers of religion. One factor encouraging subjectivity was Kant's description of the concepts of mind as *synthetic a priori* (with an inborn capacity to contribute to and organize one's sense experience). According to Kant, the mind of a human being has innate categories by which the mind actively classifies the sensory data it receives. For example, the concepts of space and time are forms of *a priori* categories that the mind imposes on sensory data. The mind is not a passive receiver of truth from the outside world but an active participant in knowledge, shaping the logical categories of judgment. This means that empiricism is not alone complete. Pure, unaltered sensory experience of the world does not exist according to Kant. The mind's action means that experience is not purely objective because the mind plays an important role.

Kant gave these existential philosophers and theologians the avenue to emphasize the inner, subjective workings of the mind as capable of generating knowledge. This concept later influenced postmodern thought, as seen in the writings of Derrida, Lyotard, Foucault, Rorty, and Jean-Luc Marion. I will not examine their positions fully here, but for the moment I want only to emphasize that, despite his influence on subjectivity, Kant may have given too prominent a role to empiricism in his theory of knowledge.

Given that Kant's thought was founded on flawed Newtonian physics, it is surprising that his influence remains so powerful in contemporary thought. In a later discussion of quantum physics I will address how certain quantum physicists hold that Kant's epistemology is undermining current moral philosophy and jurisprudence. I turn now to a closer look at Kant's theory of knowledge for the purpose of examining it in the light of our current understanding in contemporary science.

IN ATTEMPTING TO SYNTHESIZE RATIONALIST AND EMPIRICAL PHILOSOPHIES, KANT DEVELOPED AN INCOMPLETE, OVERLY RESTRICTIVE THEORY OF KNOWLEDGE.

A Prussian by birth and nature, throughout most of his adult life, Immanuel Kant lived a very structured, rational life, rising every morning at precisely five a.m. for a one-hour period of reflection. This extraordinarily gifted and disciplined university professor then worked on his classroom lectures from six to seven, taught until nine and then wrote until noon each day. His main meal was a lunch with three to four colleagues or guests, followed by a daily walk with a servant carrying an umbrella behind him in the event of rain. Prussian citizens were rumored to set their clocks by the precise time of his daily walk. Every evening he read until 10 p.m., when he retired for bed. He became the leading modern philosopher and the epitome of the Enlightenment. His *Critique of Pure Reason*, published in 1781 and revised in 1787, is perhaps the most important work of the Enlightenment.

In this book Kant set forth a new theory of knowledge that attempted to synthesize the apparently conflicting positions of rationalism and empiricism. Rationalists, such as Descartes, Spinoza, and Leibniz, were Continental European philosophers who took the position that reason is a more reliable path to knowledge than experience. Deductive philosophy was their method with particular emphasis on the use of mathematical logic as a dependable method of determining truth. Empiricists,[14] on the other hand, such as Locke and Hume, were British philosophers who maintained that all knowledge came from direct observation of phenomena. For them sense perception was the dominant characteristic of dependable knowledge. In empiricism only by means of the senses can we have access to knowledge about reality. Empiricism in the seventeenth and eighteenth century laid the cornerstone for the philosophy of logical positivism, which became a dominant philosophy for part of the mid-twentieth century.[15] Logical positivism held that not all religious and metaphysical language could be verified by the senses and was consequently meaningless. This view had such influence in twentieth century society that even theological schools began curricula with "Death of God" studies.

For Kant the two sources of knowledge are sensibility (empiricism) and understanding. Understanding proceeds from certain *a priori* categories or concepts of the mind. These concepts of understanding organize and synthesize data from the senses. They exist in the mind and participate in the process of understanding. In his attempt to synthesize the rationalists and empiricists, Kant held that experience was not a passive reception of sensations but the product of our senses and our own thought processes that reveal our sensations to us. Kant's analysis in the *Critique of Pure Reason* stunned the philosophical world. His argument was directed against any attempt to use reason to consider objects that were beyond our senses. In

Kant's new theory, empiricism held so prominent a position that he considered all of our knowledge a consequence of human understanding resulting from experiences of our senses. Consequently, for Kant, metaphysical questions, such as the existence of God, were outside the scope of human reason. In his view, reason could not be applied to matters outside of one's experience through the senses.[16] In Kantian epistemology, reason could never lead one to knowledge of God, and theological inquiry could not be made by means of rational analysis. Because God is not subject to the senses, Kant dismissed any attempt to discuss God by the use of rational concepts.[17]

Kant wrote in a ponderous Germanic style which, coupled with his tendency to invent words and phrases and the complexity of his thought, requires careful reading. His ideas were profound, brilliant, and, with respect to the rational inquiry concerning God's existence, modern science indicates that they were *overly restrictive.*

Kant did not have the benefit of the discoveries and methods of contemporary physics, so his position (based on Newtonian physics) may have seemed unassailable in his time. Nevertheless, given the discoveries in contemporary physics and science, it is astonishing how much of Kant's excessively limited theory of knowledge still pervades current thought. Developments in science in the past century issue profound challenges to his theory of knowledge, because, *inter alia*, quantum physics, particle astrophysics, cosmology, and information theory now use abstract rational concepts rather than empirical concepts to analyze objects that are beyond empirical experiences, beyond the senses. Kant's theory of knowledge is too restrictive to have a sufficient capacity to describe all that we can know. Kant's theory is too restrictive in terms of metaphysical reasoning and in terms of knowledge from personal acquaintance. In addition to reason we have "personal knowledge," as indicated in Michael Polanyi's statement: "We know more than we can tell."

Kant's position is that we can have no knowledge of a thing-in-itself and any attempt to access it by description is nonsensical. He insisted in the existence of an external reality but denied access to it. Kant distinguished between the *phenomenon* (things as we experience them) and the *noumenon* (things as they are in themselves, *das Ding an sich*). He concluded that we cannot know the noumenon but only the phenomenon. For Kant even our deepest perception of a phenomenon would be altogether different from the noumenon or the thing as it is in itself. We can only know our subjective experience of the world but nothing of the thing in itself. (One may wonder whether "nothing would do just as well as a something about which nothing can be said.")[18]

As noted above, Kant understood that not all human thought is based on empirical or sense experience. Many of our concepts are *a priori* categories of our understanding, which we use to form judgments about our sense experiences. These concepts do not come from our sense experiences but are part of the structure of our minds. But, as I noted above, Kant, influenced by a Newtonian understanding of physics that dominated science in his time, made the mistake of presupposing that these *a priori* categories of understanding can only be applied to empirical experience (i.e., experiences of the senses) in space and time. This presupposition unnecessarily excludes rational inquiry into anything beyond the senses. Contemporary science, however, indicates that the fact that one cannot directly experience something with the senses does not mean that one cannot have knowledge about something.

Contemporary physics demonstrate that one can discuss God in rational terms, even if God is outside the experience of the human senses. This merely follows accepted methods of reasoning, such as employing abstract rational concepts in quantum physics. John Polkinghorne notes the similarity in rational analysis between theological inquiry and contemporary physics:

> No one has ever seen a quark, and we believe that no one ever will. They are so tightly bound to each other inside the protons and neutrons that nothing can make them break out on their own. Why, then, do I believe in these invisible quarks? . . . In summary, it's because quarks make sense of a lot of direct physical evidence. . . . I wish to engage in a similar strategy with regard to the unseen reality of God. His existence makes sense of many aspects of our knowledge and experience: the order and fruitfulness of the physical world; the multilayered character of reality; the almost universal human experiences of worship and hope; the phenomenon of Jesus Christ (including his resurrection). I think that very similar thought processes are involved in both cases. I do not believe that I shift in some strange intellectual way when I move from science to religion. . . . In their search for truth, science and faith are intellectual cousins under the skin.[19]

In criticizing Kant's theory of knowledge, Mortimer Adler distinguished among methods of knowing about physical objects we experience. We perceive some objects *directly* through our five senses (sight, hearing, touch, smell, and taste). Other objects we perceive only *through* instruments of observation (e.g., microscopes or telescopes).

Other physical objects we do not perceive directly but by *detection*. For example, physics laboratories have the ability to detect traces of imperceptible objects. These kinds of physical objects are not directly subject to the senses but detectable by the effect they produce under certain conditions. They are thus known by detection and by rational inference. Subatomic particles, black holes, and even the universe as a whole are objects that we know by the process of detection and rational inference.

Adler argued that one can only form an *empirical concept* of a physical object that can be perceived directly and immediately or through the use of instruments of observation such as a microscope or telescope. Even though we cannot form an empirical concept of subatomic particles, we have some understanding of these physical objects. Adler distinguished between empirical concepts and what logicians call *theoretical constructs* to refer to our understanding of objects of thought beyond our immediate perceptual experience.

When one thinks of God, of course, one does so by a theoretical construct, not an empirical construct.[20] If science can validly deal with physical objects that are completely outside ordinary experience (because they are not perceptible) and can employ theoretical constructs (not empirical concepts) to know something about these objects, then one cannot be precluded from employing theoretical constructs to deal with the question of God. Reason has its limits in considering the question of God, but to eliminate any attempt at rational inquiry into objects beyond the senses is an overly restrictive epistemology. As Adler wrote in referring to Kant's theory of knowledge:

> His thundering issued from a theory of knowledge which was critical of any attempt on the part of reason to deal with objects that lie beyond the range of experience. To do so, he maintained, was an illegitimate and illusory use of reason. The empirical concepts that he thought reason must employ cannot be validly employed in thinking about non-empirical objects, the most eminently non-empirical object being God.
>
> Kant's theory of knowledge should have been discredited in the eyes of the world by the non-Euclidean geometries and the post-Newtonian physics with which he was unacquainted. That his theory of knowledge is still respected in certain quarters is quite remarkable.
>
> Be that as it may, his strictures against theological inquiry lose all their force when we recognize that theology, like nuclear physics and cosmology in

> the 20th century, uses theoretical constructs, not empirical concepts, to deal with objects that lie beyond the range of ordinary or common experience. If, for that reason, theological inquiry cannot be legitimately and validly conducted, the same reason would make nuclear physics and contemporary cosmology illegitimate and invalid enterprises.[21]

The study of quantum physics, black holes, particle astrophysics, cosmology, and information allows us to know quite a bit about things that are beyond our senses. Similarly, there is merit in rational metaphysical inquiry concerning the knowledge of God, even though that knowledge will always be incomplete and distorted on a purely human rational basis. Although we cannot know everything about God through human rational inquiry and may not be able to achieve a genuine understanding of God's essence, we can know something about God.[22]

Former Parisian and Princeton philosopher Jacques Maritain also argued that there are several valid ways of knowing, including the empirical, the metaphysical, and the mystical. Maritain followed Thomas Aquinas in acknowledging that physical objects have a reality in themselves and that we can only have a limited knowledge of these objects. We cannot know their full essence as they are in themselves, but we can know something about them.

For example, although science does not cover all areas of knowledge, it is making strides toward a more accurate knowledge of the physical world. This is what makes technology possible. Most scientists adopt a critical realist approach that fits into Aquinas's perspective. The "critical" aspect of this approach means that direct observation is not the source of knowledge, but rational inference or interpretation interacting with experiment. In this respect, a critical realist considers all human knowledge to be personal knowledge.[23]

Because how we think about God affects how we live, no one approaches this question with a completely disinterested, objective interpretation of the evidence. As philosopher Stephen Evans claims, "Human beings think as whole persons. It is human beings who reflect, not brains or minds detached from concrete human persons. Their thinking therefore necessarily reflects the shape of their human interests and habits."[24] Human thinking is not only the thinking of a finite, contingent being but also a being whose thought processes are distorted by pride and self-interest.

Although modern scientific reasoning indicates that we can discuss the concept of God in rational terms, we need to acknowledge our limitations; a finite being will not comprehend fully an infinite being. If God is infinite, any attempt to grasp such a being will be incomplete. As finite beings with a finite language, our attempts to discuss the infinite will always be inadequate. One cannot use words concerning God as one would use words to describe anything else. Our language is limited to descriptions of components of the universe or to the universe itself. God is beyond the universe and not limited to the categories of objects of our thoughts. God is beyond all categories and beyond the comprehension of the human mind. We encounter real limits in our reasoning and in our knowledge. However, as Jacques Maritain insisted, we can know something about God by combining the empirical, metaphysical, and mystical ways of knowing. The empirical way alone leads only to naturalism and denies the existence of the divine. As theologian Paul Tillich observed: "The main argument against naturalism in whatever form is that it denies the infinite distance between the whole of finite things and their infinite ground, with the consequence that the term 'God' becomes interchangeable with the term 'universe' and therefore is semantically superfluous. This semantic situation reveals the failure of naturalism to understand a decisive element in the experience of the holy, namely, the distance between finite man, on the one hand, and the holy in its numerous manifestations, on the other. For this, naturalism cannot account."[25]

Our language and finite minds are all we have, and reflection upon an infinite God can expand our awareness of reality. We can gain some valid insights by reflecting upon such a being. At the very least this reflection can show us that all of our concepts about God are too small. Just because we cannot know all of God does not mean that we cannot experience God. Our sense of awe and our understanding of reality may be enhanced as we catch even a tiny glimpse of the magnitude of God.

Each person must examine the evidence available and draw his or her own conclusions. One cannot be completely objective in this regard.[26] I want to emphasize that this book is not an attempt to construct a compelling proof for the absolute certainty of God's existence. I will consider an argument for the existence of God to show the plausible and rational possibility of God's existence. The argument I will examine is influenced by the thinking of Mortimer Adler, who believed that he had successfully modified the arguments of Aquinas and Aristotle. As noted above, Adler held that his argument proved the existence of God beyond a reasonable doubt, but not beyond a shadow of a doubt. My argument modifies Adler's discussion and also appeals to the intelligibility of the universe. I describe certain developments in philosophy and science that strengthen Adler's argument. I emphasize that the intelligibility of the universe is what makes rational and scientific inquiry possible and, *inter alia*, is demonstrated in the inherently mathematical character of the universe. One should not accept this fact too casually. It is rather astonishing that the universe is intelligible, for it could also have been a disordered chaos rather than a mathematically ordered cosmos. One should marvel that abstract mathematics can perfectly describe the counterintuitive, invisible world of subatomic quantum physics and the unexperienced, invisible macro domain of relativity. Mathematical intelligibility in a universe finely tuned for the existence of human life raises rational questions.

One can never be certain, by reason alone, that there is no God.[27] The discussion in this book will merely describe what I consider to be certain signposts or signals pointing to the divine. As I noted earlier, everyone must live with uncertainties. Perhaps our most certain method of applying reason is in the area of mathematics, but even there Kurt Gödel's famous incompleteness theorem demonstrates that one must make a leap of faith concerning the completeness or consistency of any formalized rational system.

Adler's rational argument for God's existence appeared to prepare him for a religious encounter with the divine. His experience confirms that one cannot separate reason from a faith experience. They are complementary ways of knowing. Reason without experience is dead. Experience without reason can be fantasy, as we see in much of contemporary new age mysticism or gnosticism. Reason and religious experience need to remain coupled. One's heart and one's mind must each be fully engaged in the knowing process. There are ways of knowing beyond the senses. We know as complete persons, not only as sensory tissue.

LEIBNIZ'S BASIC QUESTION IS STILL ESSENTIAL: WHY IS THERE SOMETHING RATHER THAN NOTHING?

Gottfried Wilhelm Freiherr von Leibniz (1646–1716) was a man of many parts with a broad knowledge in the areas of philosophy, mathematics, science, law, and theology, but his focus was on the philosophical arguments for the existence of God. His only published book was on that subject and entitled *Theodicy: Essays on the Goodness of God, the Freedom of Man, and the Origin of Evil*. Like his father, he was a professor of philosophy at the University of Leipzig and a committed Lutheran. Leibniz studied law and received a Doctor of Law from the University of Altdorf. Through his study of law, he encountered the archbishop-elector of Mainz, who became his mentor, employing Leibniz in the role of a political adviser. This political position required him to study international politics and travel to various European cities. His travels on political assignments also allowed him to meet some of the substantial scientists and philosophers of his time, including Isaac Newton and Benedict Spinoza. Leibniz entered into a correspondence with many of these leading thinkers and attempted to apply a systematic thought process to his understanding of science, mathematics, and philosophy. In 1673, after the death of his mentor and employer, the archbishop-elector of Mainz, he was employed by the Duke of Brunswick and Hanover. Leibniz continued his philosophical thought and worked as part of the Hanoverian family for the last three years of his life, dying in 1716.

As noted above, contemporary science and mathematics raise certain questions concerning Kant's prohibition against any attempts to use theoretical reason to deal with nonempirical objects. For the purpose of this book, I want to focus on an important question articulated by Leibniz. Leibniz raised a basic question that remains unanswered in Kant's epistemology: "*Why is there something rather than nothing?*" We know that there is something. Why does it exist? Why is there anything at all? We know that nothing comes from nothing. *Ex nihilo nihil fit*. We know that there is something. Something could not have come from nothing. Why is there something?

Leibniz's question is based on the principle of sufficient reason: No fact can exist without a sufficient reason for its existence. This principle is necessary when one considers the intelligibility of the universe. This intelligibility was the fact that most amazed Albert Einstein. As I emphasize many times in this book, science could not proceed without this intelligibility. Stephen T. Davis, professor of philosophy at Claremont College, asks us to imagine a world without a principle of sufficient reason. He notes that we would all live with the concern that dangerous animals, such as a saber-toothed tiger, could at any time pop into existence and devour us. Even if we barricaded ourselves in a protected shelter, we would find no protection, because dangerous chasms, beasts, or bombs could at any time pop into existence inside the shelter without any reason and destroy us.[28]

British philosopher Bertrand Russell held to the position that the universe simply exists as a brute fact. He refused to address Leibniz's question why there is something (a cosmos) rather than nothing. But what would be his reason for holding his position, given the scientific understanding we now have concerning the universe? Unless he could distinguish the universe from other contingent things, he would have to explain why hotels, airplanes, and chemicals cannot come into existence without a cause, but the universe can just pop into existence out of nothing. An appeal to quantum physics would not suffice, because a quantum vacuum is not nothing, but a precisely balanced series of conditions with a context of space/time, precise characteristics of mass and energy, complete with complex physical laws. Anyone appealing to a quantum vacuum would only move the question one step back; a quantum vacuum is a something and requires an explanation for its existence. I will explore this concept in more detail later in the book.

No one lives as if the principle of sufficient reason is false. The principle presupposes the existence of reason. When one argues against the principle, he or she begins to question the existence of reason itself. The conundrum of using reason to argue against the existence of reason appears odd if not self-defeating. The intelligibility of physical reality appears to require the principle of sufficient reason.

EVERYTHING THAT EXISTS IS EITHER CONTINGENT OR NECESSARY.

When we consider the basic fact of existence, we can understand that whatever exists, including the universe as a whole, either has its existence in, through, and from itself or its existence is dependent on the existence of something else. In other words, everything that exists is either contingent (dependent on something else) or necessary (independent). A *contingent* thing depends on something else for its existence.

An example of a contingent existence is Toby, my golden retriever. Toby is the result of a particular mating between two adult golden retrievers. These two golden retrievers may never have met. The existence of Toby depended upon the mating of these two retrievers. Toby's existence is contingent (dependent) upon his parents having met. His continuing existence is also dependent, among other things, upon the frozen turkey dinners he devours each evening. Moreover, Toby's existence is not an *indefeasible* existence; his existence can be taken away from him.

In addition to Toby, the list of contingent things is almost endless. Other examples include our parents, my pen, the earth, our solar system, stars, and galaxies. All of these contingent things are not endowed with their particular existence indefeasibly.

In contrast to a contingent thing, a *necessary* thing has its existence in, through, and from itself and does not depend on anything for its existence.[29] A contingent thing can be otherwise, but a necessary thing cannot be otherwise.[30] A necessary thing cannot be anything except what it is;[31] its existence is indefeasible and cannot be taken away.

DO CONTINGENT THINGS IN OUR UNIVERSE DEPEND UPON SOMETHING NECESSARY AS THE CAUSE OF THEIR CONTINUING EXISTENCE?

I have described the distinction between contingent and necessary things because this distinction is central to an understanding of the argument for a necessary cause continually sustaining and preserving the cosmos. In the traditional argument for God from contingency (Thomas Aquinas), contingent things have their existence from, through, and in another. As noted, their existence is not in themselves. When they come to be, they are not endowed indefeasibly with their existence. Their existence can be taken away. They are not completely independent. Contingent things come to be, but their coming to be does not make them necessary, independent things.

Adler made the distinction between *causa essendi* and *causa fieri*. Toby's mother may be *causa fieri* (the cause of coming into existence) of Toby, but she does not act as *causa essendi* (an efficient cause of continuing existence) of Toby. Toby's mother passed away while Toby continues to inhabit the earth. She cannot be the cause of his continuing existence. A match may be *causa fieri* of a flame, but oxygen acts as a required condition for the continuing existence of the flame. Although oxygen is one of the required conditions for the flame, it is not *the efficient cause of the continuing existence* (*causa essendi*) of the flame.

The contingent components of the universe always act as *causa fieri*. Their actions as causal agents affect the generation, becoming, motion, changes, corruption, and perishing of other contingent things. They do not cause the continuing existence of the products of their actions or being. In other words, they never function as *causa essendi* or the *efficient* cause of the continuing existence of other contingent things.

Adler could not think of any contingent component in the universe that would cease to exist absolutely. He held that everything in the universe is *superficially* contingent. When a contingent component of the universe ceases to exist, it is not reduced to absolute nothingness. It is important to note the distinction between *superficial* contingency and *radical* contingency. When an individual contingent thing has a superficial contingency, after it passes out of existence it is transformed into another form or condition. But something with a *radical* contingency would simply cease to be and be replaced by absolute nothingness (annihilation).

To understand the concept of superficial contingency, picture in your mind's eye a log burning in a fireplace. The log is consumed by flames and transformed into ashes. The log ceases to exist, but it is not replaced by absolute nothingness. It is not annihilated. Similarly, the cremation of a human body reduces the body to ashes; it is not reduced to absolute nothingness. In the natural corruption of the contingent physical components of the universe, no thing is reduced to absolute nothingness. All superficial contingent things are transformed, but not annihilated. In the *Summa Theologiae*, Aquinas asserted that God did not annihilate anything, but transformed it. No one has any experience of a component of the universe having been annihilated or exnihilated (coming to be out of nothing).[32]

In what Adler described as the best traditional argument for the existence of God, a central conditional premise was that a contingent being required a cause of its continuing existence at every moment of its existence. Adler rejected this premise, which was based on Aristotle's concept that the continuous motion of a body requires a continuing cause to perpetuate its motion. His rejection of Aristotle's (and Aquinas's) concept was based on a potential inherent perpetuation seen in the principle of inertia (a body set in motion continues until a counteracting cause stops it). Adler held that an "inertia of being" might continue the existence of a contingent thing.[33]

However, Adler was convinced that the *continuing existence of the universe* required a supernatural sustaining cause. Without this sustaining cause the universe would vanish into complete, absolute nothingness. It would be annihilated. Adler did not believe that the *entire universe* (all physical reality) contained its own explanation for its existence. I move now to a portion of the argument that has some further confirmation in contemporary astrophysics, particularly when one considers the radically contingent nature of the entire universe.

ALTHOUGH THE COMPONENTS OF THE UNIVERSE ARE ONLY SUPERFICIALLY CONTINGENT, THE UNIVERSE AS A WHOLE IS RADICALLY CONTINGENT, BECAUSE THE UNIVERSE IS ONLY ONE AMONG MANY POSSIBLE UNIVERSES.

As mentioned above, the obstacle presented by only superficially contingent things was that they did not cease to be absolutely, so there was no need for a *causa essendi*, an efficient cause of their continuing existence. They actually continued to exist in a different form. However, when one considers the universe as a whole, one is confronted by a *radical* contingency that does require a *causa essendi* to prevent its vanishing or annihilation into absolute nothingness. When we move from a consideration of the superficial contingency of the components of the universe to the question of an efficient sustaining cause of the universe as a whole (cosmos), we are moving from an argument from contingency (Thomas Aquinas) to a truly cosmological argument.[34]

The universe is radically contingent because it is one among many *logically* possible universes. For the argument I am considering to be valid, one does not need evidence of a different kind of universe, but only the *logical possibility that there could be another kind of universe.* In other words, no other universes need *actually* exist. It is sufficient for the validity of the argument if they only can exist as a matter of logical possibility. Adler does not argue for the *actual existence* of other universes but only for their *possible* existence.

We can conceive of other universes that could exist with different characteristics and different physical laws than our universe. Because other universes are possible, this universe is not the only universe that could ever exist. It is not a *necessary* universe. Because it is merely a *possible* universe and not a necessary universe, its existence is not necessary in and through itself.[35] The universe could be other than what it is. A universe that could be other than what it is might not be at all. Such a universe has only a possible, not a necessary, existence.[36] *Such a universe also has the possibility or the potential for nonexistence.*[37]

A MERELY POSSIBLE UNIVERSE MIGHT NOT EXIST; IT HAS THE POTENTIAL TO BE REDUCED TO NOTHINGNESS (ANNIHILATION) AND DEPENDS UPON A NECESSARY EXNIHILATING CAUSE OF ITS CONTINUING EXISTENCE.

A universe that has the potential for nonexistence is a *radically contingent* universe, not a necessary universe. Anything that is radically contingent requires an efficient cause of its continuing existence; it depends upon something else for its existence. This merely possible universe is contingent and depends upon a cause of its continuing existence to prevent the possibility of nonexistence. This merely possible radically contingent universe requires a preservative cause of its continuing existence to protect it from the possibility of annihilation (its reduction to nothingness). This preservative activity is an action of exnihilation (existence coming out of nothing) as it is juxtaposed to an action of annihilation (vanishing into absolute nothingness).

Hume suggested that the universe was eternal. As discussed below, the universe appears to have had a beginning. But even assuming that the universe is eternal, because of its radically contingent nature, it requires a cause for its continuing existence.[38] To prevent the universe from vanishing into nothingness, the cause of its continuing existence cannot be a natural cause because natural causes are themselves contingent things. They depend upon something else. They may act as a necessary *condition* of continuing existence (like water for animal life), but they never act as *causa essendi* (an efficient cause of continuing existence) that prevents the annihilation of a radically contingent cosmos.

GOD IS THE NECESSARY CAUSE OF THE CONTINUING EXISTENCE OF THE UNIVERSE AND ALL OF ITS COMPONENTS, EVEN IF THE UNIVERSE DID NOT HAVE A BEGINNING.

If we define the concept of God as a necessary rather than a contingent being, God cannot be part of the universe, because the universe and all of the individual things in it are contingent in their existence. A necessary existence means that such an existence is uncaused, independent, unconditioned, and infinite. In this concept God has a necessary existence as a preservative cause of the existence of the universe. As a cause of its continuing existence, God would not be simply a cause that began or wound up a universe and then left it to run on its own, but a cause that intimately and constantly preserves the universe.

The important premise in this argument is that the universe is radically contingent and not necessary.[39] Because other universes are possible, our universe is not necessary in and through itself. If it is not necessary, it is contingent. If it is contingent, at every moment it has the potential for annihilation. If it has the potential for annihilation, it needs a sustaining cause to exist. The continuing existence of the universe is *radically* different from the continuing existence of any component of the universe. When something radically contingent ceases to be, it does not become something else but is replaced by sheer nothingness.[40]

If the universe is contingent, we do not have an explanation in terms of noncontingent natural laws from which the universe's existence follows.

And we do not have an explanation *why* the universe exists. This indicates the requirement of a personal explanation based in the *intentions* of a sustaining necessary cause of its existence. We know of no natural explanation for the existence of the universe in terms of noncontingent laws or principles that would cause its existence.[41] If no laws or principles can offer a natural explanation, a personal explanation is required. A personal explanation addresses the requirement of an *intentional* act of a sustaining necessary cause of the universe's continuing existence.

The universe cannot explain its own existence because it is merely a possible universe. As such, the explanation for its existence must come from outside the universe. Because the universe is the totality of all physical reality, the explanation must reside in a nonphysical reality. One could argue that the universe came into existence without any cause and for no sufficient reason. But to set forth that proposition, one would have to deny the scientific method and the results of this method in the production of technology that works in the physical world. There is then no reason to believe that our cognitive thoughts give us any ability to invent a laser, fly to the moon, or use information technology. Given the success of science in practice, the burden of proof appears to be on anyone claiming that there is no sufficient reason for the universe as a whole.

One may object that the conclusion to this argument is not the God of Abraham, but, under the cumulative case I am setting forth, the evidence points to an immaterial, simple, and infinite personal being. Philosopher Bruce Reichenbach set forth a rationale for the conclusion that the cause of the universe is a personal necessary being. I will address other issues relating to this concept when I discuss some of the writings of Sören Kierkegaard. For now I merely want to agree with Reichenbach's argument:

> Defenders of the cosmological argument suggest two possible kinds of explanation. *Natural explanation* is provided in terms of precedent events, causal laws, or necessary conditions that invoke natural existents. *Personal explanation* is given "in terms of the intentional action of a rational agent" (Swinburne, 1979, 20). We have seen that one cannot provide a natural causal explanation for the initial event, for there are no precedent events or natural existents to which the laws of physics apply. The line of scientific explanation runs out at the initial singularity, and perhaps even before we arrive at the singularity (at 10^{-35} seconds). If no scientific explanation (in terms of physical laws) can provide a causal account of the origin of the universe, the explanation must be personal, i.e., in terms of the intentional action of a rational, supernatural agent.[42]

The laws of physics are insufficient to serve in the role of a necessary thing sustaining the universe. They do not explain their own existence. They do not explain their mathematical characteristics. They do not explain why the world is intelligible to us. They are mere equations and do not explain why a physical world exists at all. They do not explain the fine-tuning of the universe that allows for the development of conscious life. They also appear to not exist prior to Planck time (an extremely small fraction of the first second of the initial event of the universe). Hence, they appear to be finite and consequently contingent and not necessary.

This is consistent with the reasoning of physicist John Wheeler, who worked with Einstein at Princeton's Advanced Institute. In commenting on the breakdown of the laws of physics that occurs in a singularity (a point of infinitely curved space and finite density found at the core of a high mass star's collapse into a black hole or in the initial event of the Big Bang), Wheeler wrote in his autobiography, *Geons, Black Holes & Quantum Foam*, that such a singularity "teaches us that space can be crumpled like a piece of paper into an infinitesimal dot, that time can be extinguished like a blown-out flame and that the laws of physics we regard as 'sacred,' as immutable, are anything but."[43]

The laws of physics are merely contingent components of the universe; their contingent characteristics do not allow them to serve as the necessary sustaining source of the universe. The cause of the universe appears to require a personal explanation.

MANY GENERATIONS OF PHILOSOPHERS HAVE MADE THE MISTAKE OF ASSUMING HUME AND KANT'S OBJECTIONS DISPOSED OF THE COSMOLOGICAL ARGUMENT

Many generations of philosophers have proceeded under the false conception that Hume and Kant closed the door on the cosmological argument for a necessary being. Not only has new evidence from contemporary science strengthened the argument but also new insights in philosophical thought have discovered flaws in Hume and Kant's reasoning, so that one finds the cosmological argument not only alive and well but also increasingly invigorated.

IN RECENT THOUGHT PHILOSOPHERS HAVE NOTED THAT DAVID HUME MISUNDERSTOOD THE TERM *NECESSARY* TO MEAN A "LOGICAL NECESSITY" AS OPPOSED TO A "CONDITIONAL NECESSITY"; A "CONDITIONAL NECESSITY" IS THE RESULT OF VALID DEDUCTIONS FROM PREMISES AND CONDITIONS. HUME'S OBJECTION DOES NOT STAND WHEN APPLIED TO A CONDITIONAL NECESSARY BEING WHO IS WITHOUT BEGINNING OR END AND IS INDEPENDENT OF ANYTHING ELSE.

David Hume insisted that the term *necessary* could not be used to describe a being. He reasoned that whatever one could conceive as existing, one could also conceive as not existing. Consequently, Hume argued, no being's nonexistence implies a contradiction and, *ergo*, there is no necessary being whose nonexistence implies a contradiction. Thus, according to Hume, no being is necessary in our universe.

I want to take some time to clarify Hume's mistake in his attempted refutation of the argument for a necessary being. Because Hume misunderstood the concept of a necessary being, the existence of something rather than nothing presents a legitimate question. I will quote the most relevant sections of Hume's presentation of the argument for a necessary being, which is explained by the person of Demea in Hume's *Dialogues Concerning Natural Religion,* published in 1779, three years after Hume's death. Demea speaks as one defending the orthodox Christian faith. I will then quote the speaker Cleanthes, who sets forth Hume's classical refutation, holding that the term "necessary" *cannot coherently be used to describe a being.*

Demea presents the argument for a necessary being as follows:

> The argument, replied Demea, which I would insist on is the common one. Whatever exists must have a cause or reason of its existence; it being absolutely impossible for any thing to produce itself, or be the cause of its own existence. In mounting up, therefore, from effects to causes, we must either go on in tracing an infinite succession, without any ultimate cause at all, or must at last have recourse to some ultimate cause, that is *necessarily* existent. . . .[1]

Demea then denies that an infinite succession of causes can provide a reason why the whole chain of causes is what it is or is at all, and concludes:

> We must therefore, have recourse to a necessarily existent Being, who carries the reason of his existence in himself; and who cannot be supposed not to exist without an express contradiction. There is consequently such a Being, that is, there is a Deity.[2]

Cleanthes then refutes Demea's argument as follows:

> Nothing is demonstrable, unless the contrary implies a contradiction. Nothing that is distinctly conceivable implies a contradiction. Whatever we conceive as existent, we can also conceive as non-existent. There is no Being, therefore, whose non-existence implies a contradiction. Consequently there

is no Being, whose existence is demonstrable. I propose this argument as entirely decisive, and am willing to rest the whole controversy upon it.[3]

In other words, Hume (through the speaker Cleanthes) argues that there is no being that we cannot conceive as not existing. It contradicts Hume's understanding of the definition of a necessary being to say that a "necessary" being does not exist. Under his definition a necessary being means a being that we cannot conceive of not existing without implying a contradiction. But the contradiction merely follows from his definition. Hume considers such a concept to be incoherent because we can conceive of the nonexistence of such a necessary being. He is "willing to rest" his whole refutation on this understanding of necessary being.

However, this is not the meaning of the term *necessary being* in the argument I am explaining concerning the existence of contingent, finite things or beings. In my argument the term *necessary* is not incoherent, because I mean a being without beginning or end and not dependent on anything. Such a being has its existence in and through itself and does not need anything else for its existence. For reasons given in this argument, such a being is required to explain even an infinite series of contingent beings or things.

This definition of necessary being *does not imply a contradiction.* We can conceive of the nonexistence of such a being without contradicting the definition of such a being. This definition is not intrinsically incoherent, i.e., this definition does not mean that such a being must exist. If such a being does exist, its existence is necessary (required) to explain the existence of contingent things or beings.

When one uses the term "necessary being" in this non-Humean sense, then the existence of contingent things, the existence of something rather than nothing, requires an explanation. This explanation cannot be an infinite series of things for many reasons. One reason is that the whole series of an infinite succession of contingent causes requires an explanation, and *this explanation cannot be made by reference to the contingent members of the series.* In other words, if the series is made up of only contingent members, none of these members can give an existential explanation for the existence of the whole series.

Up until the latter half of the twentieth century, Hume's argument was considered conclusive. But in the last decades philosophers have noted that Hume was using the term *necessary* to mean a "logical necessity." I am not using the term *necessary* to mean *logically* necessary but rather to mean something that has its existence in and through itself, without a beginning or an end and without any dependence on anything else. Hume's objection is valid only if the nonexistence of something necessary involved an internal contradiction.

In his book, *The Cosmological Argument: A Reassessment*, Bruce Reichenbach wrote a courageous and logically brilliant fresh analysis of the cosmological argument. In this work he distinguished between logical necessity and conditional necessity. Hume and Kant made the mistake of interpreting "necessary" to mean logically necessary. Reichenbach demonstrated quite clearly that the cosmological argument uses conditional necessity, not logical necessity. Conditional necessity follows from the premises and conditions of the argument, not from the supposition of logical necessity. A being exists necessarily because the concept of such a being is the result of valid deductions from these premises and conditions. This argument does not confine its rationale to the meaning of the terms contained within a definition. It is not an attempt to define a necessary being into existence. The conclusion of a necessary being is required in the sense that it is drawn from certain conditions and premises. Thus, in this argument, the necessity is a conditional, not a logical necessity. Once this distinction is made, no contradiction remains.[4]

Philosophers David Conway and John Haldane have correctly argued that Hume's objection fails when one defines a necessary being as a being with no beginning and no end, who is not dependent upon anything. As noted, under this definition of the term *necessary*, the thought of the nonexistence of such a being does not involve an internal contradiction.[5] When the term *necessary* is used in this way, philosophers who have understood the recent arguments realize that the term *necessary being* is not incoherent. Hume's objection then cannot stand.[6]

KANT FOLLOWED HUME'S ERROR SO THAT HIS OBJECTION TO THE COSMOLOGICAL ARGUMENT DOES NOT STAND.

Immanuel Kant asserted "that there is nothing of whose existence we may form an idea of whose non-existence we can equally form the idea without any internal incoherence being involved in our notion of that thing's non-existence."[7] However, as David Conway and others have pointed out, it does not follow from Kant's assertion that a notion of nonexistence is incoherent when combined with a contingent universe.[8] Kant thought that the cosmological argument was based on the ontological argument. In the ontological argument the *existence* of a necessary being is required by the *essence* of such a being. The ontological argument can be seen as a mere tautology: God is a necessary being, therefore God's essence requires God's existence.

Kant objected to the argument, because he held that categorical judgments (propositions) must contain a subject *and* a characterizing predicate. Kant's basic argument was expressed in the phrase "existence is not a predicate." In the statement, "Tiger Woods is a great golfer," the predicate "great golfer" characterizes the subject "Tiger Woods." In Kant's analysis it is a "real predicate." But, he argued, to attempt to prove that God exists because God's essence is existence assumes the question of the subject's (God's) existence in the predicate. In other words, for Kant, "existence" is not a characteristic (property) and, consequently, cannot be a real predicate.

But, as noted above, Kant (and Hume) considered the concept of "necessary" as one referring to a logical necessity. In their usage, the term *necessary* relates to "propositions" rather than "beings." Thus, they argued that a proposition may be logically necessary, but a "being" could not be. I am not using the term *necessary* as a relation between propositions (statements), but as a real predicate, i.e., something with characteristics or properties. In my usage I mean a necessary being with the following properties: independence, infinity, without beginning and without end.

These characteristics constitute a real predicate in Kant's language. They mean a necessary being that has an indefeasible existence, in, through, and from itself alone. Hume and Kant's objections do not stand against this characterizing meaning of the term *necessary*.

Hume and Kant's claims to have refuted all possible arguments for the existence of God have suffered severe setbacks by new insights in philosophy and in contemporary science. Kant assumed that the universe had an infinite past. As I shall discuss, a recent proof by physicists Arvind Borde, Alan Guth, and Alex Vilenkin indicates that any universe (or multiverse) "with a positive average expansion rate" had a beginning. Our universe has such an expansion rate. Kant was wrong in his assumption of an infinite past. The evidence indicates that the well-established theory of relativity requires that any universe with this positive average expansion rate had a beginning. One can no longer merely invoke the arguments of Hume and Kant as limits on the boundaries of our knowledge.[9]

A UNIVERSE WITH AN INFINITE PAST WOULD STILL REQUIRE A NECESSARY BEING TO SUSTAIN ITS EXISTENCE

A universe with a finite past is not a condition precedent to the requirement of a necessary being to act as the efficient cause of the continuing existence of the universe. The concept of creation may refer to *creatio ex nihilo*, but, more fundamentally, to *creatio continua*. As noted, we do not know what happened in the quantum universe prior to Planck time (10^{-43} of the first second of our universe's existence). The terms *before*, *prior*, or *pre* in relation to Planck time are nonsensical, because time begins at Planck time, which is time zero. Nevertheless, as I discuss below, the initial singularity of the Big Bang bears the earmarks of an *ex nihilo* coming to be. The Second Law of Thermodynamics indicates that the universe had a finite past, and recently, three physicists have provided evidence that the Second Law is correct, because any universe (or multiverse) with an average positive expansion rate, to avoid a contradiction with the well-established theory of relativity, had to have a beginning. I will discuss this in more detail in chapter 5, but for now I want to note that a universe with an infinite past would still not defeat the argument under consideration.

The universe and all that exists depends now and always on the sustaining will of a necessary being. This includes the laws of physics themselves and whatever laws, if any, functioned in the quantum cosmos "pre" Planck time. Stephen Hawking asked: "Where do the laws of physics come from? What is it that breathed the fire into the equations and made a universe for us to describe?"[1] The fundamental question with which we began our inquiry is most relevant: Why is there something rather than nothing? The remote possibility of the universe not having a beginning is not dispositive of the question. Don Page, one of Stephen Hawking's collaborators, understands this issue well and uses the example of an artist's drawing of a circle to illustrate that the absence of a beginning or an end does not remove the artist as the cause of the circle.

One could hypothesize that the laws of physics are necessary, existing from infinity, but they are not good candidates for a necessary thing that has its existence in, through, and from itself. We know that all laws of physics break down at Planck time. There are no particles and no time in which the laws could act in any classical understanding. As affirmed above in physicist John Wheeler's conclusions, the idea that the laws of nature could be a necessary thing becomes implausible when one notices their insufficient and incomplete character. Cambridge physicist John Polkinghorne notes the theological implications of such conclusions:

> What has given rise to the revival of natural theology is the insight that the laws of nature possess certain characteristics that have resulted in their being seen not to be sufficiently intellectually satisfying and complete in themselves alone. Instead, their form raises questions going beyond science's power to answer, so that they are felt to point beyond science to the need for a deeper and more comprehensive understanding. This feeling is induced by two insistent metaquestions to which we now turn: "Why is the physical world so intelligible to us?" and "Why are its laws so finely tuned to the possibility of a fruitful history?" Putting it more briefly, "Why is science possible?" and "Why is the universe so special?"[2]

One of the most interesting aspects of discoveries concerning physical laws is that the discoveries move in the direction of deeper, more profound, and more beautiful explanations. For example, a physicist may discover a law that controls the movement of certain particles and their interaction with other particles. This law may be expressed in terms of a mathematical formula. Subsequently, another physicist may discover that this formula in turn is the result of a more fundamental and more beautiful rule of physics. Later, a third physicist may discover that this new rule is the result of a deeper set of laws that have an even more beautiful and elegant mathematical structure. Mathematical beauty and elegance seem to point in the direction of more profound and deeper truths. In considering a certain manifestation of order in the universe, scientific explanations account for that order by discovering more underlying order.[3] This deepening intelligibility is described by Professor Thomas F. Torrance:

> . . . the more deeply scientific inquiry penetrates down to the rock-bottom structures of nature, such as *quarks*, which are not self-explainable, the more it seems to be putting its finger upon the very edge between being and nothing, existence and creation, establishing contact with a state of affairs and intelligibility which calls for a sufficient reason beyond itself. That is to say, quantum theory has the effect of forcing out into the open the contingent nature of physical reality in such a way as to make a genuine doctrine of creation pertinent in its own field.[4]

We do not know the deepest physical laws. But we know that these laws will reveal even greater order, beauty, and symmetry. When the ultimate, fundamental mathematical physical laws are finally known in all of their profound beauty, symmetry, and order, one can no longer appeal to a deeper scientific explanation. At that time, the questions will be: Why do these laws exist? Where did they come from? And why are they here?

Physicists are now in search of a *Theory of Everything* (TOE) which will unify diverse areas of knowledge about the physical world.[5] *But TOE will only be an equation.* It will not explain why there is any physical thing. One may have an equation (recipe) for a cake, but where do the physical ingredients to make the cake come from? This is a question that deeply disturbs Stephen Hawking. A physical theory could only achieve a self-consistency; it cannot have a self-sufficiency. An equation will not answer why there are things that work in a particular way. Hawking realizes that even if a TOE is developed, it would only be a set of rules or a formula. It will not answer why there is a physical something.

The question of whether the universe had a beginning may not be the most fundamental question concerning its existence even though powerful proofs indicate that it had a beginning. A more basic question is Why does the universe exist? Why is there something rather than nothing, and why is that something intelligible? Why is the universe inherently mathematical? Why does that something have such a remarkable set of laws that allow for the existence of life and consciousness? Where did these laws come from?

It is not rationally sufficient to shrug one's shoulders and simply say that the laws just are the way they are for no intelligent reason. If one is to be rational, one must push on with the inquiry and ask for an explanation for their existence. Physicist Paul Davies understands the irrational nature of the claim that they exist in their present form for no reason:

> The most refined expression of the rational intelligibility of the cosmos is found in the laws of physics, the fundamental rules on which nature runs. The laws of gravitation and electromagnetism, the laws that regulate the world within the atom, the laws of motion—all are expressed as tidy mathematical relationships. But where do these laws come from? And why do they have the form that they do? . . . Over the years I have often asked my physicist colleagues why the laws of physics are what they are. The answers vary from "that's not a scientific question" to "nobody knows." The favorite reply is, "There is no reason they are what they are—they just are." The idea that the laws exist reasonlessly is deeply anti-rational. After all, the very essence of a scientific explanation of some phenomenon is that the world is ordered logically and that there are reasons things are as they are. If one traces these reasons all the way down to the bedrock of reality—the laws of physics—only to find that reason then deserts us, it makes a mockery of science.[6]

When one reflects that the laws of physics, the most basic laws of our universe, are orderly mathematical interrelations that are not self-explanatory, one borders on superstition if one merely accepts their existence as a brute fact. Their inherent mathematical nature cries out for an explanation. Why fail to address the reason for their existence? Why stop one's thinking at the laws of physics? These laws appear to be only contingent components of the universe. In examining the contingent characteristics of the laws of physics as they fail to apply in singularities (e.g., black holes), as noted above, John Wheeler (who coined the term "black hole") concluded that "the laws of physics that we regard as 'sacred,' as immutable, are anything but."

BECAUSE THE UNIVERSE (OR MULTIVERSE) HAD A BEGINNING, IT IS CONTINGENT AND HAS A CAUSE FOR ITS COMING INTO EXISTENCE

Having concluded (1) that the laws of physics are not sufficient candidates for a necessary being (an independent being that has its indefeasible existence completely in, through, and from itself) and (2) that a necessary being is a rational explanation for a required preservative cause of the continuing existence of the universe, I turn to the question whether the universe had a beginning and came into existence out of nothing. If the universe had a beginning out of nothing, it had a cause of its coming to be. Moreover, because a creation out of nothing is not within the power of natural causes, one can rationally conclude that, if the universe began to exist, it had a supernatural cause. There are some relatively recent discoveries and proofs that strongly indicate that the universe had a beginning.

IF THE UNIVERSE HAD A BEGINNING, IT HAS A CAUSE OF ITS COMING INTO EXISTENCE.

In 1929 Edwin Hubble, a lawyer turned astronomer, working at the Mount Wilson Observatory in Pasadena, California, discovered that the universe was expanding. Using the observatory's 100-inch telescope, Hubble observed that the galaxies are expanding away from one another at a velocity directly proportional to their distances apart. The galaxies close to one another do not actually expand due to gravitational forces between them, but the space between these galactic clusters expands. The universe's expansion is actually the expansion of space itself (a concept that Hubble never really understood). An expanding universe implies that the universe was previously smaller. If the rate of expansion were reversed, all of the matter in the universe would be compressed to an infinitely dense singular point smaller than a proton. The Big Bang emerged from such a singularity, in which the space-time fabric is subject to an infinite curvature and does not exist in any terms that can be described by the known laws of physics.

As mentioned above, the radically contingent nature of the universe (cosmos) follows from its merely possible existence. Its contingent nature also follows from the finite past of the universe. This concept brings us to the *kalam* cosmological argument that adds further weight to the modified argument of Adler described previously. It adds support for that argument by pointing to an initial cause transcending finite reality. The principal proponent of this argument in recent years has been William Lane Craig. His detailed analysis of the argument in light of contemporary scientific discoveries has modified and strengthened the argument so significantly that perhaps it should now be referred to as the *Craig* cosmological argument. For an example of his thinking see *Theism, Atheism, and Big Bang Cosmology*, written with Quentin Smith.[1]

The essence of his argument is as follows:

1. Anything that begins to exist has a cause of its existence.
2. The universe began to exist.
3. Therefore, the universe has a cause of its existence.

Craig begins his defense of the argument by addressing the initial singularity. In emphasizing the *ex nihilo* origin of the universe out of an absolute nothingness, Craig argues that the universe has a finite past. He quotes John Barrow and Frank Tipler[2] to emphasize that not only did energy and matter come into being in the initial singularity but also space and time themselves. There is no "earlier" space-time. This appears to be about as close to a beginning out of nothing as any of our physical reasoning has ever encountered.

In *A Case Against Accident and Self-Organization*, I wrote a section entitled "The curtain at Planck time" (Section 5.3.21, pp. 152–54). In that section I noted that we cannot move our observations of the universe backwards in time beyond Planck time or 10^{-43} of the first second after the Big Bang. Before Planck time the universe would still be smaller than a proton, the temperature would be 10^{32} degrees Kelvin (10 trillion trillion times hotter than the center of our sun), and the particles of quantum physics could not have existed. As indicated previously, technically, we cannot even use the terms *before*, *prior*, or *pre* in relation to Planck time because time begins at Planck time, which is time zero. We simply cannot look behind the curtain and tell whether this universe was pinched off from some other universe or a "blister" on some other preexisting space or precisely what was going on.[3] However, this may not matter for Craig's argument, given recent developments in science.

Craig's persistence in affirming his argument has received some confirmation in a relatively new physical proof. It is my understanding that Craig is about to publish a work with physicist James Sinclair calling our attention to a proof by physcists Arvind Borde, Alan Guth, and Alexander Vilenkin that implies that any universe (or multiverse) "with a positive average expansion rate" has a cosmic beginning. In other words, under Craig's argument, the universe began to exist, and consequently, needs a nonphysical cause to explain its existence (nonphysical because in this argument the term *universe* includes all physical matter/energy).

In their published paper in the April 2003 *Physical Review Letters*, entitled "Inflationary Spacetimes Are Incomplete in Past Directions," these physicists proved that an infinitely old universe is not consistent with Einstein's well-established theory of relativity.[4] Their proof has profound implications because it applies in all instances irrespective of the state of the universe "pre" Planck time. Even if our universe is only a blister on a larger universe, according to their proof, the fact that we have an average expansion rate means that our universe or multiverse has a finite past. It has a beginning and requires a nonphysical cause of its coming to be. In other words, if everything that exists must have a cause, our universe requires a nonnatural or a supernatural cause.

As I noted above, we do not know exactly what happened in the quantum universe "prior" to Planck time, but the Borde Guth Vilenkin proof ("BGV proof") applies to any kind of universe with an average expansion rate, *even if we cannot give a physical description of such a universe "before" Planck time.* We know that our universe (or multiverse) has a positive average expansion rate. Although he is not fond of the theological implications of his work, Vilenkin demonstrates (1) that "a past-eternal inflation without a beginning is impossible," and (2) that a cyclic universe with alternating contractions and expansions cannot escape the BGV proof (because even a cyclic universe would be expanding on average).

Vilenkin has given a useful illustration of the BGV proof, which I will try to describe in a simple summary. I recommend reading his recent book, *Many Worlds in One*, and particularly the chapter entitled, "Did the Universe Have a Beginning?" Because an expanding universe involves the expansion of space itself, one could conceive of the expansion by picturing a balloon with stars drawn on it increasing in size. As the balloon inflated the stars would move further apart. Another helpful image is that of a loaf of bread full of raisins. As the loaf is baked, the bread expands and the raisins move further apart.

Now to follow Vilenkin's illustration of the BGV proof, assume an expanding universe with trillions of observers ("Watchers") scattered like dust throughout the entire space-time of the universe (or multiverse). These Watchers are in motion filming everything they see with sophisticated video cameras that record time and the velocity of passing objects. As the universe expands, these Watchers observe that they move away from each other. Also assume that Elton John's Rocket Man has been traveling through the universe for eternity wearing a completely accurate wristwatch that never needs a battery or any winding to function. Assume also that his rocket engines are not on, because he is traveling by inertia. As he passes a Watcher, the Watcher records Rocket Man's velocity on film. Because the universe is expanding, the Watchers observe that they are moving away from each other as noted. As Rocket Man travels past each Watcher, his velocity relative to each Watcher will be less than his velocity relative to the previous Watcher's measurement of his velocity. But this means that if Rocket Man's velocity decreases as he moves into the future, his velocity should be greater and greater when we compare the previous Watchers' measurements of his velocity. If we follow his history into the past, as his velocity increases he will approach the speed of light.

As we follow Rocket Man into the past and approach infinity, the time measurement he makes on his wristwatch would still be finite. According to the theory of relativity, however, as Rocket Man's velocity increases toward the speed of light, his wristwatch stops from the Watcher's perspective. They thus see Rocket Man "stuck" for eternity in time.

This solves the problem of the "infinite past" for the Watchers, but not for Rocket Man. Like the watches in the old Timex commercials, his watch "keeps on ticking." The theory of relativity thus leads to a contradiction: The Watchers observe that Rocket Man is "frozen in time," but he begs to differ. His wristwatch has been recording a finite amount of time for his voyage, which does not make sense if he has really been traveling from "eternity past." In other words, we cannot give a noncontradictory explanation to the Watchers why Rocket Man's history, as measured by his wristwatch, is finite.

Vilenkin points out that the implication of a beginning to the universe (or multiverse) is unavoidable. He wants to see this simply as an unexplainable logical paradox and not as evidence for the existence of God. This is a purely metaphysical choice on his part; it does not follow from his own proof. What follows is a confirmation of Craig's argument. If the universe had a beginning, it had a cause of its coming to be. Vilenkin dismisses the concepts of a past eternal inflation of the universe or the idea of a cyclic contracting and expanding universe and confirms that there is no escape from a cosmic beginning: "It is said that an argument is what convinces reasonable men and a proof is what it takes to convince even an unreasonable man. With the proof now in place, cosmologists can no longer hide behind the possibility of a past eternal universe. *There is no escape: they have to face the problem of a cosmic beginning.*"[5]

This corroborates Craig's argument and indicates that an expanding universe or multiverse requires a space-time boundary. Even given the pre-Planck time cloud of quantum uncertainty, the cosmos requires a beginning. Craig's argument has taken on more force as science continues to confirm his explanation of this branch of the cosmological family of arguments.

I turn now to a discussion of the Second Law of Thermodynamics, which also provides evidence for time's arrow and the proposition that the universe had a beginning.

THE SECOND LAW OF THERMODYNAMICS REQUIRES THAT DISORDER IN THE UNIVERSE TENDS TOWARD A MAXIMUM; THE UNIVERSE COULD NOT BE DISSIPATING FROM INFINITY OR IT WOULD HAVE RUN DOWN BY NOW; CONSEQUENTLY,

THE UNIVERSE APPEARS TO HAVE HAD A BEGINNING THAT HAD TO BE HIGHLY ORDERED.

Thermodynamics is the study of the interrelation between heat and other forms of energy. The First Law of Thermodynamics states that energy and matter can neither be created nor destroyed. The Second Law of Thermodynamics requires that entropy or disorder in the universe tends toward a maximum. The contents of the universe are becoming less ordered, and as the universe becomes more disorganized, less of its energy is available to perform work. Because the universe is running down, it must have had a beginning. The universe could not be dissipating from infinity, or it would have run down by now. In light of the observed process of dissipation, the Second Law of Thermodynamics requires a beginning, and a very highly ordered beginning (one with low entropy).

Oxford mathematician Roger Penrose calculates that, given the present ordered nature of our universe, the accuracy necessary to begin the universe in the highly ordered state in which it must have begun would be a remarkable 1 part in $10^{10^{123}}$. This is an enormously large number, possibly the largest you have ever seen. If one were to write a zero on every proton, electron, and neutron in every atom in the known universe, there would still not be enough matter to even write the number down using the ordinary denotation of zeros.[6]

ONE COULD HYPOTHESIZE THAT THE UNIVERSE CAME ABOUT THROUGH A SERIES OF ENDLESS PAST CONTINGENT EVENTS THAT STRETCH BACKWARD THROUGH INFINITY, BUT SUCH A SERIES MAY NOT BE POSSIBLE IN REALITY, AND THE CAUSAL EXPLANATIONS OF EACH PART OF SUCH AN ENDLESS SERIES CANNOT BE A CAUSAL EXPLANATION OF THE WHOLE SERIES.

One might propose that the universe did not have a beginning but that the reason for its existence is an actual infinite number of past events. From Aquinas to W. L. Craig, there is a long history of philosophers who question the possible actual instantiation of such a series of past events. If one adds or subtracts any number from infinity, one still is left with infinity. Craig is particularly persuasive in his descriptions and illustrations.[7] An actual infinite has no room for growth. One cannot count an infinite series of events no matter how long he or she counts, because one will always be at some specific number that could be increased by simply adding another number. One cannot count an actual infinite series of past events. It would be like attempting to leap out of a bottomless pit.

This raises the interesting problem of how we ever arrived at the present moment. This problem becomes apparent when we realize that one attempting to move forward from the past can never really get started in an attempt to progress forward to the present. The reason is that to arrive at any particular point in time in a series of infinite events, one must already have counted an infinite number of events to get to that point. In essence, one attempting to move forward in the past could never begin counting forward to arrive at the present moment.

To understand this concept, think of the future as a series of infinite events. Let's start counting 1, 2, 3, . . . ten trillion, . . . a trillion trillion . . . . We will never be able to stop counting, because we can never count an infinity of future events.

Now think of the past as an infinite series of events. So we start counting past events going backwards. Again, we realize that we will never be able to stop counting to reach infinity backwards because, as in the case of an infinite series of future events, we can always add an additional event. Now realize that an infinite series of past events never allows us to start counting forward to get to the present moment. We always have another past event to add before we can begin counting forward. We will never be able to start counting forward.

Think of attempting to move forward by walking "up" an endless, extremely fast, "down" escalator. We can't even begin to move forward. We cannot get started because there is always another step preventing us from taking a step forward. If we think of the steps as "events," an infinity of steps moving backwards never allows us to start. So how do we get to the present moment? Yet we know that the present moment exists and that past events have occurred. But if there were an infinite number of past events, we also know that we could never start moving forward to get to the present moment. We always have another past event being added to the number of past events to prevent our moving forward and arriving at the present. *But we are at the present*, and we know that there have been at least some past events. The only apparent solution is that past events may not stretch into infinity. They may have had a beginning.[8]

Mathematicians may argue that toward the end of the nineteenth century Georg Cantor came up with a logically consistent theory of the actual infinite by beginning with a unique representation of a function as a trigonometric series. Although in theory his construction was logically consistent, very few philosophers and mathematicians believe in an actual infinite regression of events instantiated in reality. The concept of an infinite past with a beginningless series of past events existing through an infinite amount of "time" until the present moment presents serious practical problems.

Assume that you discover a golf pro shop that sells only Titleist and Pinnacle golf balls. But this is not so limited if you also discover that the shop has an actual *infinite* number of Titleist golf balls and an *infinite* number of Pinnacle golf balls. For every Titleist golf ball there is a Pinnacle golf ball; and for every Pinnacle golf ball there is a Titleist golf ball. Consequently, the pro shop contains as many Titleist golf balls as the entire number of golf balls available for sale. However, the pro shop must also contain as many Pinnacle golf balls as Titleist golf balls. *And* the number of Titleist balls must equal the combined number of Pinnacle and Titleist golf balls. However, this is an absurd concept. How can the number of Titleists equal the number of Titleists and Pinnacles *combined* when there are an infinite number of Pinnacles? Although one may conceive of an actual infinite, any attempted actual instantiation appears to be absurd.

As discussed above, we have good evidence that time/space in this universe began at Planck time of the initial singularity. We cannot look backward "before" Planck time so we do not know the cause of the singularity, but we know that because of the infinite density and the absence of any physical reality of space/time it is unlikely that any physical thing could go through that singularity into this universe. In other words, it is unlikely that another preexisting space could be the cause of the beginning of space and time at the Planck time of our universe.

The impossibility of an actual infinite series of past events and the Second Law of Thermodynamics indicate that there was a beginning, and the Big Bang appears to be consistent with such a beginning. If the universe had a beginning, it needs a cause of its beginning to exist, because nothing comes from nothing. If the universe and matter began to exist, it had a cause of its coming to be. There are very plausible reasons to think that the universe had a beginning. Consequently, in addition to a necessary cause for its continuing existence, the universe may also need a cause of its becoming.

Moreover, as noted above, with respect to an endless series of contingent things or beings, David Conway noted that Hume's objection fails to explain the existence of the whole series of contingent things: . . . "the causal explanations of the parts of any such whole in terms of other parts cannot add up to a causal explanation of the whole, if the items mentioned as causes are items whose own existence stands in need of a causal explanation."[9] For example, a computer software virus that has the capacity to replicate itself throughout the World Wide Web could appear on all of the world's computers. But the fact that it then exists throughout the entire Web connection of computers does not explain the existence of such a virus.

A QUANTUM FLUCTUATION DOES NOT RESULT FROM TRUE NOTHINGNESS.

As discussed briefly above, some scholars speculate that the universe began as a quantum fluctuation in a quantum vacuum. But a quantum vacuum is not nothing. The speculation only moves the question of the explanation for the universe's existence back to another similar question for the source of the necessary conditions for a quantum vacuum. As Oxford philosopher Keith Ward writes: "On the quantum fluctuation hypothesis, the universe will only come into being if there exists an exactly balanced array of fundamental forces, an exactly specified probability of particular fluctuations occurring in this array, and an existent space-time in which fluctuations can occur. This is a very complex and finely tuned nothing!"[10]

Quantum cosmologists have much to explain: Quantum fluctuations need a context of space and time, a perfectly balanced zero net energy from a matching negative gravitational energy and a positive kinetic and rest mass energy, a quantum field with certain characteristics of mass and energy, and the laws of quantum mechanics that dictate precise probabilities to fluctuations in this background.[11]

To be rational the atheist must show how something comes from nothing. Otherwise, the existence of something is not explained, unless that existence is a necessary existence, independent of anything else. One has to have a starting point, and if an atheist is not going to beg the question why her starting point exists, she must begin from *really* nothing—what Francis Schaeffer called *nothing-nothing*. This means no laws, no quantum fields, no wave functions, no observers, no energy, no particles, and no motion. All proposals of something coming from nothing actually start with the assumption of something. An atheist's definition of "nothing" always starts with "something" (either a vacuum, a field, energy, matter, potentials, etc.).

6

THE PHILOSOPHY OF NATURE SET FORTH IN THIS BOOK EMPHASIZES THE INTELLIGIBILITY OF THE UNIVERSE NOTED IN EINSTEIN'S STATEMENT: "THE MOST INCOMPREHENSIBLE THING ABOUT THE WORLD IS THAT IT IS COMPREHENSIBLE." A SIGNIFICANT ISSUE IN EXAMINING THE "SOMETHING" THAT EXISTS IS WHY IS IT INTELLIGIBLE?

A central aspect of my cumulative argument is founded on the essential intelligibility of the physical universe and the laws operating within the universe. My aim is to complement what we know from science rather than to present a view that is antagonistic to science. Science and theistic belief are not only compatible but also science gives supportive evidence to many aspects of faith. In order to conduct science one must believe in the intelligibility of the laws of nature. Nature proceeds in accordance with laws that can be described by abstract mathematical principles. We did not invent these laws, but, amazingly, we find that abstract mathematics allows us to discover their existence.

Science presents a question concerning the reason for this intelligibility, which by definition appears to be outside the capacity of science to address. This intelligibility and rationality also avoids the objections made by

David Hume because it does not assert an analogy between God's creativity and the visible manufacture of a human artifact, such as a watch. Hume objected to the anthropomorphic nature of an argument that contained any analogy whereby a human construction was compared to the creative act of God. The arguments contained herein do not employ such an analogy but emphasize the inherent rationality, intelligibility, and order in the universe with particular attention given to the phenomena of abstract mathematical concepts accurately describing physical reality. For example, Einstein took the concept of an abstract mathematical idea, the curvature of space-time, and matched it with the structure of the physical universe. His work indicates that the universe is *inherently* mathematical. We need to ask why, in the most effective scientific theories; we do not create but rather *discover* the mathematics that is already present in nature. As John Polkinghorne comments: "Some have suggested that humans happen to have a taste for mathematics and so they mould their accounts of physics into forms that gratify this preference. Previous discussions of the difficulty of theoretical discovery, and the way in which the universe resists our prior expectation encourage the contrary realist view that these beautiful mathematical patterns are read out of, and not read into, the structure of the world."[1]

THE UNREASONABLE EFFECTIVENESS OF ABSTRACT MATHEMATICS IN DESCRIBING THE PHYSICAL WORLD IS AN EXAMPLE OF INTELLIGIBILITY THAT REQUIRES AN EXPLANATION.

Why are the physical laws mathematical? And why does abstract mathematics work so effectively in explaining the physical world? To our amazement we find the universe to be mathematical. And, as I emphasized, not just mathematical in the sense that we can impose some mathematical equations on what we see, but inherently mathematical; mathematical, whether we see it or not. Hence, we discover the mathematics that is already present in nature prior to our quantitative study. One should be struck by the mathematical character of inanimate matter and be amazed that the universe is intelligible in the sense that scientists can follow a rational scheme in developing our understanding of the physical universe. The universe did not have to be this way. It could have been a chaos without a rational form. Paul Davies also dismisses the argument that the brain imposes mathematical order that does not actually exist in the real physical world; abstract mathematics is too accurate in practical, physical applications not to reflect the real nature of the physical world.[2] He writes: "The fact that 'mathematics works' when applied to the physical world—and works so stunningly well—*demands* explanation, for it is not clear we have any absolute right to expect that the world should be well described by our mathematics."

The quantum world is something we cannot see at all, but it is intelligible to us through the use of mathematics. Our ability to understand the quantum world exceeds anything that could be required for the purposes of our survival. How can we explain the astounding agreement between abstract mathematics and the laws of the physical world? Abstract mathematics has predicted counterintuitive phenomena to a remarkable precision. For example, the agreement between the counterintuitive theory of general relativity and the physical world has been confirmed by experience to more than one-trillionth of a percent. Precision to this degree cannot be explained by chance alone.

Before Einstein performed his calculations, the observed universe was explained by Newtonian physics with its Euclidean geometry and mysterious gravitational force. These concepts were derived from man's observance of the world around him. Thus, the image of Newton discovering the law of gravity by watching an apple fall to earth seemed perfectly reasonable from our observance of the action of the gravitational force on falling objects. When the apple left the branch of the tree, one reasoned that it fell to the earth because of the earth's gravitational attractive force. Space was flat, and the curved orbits of the planets moved under the influence of the attractive force of gravity. There was nothing useful for survival that required any radically different thought processes. Newtonian physics worked in the world we experienced. Einstein, however, was able to discover, not create, a theory that improved on Newton's physics. Roger Penrose emphasizes that Einstein discovered the existence of a precise mathematical framework inherent in the structure of space and time: "Einstein was not just 'noticing patterns' in the behavior of physical objects. He was uncovering a profound mathematical substructure that was already hidden in the very workings of the world."[3]

How is one to explain the exceptional performance of abstract mathematical functions in reflecting the real structure of the physical universe? Abstract mathematics, like musical ability, has little survival value. What explains the "unreasonable effectiveness" of abstract mathematics matching the physical universe?[4]

THE RELATIONSHIP OF MATHEMATICAL TRUTH AND BEAUTY ENHANCES THE DRAMATIC INTELLIGIBILITY OF THE UNIVERSE.

The unreasonable effectiveness of mathematics in describing our universe is even more remarkable when one considers the relationship of beauty to the inherent mathematical nature of the universe. Physics Nobel laureates Paul Dirac and Richard Feynman were convinced that mathematical truth can be recognized by its beauty. Beauty points toward truth. Dirac was more concerned with the beauty in an equation than whether the equation matched an empirical experiment because he had discovered that beauty was a more accurate indicator of truth. He credited his sense of beauty with allowing him to find the equation for the electron, that, coupled with Maxwell's equations, forms the basic foundation for the very successful quantum field theory of quantum electrodynamics. Almost every contemporary physicist knows that beauty is the fundamental indicator of truth in his or her analysis.[5]

Oxford mathematician Roger Penrose also emphasizes that aesthetic criteria, not only in visual appearance but also in inherent mathematical qualities, are extremely important in his discovering truth. He notes that a beautiful concept has a greater likelihood of being true than an ugly one. An ugly idea lacks unity, proportion, and wholeness and misleads a mathematician in his or her search for truth. In this sense, something repulsive, in a negative way, confirms the idea that beauty indicates truth. Penrose finds a sense of beauty to be an indispensable means of discovering truth. He comments on his use of aesthetic criteria in his work: "It seems clear to me that the importance of aesthetic criteria applies not only to the instantaneous judgements of inspiration, but also to the much more frequent judgments that we make all the time in mathematical (or scientific) work."[6]

To Penrose the Platonic world of perfect mathematical forms (and other forms) is primary, whereas our physical world is only a shadow of its existence. This other world is the source of the inherent mathematical structure of our physical environment, and it is more real that our known world. Beyond mathematics, this other world is more perfect and more real and includes more ideal and perfect ethics and beauty. In some ways, the world he describes sounds like the Judeo-Christian concept of heaven and perfection. Based on his experience in mathematics, he argues for the existence of a more real world than our physical world with perfect mathematical absolutes, beauty, and good. His thinking raises the question of whether our physical and mental worlds are not ultimate reality, but only shadows of what lies beyond them.[7]

Closely related to beauty as an integral part of mathematical truth, the classical idea of the beautiful relates to radiance, unity, proportion, wholeness, and harmony. For example, beautiful classical music appears to have an inherently mathematical nature. In contrast to dissonance, unity, harmony, and proportion are the foundation for the beauty of classical music. Form is perhaps the first classical requirement. The beauty of form is not only the perception of it but also appears to be inherent, radiating out from the form's interior. Thomas Dubay discusses this quality in the performance of classical music:

> A performance of classical music is a melodic unity whose harmonies are in exquisite proportion—which are two reasons why it is beautiful (unity and proportion). Coming from the Greek, *sym-phony* means "sounding together." The instruments of an orchestra sound together not simply through simultaneous noises with all their differences of qualities and notes and regular patterns, but only when a composing mind bestows on them a melodic unity, a radiant form. . . . Beethoven's inability to hear the very music he was composing vividly underlines what is true of any beautiful form: it must preexist in a mind before it can be concretized in reality. Thousands upon thousands of notes in all their fine precisions and varied interrelationships must somehow have a mental existence before they can be placed on paper and be heard thrilling an appreciative audience.[8]

Consistent with Penrose's idea that a more perfect and more real world has a more profound and more beautiful reality, the beauty of music seems to come from a more sublime reality. As Cardinal John Henry Newman claimed, "Mysterious stirrings of heart, and keen emotions, and strange yearning after we know not what, and awful impressions from we know not whence . . . have escaped from some higher sphere; they are the outpouring of eternal harmony in the medium of created sound; they are echoes from our Home."[9]

Perhaps beauty is more objective than we acknowledge; it is not merely in the eye of the beholder. Beautiful music, fine art, and nature itself have splendor in themselves and not because of the learned opinion of persons. In a recent study Dr. Alan Slater, a developmental psychologist at the University of Exeter, demonstrated that newborn babies who were less than one week old had an inherent trait that attracted them to prefer beautiful people. Our concept of beauty appears to be largely inborn and not learned. The infants were shown photographs of a selection of faces taken of attractive persons, interspersed with photographs of pictures of persons whom office workers judged to be unattractive. Almost all of the babies preferred to look at the attractive faces. On average, they spent a remarkable 80 percent of their time staring at the attractive faces. "Attractiveness is not simply in the eye of the beholder," Dr. Slater maintains. He continues, "It is in the brain of the newborn infant right from the moment of birth." Dr. Slater presented his findings in the autumn of 2004 to the British Association for the Advancement of Science. Beauty appears to have an inherent objective standard. It is not as subjective as one may like to think. This may appear to be unfair in some respects, but beauty is not confined to the physical. Many persons think beautiful thoughts, produce beautiful music, form beautiful equations, and write beautiful literature.

There appears to be an objective aspect of beauty that lies beyond formal human constructs. Great artists commonly feel that their best work reveals eternal truths that have some kind of prior real existence. Great works of art have an inner splendor that, like the universe itself, fills us with wonder and delight. These works contain a quality from their inner elements that is inherent in the beauty of the form and radiates out from its interior. Beauty manifests itself in the external aspect of the art but also transcends the external and flows from the interior depth of the art.

We are bathed in beauty in this world from so many different perspectives and manifestations. Our universe is wondrously and beautifully elegant. As I have repeatedly stated, it did not have to be this way; it could have been a displeasing chaos, completely unintelligible. It could have been a chaos in which there is no ability to comprehend its order and no ability to do science or mathematics. You and I behold a universe that is like a great work of art made with love. What is the source of this beauty? David Hume ignored the beauty of the universe and its intimation of what might exist outside the boundaries of space and time. Yet, as Plato noticed, beauty is suggestive of another reality, a more real and even more beautiful reality.

Hans Urs von Balthasar was one philosopher/theologian who attempted to examine some of the deep reaches of beauty. He was a Swiss Catholic priest with a doctorate in German literature. He served as chaplain at the University of Basel. After he married a medical doctor who had a mystical orientation, von Balthasar left the priesthood and began to write a theological trilogy concerned with the transcendental aspects of beauty, goodness, and truth. He wrote in these three areas consciously in opposition to Kant's three critiques of pure reason, practical reason, and judgment. For von Balthasar the call of God is expressed in beauty. When one encounters the divine in the beautiful, one's response is to turn away from a focus on one's self and live out the relationship with the Beautiful in a committed action. Reason alone does not produce such a response; it is elicited by a revelation of the Beautiful.

One cannot dismiss von Balthasar's writing under a purely scientific analysis. Our survival does not appear to be related to the beauty of the Earth or of the universe. We do not have to have beauty in our environment for us to survive—at least not all of the beauty. When one sees the snow-covered Swiss Alps, a beautiful river valley, lakes, oceans, or a colorful sunset, one may realize that it could have been otherwise.[10]

THE RATIONALITY, ORDER, AND FINE-TUNING IN THE UNIVERSE ARE CONSISTENT WITH THE ASTONISHING INTELLIGIBILITY OF THE PHYSICAL WORLD.

Closely related to Leibniz's question is the issue of explaining the fine-tuning in the universe that allows for the development of a life so conscious that it is aware of the universe, can think about the issues of its own development, and, indeed, think about thinking itself. Our initial question becomes more deep and profound when we ask not only why there is something rather than nothing but also ask why this something is so apparently fine-tuned to allow for conscious beings who think about Leibniz's question. Why does this something contain features at its most basic level (the level of physics) that are exactly what is required for the existence of conscious life in the universe? If these features were any different, life could never have formed and conscious beings such as you and me would not be here to wonder about such issues.

Contemporary physics has discovered that the physical universe burst into being with structural values precisely fine-tuned in numerous ways to accommodate the formation of life. At the very outset of the Big Bang, the mass of the elementary particles, the strength of the four forces, and the values of the fundamental constants were very precise. Imagine that you are selecting the values for these natural quantities by twiddling a vast number of knobs. You would find that almost all knob settings would render the universe uninhabitable. All these many knobs would have to be fine-tuned to enormous precision if life is to flourish in the universe.

In fact, our universe is so remarkably fine-tuned to allow for the origination of life that one may think of it as a finely sharpened pencil standing vertically on its graphite point in a precarious balance. Any deviation in a myriad of physical values would cause the pencil to tilt, fall, and preclude the formation of life. The fine-tuning is exactly what is required not just for one reason but for two or three or five reasons. Accidental processes could not plausibly tune these fundamental astrophysical values first one way and then another to satisfy conflicting requirements for the development of life.

There are many examples of this extraordinary fine-tuning, but consider only a few.

Fine-tuning appears in the formation of carbon.

Life would be impossible without carbon, and yet because of the precise requirements for its existence, the carbon atom should be very scarce. The formation of a carbon atom requires a rare triple collision known as the triple alpha process. The first step in the triple alpha process occurs when a helium nucleus collides with another helium nucleus within a star. This collision produces an unstable, very ephemeral isotope of beryllium. When the unstable, short-lived beryllium collides with a third helium nucleus, a carbon nucleus is formed. The triple alpha process works basically as follows: In the initial stage of the Big Bang, atomic nuclei of four particles, two protons and two neutrons, were forged to form helium 4. These particles are known as alpha particles and have a strong affinity for each other. They reject the addition of a fifth particle and will not form stable nuclei with five to eight particles; they will naturally remain with only 4 nuclei. This is true even when in the interior of a star a helium 4 nucleus collides with another helium 4 nucleus. The two helium 4 nuclei will collide into each other but not remain together, except for an extremely short period of time equal to about a hundred-millionth of a billionth of a second. During that very short time period if a third helium 4 nucleus collides with this short-lived combination of two helium 4 nuclei, a stable nucleus will form as the chemical element carbon 12. The existence of carbon 12 allows for other heavier elements to begin to form.

Stephen Barr points out that physicists were puzzled by the abundance of carbon in nature when its existence should be very rare, given the extraordinary triple alpha process and the brief time interval of a hundred-millionth of a billionth of a second for the process to take place. How could nature contain so much carbon with such a rare triple collision required for its formation?

Astrophysicist Sir Fred Hoyle provided the solution to the puzzle and predicted the resonances (or energy levels) of the carbon and oxygen atoms. The resonance of the carbon nucleus is precisely the right resonance to enable the components to hold together rather than disperse. This resonance perfectly matches the combined resonance of the third helium nucleus and the beryllium atom.

Hoyle admitted that his atheism was dramatically disturbed when he calculated the odds against the precise matching required to form a carbon atom through this triple alpha process. He said the number he calculated from the facts is so overwhelming as to put almost beyond question the conclusion that a superintellect had monkeyed with the laws of physics.

Fine-tuning appears in the explosive power of the Big Bang's precision, matching the force of gravity.

The matching of the explosive force of the Big Bang and gravity had to match to 1 part in 10^{60}, or a universe with the capacity of conscious life would not have come into existence. If the explosive force were only slightly higher, the universe would consist of gas without stars or planets. If the force were reduced by one part in a thousand billion, the universe would have collapsed back to a singular point after a few million years.

Fine-tuning appears in the strong and weak nuclear forces.

The strong force that binds the particles in an atom's nucleus must be balanced with the weak nuclear force to a degree of 1 part in 10^{60}. If the strong force were any weaker, atomic nuclei could not hold together and only hydrogen would exist. If the strong force were only slightly stronger, hydrogen would be an unusual element, the sun would not exist, water would not exist, and the heavier elements necessary for life would not be available.

Fine-tuning appears in the electromagnetic force and in the ratio of electron mass to proton mass and proton mass to neutron mass.

Any deviation in the strength of the electromagnetic force would also preclude the molecular formation necessary for life. The electromagnetic force must be precisely balanced with the ratio of electron mass to proton mass. The proton is 1,836 times heavier than the electron. This fundamental ratio must be very finely adjusted to make life possible. Moreover, the mass of the proton and the mass of the neutron are meticulously balanced. The emergence of life depended on an astounding precision among the masses of these three particles.

Fine-tuning appears in the cosmological constant.

The cosmological constant is a characteristic of the space-time fabric of the universe related to its stretching energy (space energy density). The more the universe expands, the greater this stretching energy or "springiness" becomes. This means that the stretching energy increases and has the effect of moving bodies of mass that warp the space-time fabric farther apart. When the fabric of space-time stretches, the bodies of masses, such as the galaxies, move farther apart. This gives the appearance that the galaxies are repelling each other, but actually space is stretching, as illustrated earlier in the example of stars on an inflating balloon.

The cosmological constant is in effect a pulling property that works against gravity as the universe expands. Gravity inhibits the expansion of the universe, but the cosmological constant increases the self-stretching property of space. At the beginning of the universe, gravity's effect on the universe was quite large. As the universe expands from the explosive force of the Big Bang, the cosmological constant's self-stretching effect increases. In a large universe the effect of the cosmological constant is much stronger and, consequently, the rate of expansion of the space-time fabric increases.

For space to expand at a rate that would allow for the development of life, the strength of the cosmological constant had to be extremely close to Newton's constant, which indicates the strength of gravity. If the strength of gravity is exactly 1, the size of the cosmological constant (space energy density) must be very close to zero, but not quite zero. The cosmological constant's value, in fact, must be less than 10^{-120}. The fine-tuning of this constant is extraordinary and represents the most extreme fine-tuning of any known constant in physics.

If the value of the cosmological constant was -1, the universe would have expanded and collapsed in less than 10^{-43} or Planck time. This is so short a length of time that the time it takes for light to cross an atomic nucleus (10^{-24} seconds) is huge by comparison. Or if the cosmological constant had been negative at, say −0.000001, the universe would have only lasted for ten-thousandth of a billionth of a billionth of a billionth of a billionth of a second.[11] Either of these scenarios, of course, would not allow for life.

If the cosmological constant was a small positive number, say 1, then the expansion would have been so dramatic that the universe would have doubled in size every ten-millionth of a billionth of a billionth of a billionth of a billionth of a second.[12] The constant had to be exactly what it was to an accuracy of one part in 10^{-120}.[13]

Fine-tuning appears in the order at the initial Big Bang.

As noted above, the Second Law of Thermodynamics requires that disorder in the universe tends toward a maximum. Because the universe could not have been dissipating from infinity or it would have run down by now, it must have had a beginning–a very highly ordered beginning. If the Big Bang is regarded as only an impressive accident, there is no explanation why it produced a universe with such a high degree of order, contrary to the Second Law. As described above, Penrose calculated that at the very beginning of the Big Bang, the precision required to set the universe on its highly ordered course in which life could develop was staggering: "an accuracy of one part in $10^{10^{123}}$."[14]

Because the mathematical probabilities against the conditions allowing for life are so overwhelming in our universe, some scientists are attracted to the concept of an "oscillating" universe in which, crudely put, there is an infinite cycle of Big Bangs and Big Crunches as the universe expands and contracts. This would permit an infinite number of beginnings. Stephen Hawking and Roger Penrose, however, have demonstrated that the gravitational force in a collapsing universe would produce a Big Crunch that would be totally chaotic, and the entropy at the Crunch would be so large that it would preclude another expansion. An oscillating universe is not possible.

We cannot tell if there are an infinite number of planets, because we can only look out over our horizon of about 15 billion light years.[15] Because in infinity almost anything or everything can happen, one who wishes to avoid the theological conclusion to which scientific evidence points can hypothesize infinities. Accordingly, with respect to the fine-tuning of the universe, one can appeal to unobservable infinities of universes to avoid the conclusion that God is behind the just right nature of our universe. But there is no evidence that such universes exist and no possibility of confirming the speculation. Even assuming the possibility of their existence, one must also ask why they exist.[16]

With respect to the fine-tuning of the basic laws of physics that allows for the emergence of conscious life (the anthropic principle), Antony Flew contends that there can be only two explanations, either a multiplicity of universes exists or God exists. He criticizes proponents of the multiverse for using an awkward "blunderbluss" in speculating that all possible universes exist. He agrees with Oxford philosopher Richard Swinburne that this is a "vacuous claim":

> Three things might be said concerning the arguments about fine tuning. First, it is a hard fact that we live in a universe with certain laws and constants, and life would not have been possible if some of these laws and constants had been different. Second, the fact that the existing laws and constants allow the survival of life does not answer the question of the origin of life. This is a very different question, . . . these conditions are necessary for life to arise, but not sufficient. Third, the fact that it is logically possible that there are multiple universes with their own laws of nature does not show that such universes do exist. There is currently no evidence in support of a multiverse. It remains a speculative idea. What is especially important here is the fact that existence of a multiverse does not explain the origin of the laws of nature.[17]

THE ARGUMENT FOR A NECESSARY BEING, COUPLED WITH THE ISSUES OF INTELLIGIBILITY, RATIONALITY, ORDER, AND FINE-TUNING IN THE UNIVERSE AND THE UNREASONABLE EFFECTIVENESS OF MATHEMATICS AND BEAUTY IN DESCRIBING THE PHYSICAL UNIVERSE, AVOIDS THE GOD OF THE GAPS FALLACY.

I am noting that the universe is *inherently* mathematical and rational. My point is based on what is given by science and is not based on something that could be changed by further scientific discovery. Because my argument is based on the scientifically given rather than on the scientifically open, it is not subject to the god of the gaps fallacy. The god of the gaps fallacy was used to fill in what science had yet to discover. This argument proceeds from an area beyond science; it proceeds from the need to explain the basis of the intelligibility, order, and rationality inherent in the universe that is the foundation for science. Science is unable to address this question, because by definition the answer must come from outside of science.[18]

The question I am examining concerns whether a self-sufficient universe just exists or whether a self-sufficient universe exists because God causes it to exist and holds its existence in being.[19] The problem with the god of the gaps approach is the failure to understand the transcendent nature of the divine. As the term *God* is used in this book, God is not a being that can be placed in a category of beings that may have natural causes for their existence. The fact that one can hypothesize completely natural causes for physical nontranscendental processes does not mean that there is no God. Natural causes for natural processes are compatible with the existence of a transcendent God. In other words, there is nothing mutually exclusive about the existence of a self-sufficient natural world and the existence of a transcendent God.

Leibniz made a profound distinction between natural causes as explanations of natural processes and the inference of a transcendent God from the existence of the world. The inference of a transcendent God from the existence of the world is not on the same plane as the explanation of natural processes by natural causes. To put the arguments on the same plane is to ignore the transcendence of God, who is not a part of the universe, not a category among categories, and not a being among beings.[20] Newton and others have been wrong in inserting God into gaps in scientific knowledge. God is not that small. The transcendent nature of God as the source of the existence and continuing existence of all that is contingent cannot be mixed into an examination of natural processes. The existence of God as the basis for the existence and order of nature is not an argument that erroneously mixes natural physical processes with transcendence. The important implication and conclusion in all of this is that the universe's existence raises a legitimate question.[21]

7

EVOLUTION IS NOT DISPOSITIVE OF THE QUESTION OF WHY THERE IS SOMETHING RATHER THAN NOTHING AND WHY THE UNIVERSE IS RATIONAL AND INTELLIGIBLE

Ever since my sophomore year of college when I took a course on physical anthropology, I have never considered the process of the gradual evolution of life as inconsistent or disruptive of faith in the existence of God. From a theist's perspective the important claim to be examined is *whether God made time itself and then made human beings (whether over a long period or a short period of time) for the purpose of entering into a transforming friendship with the divine life.* This claim is consistent with my earlier writings and is central to the issues addressed in this book. The more important issues are the reasons for the rationality, intelligibility, and existence of a contingent nature.

NATURAL SELECTION DOES NOT EXPLAIN EXISTENCE, THE UNREASONABLE EFFECTIVENESS OF MATHEMATICS, FINE-TUNING OF THE PHYSICAL LAWS, OR THE INTELLIGIBILITY OF THE UNIVERSE; IT IS ONLY A CONTINGENT COMPONENT OF THE UNIVERSE.

Evolution does not address the far weightier issues that I have raised above concerning God's existence. Evolution does not do away with the argument for belief in a Supreme Being. For example, evolution does not address why there is something rather than nothing. It does not address existence. It does not address the intelligible nature of physical laws. It does not address why abstract mathematics match the physical universe. It does not address the fine-tuning of the universe. Natural selection is only a component of the universe. As merely a component of the universe, it is not an explanation for the universe. Darwin's theory, for all its merits, does not explain or even address why something exists or why it is intelligible, rational, and mathematical, nor does it address why beauty in abstract mathematics points toward truth in the physics of the universe.

Science gives us wonderful knowledge, but it has its limits. It cannot provide the answer to the question of the existence of the universe, because an examination of the components or members of the universe cannot explain the existence and the order of an intelligible universe. When one engages in science, he or she engages in looking at the relationship among the members of the universe. This is not sufficient to address the question of why the universe exists at all, why it is intelligible, or why it has the particular collection of members that comprise the whole of the universe.

RICHARD DAWKINS COMMITS THE ELEMENTARY LOGICAL FALLACY OF CIRCULAR REASONING IN HIS PRINCIPAL ARGUMENT FOR THE NONEXISTENCE OF GOD.

Mortimer Adler demonstrated that, like Gödel's incompleteness theorem in mathematics, our ability to disprove an existential proposition has limits. Although one may think that a belief in a purely spiritual being conflicts with our knowledge derived from physical science, the conflict is not with scientific knowledge of the physical universe but with a dogmatic materialism assumed in contemporary philosophy. Spiritual beings may not exist, but the existence of spiritual beings is not impossible. No proof can be set forth for the proposition that only material things exist.

Logical disproof faces severe rational limitations. Although one can prove an affirmative existential proposition, one cannot prove a negative existential proposition. In other words, one cannot prove that something does not exist. No one has been able to structure a logically valid argument that God does not exist. Although the logical arguments for God's existence may not support a conclusion beyond a shadow of a doubt, Adler formed a logically valid argument that supports an affirmative conclusion for God's existence beyond a reasonable doubt. (As discussed in this book, discoveries in philosophy, physics, cosmology, and algorithmic information theory strengthen Adler's position.)

Adler asks the question: What can an atheist offer, if an atheist cannot prove a negative existential proposition, such as God does not exist? He notes that the atheist can only offer rhetorical, not logical, arguments. These rhetorical attempts may not even rise to the level of arguments, since they are mostly attempts to discredit religious belief with attacks full of ridicule but lacking substance. Adler cited the manner in which Voltaire in *Candide* could only ridicule Dr. Pangloss, whom he portrayed as a follower of Leibniz. Voltaire used rhetoric and ridicule, but he made no logical, substantive arguments to disprove religious beliefs. In order to construct an argument that disproves, rather than ridicules, religious belief, one must develop a substantive argument with logical force, not one that attempts to persuade with mere rhetoric.[1]

In his book, *The God Delusion*, Richard Dawkins attacks religion using ridicule, mockery, and vitriolic statements to persuade his readers; he provides very little substantive, logical analysis for his position. The analysis that he does provide lacks rigorous critical thinking and commits elementary errors in logic. By employing an argument with only rhetorical force, he attempts to discredit religious belief. His evidence fits the mold of Joseph Campbell's attempt in the twentieth century to reduce all religions to mythologies. Adler's comments on Campbell's reasoning may be applied to Dawkins's invalid syllogisms today: "Valid logical arguments that constitute proofs or disproofs are intellectually convincing. Rhetorical arguments, if effective, are persuasive, emotionally or intellectually, but never convincing."[2]

Alvin Plantinga has written a compelling refutation of Dawkins's attempt to form a rational argument.[3] I will draw on Plantinga's insights concerning Dawkins's principal argument in his book, *The God Delusion*. In this book Dawkins considers his chapter entitled "Why There Almost Certainly Is No God" to contain the central argument of his book. Clearing aside the bombastic rhetoric, his central argument is as follows. Without giving any quantitative basis for his premise, Dawkins assumes that if God exists, he would have to be so complex that his existence would be astronomically improbable. He assumes that God is complex, and he assumes that something complex is improbable. Calling his assumed improbability the "Ultimate Boeing 747 gambit," he refers to the well-known statement that the probability of life just occurring (by random processes) is "as unlikely as a typhoon blowing through a junkyard and constructing a Boeing 747."[4] His basic point is that if God created the universe, he would have to be extremely complex to make something so complex. Because Dawkins assumes that complexity is inversely related to probability, God, *ergo*, is extremely improbable.

One exploring the logic of Dawkins's reasoning must ask what Dawkins means by the term *complex.* Valid reasoning requires a consistency within the context of terms, especially when one uses the term *complexity*. Among persons studying the term *complexity,* over thirty different definitions are used. Complexity is at the heart of Dawkins's argument, so we need to understand as precisely as possible what he means by this term.

In his book *The Blind Watchmaker* Dawkins set forth his definition of complexity in a rambling series of paragraphs, which he admits is a "long, drawn-out argument":

> So, what is a complex thing? How should we recognize it. . . . Let us try another tack in our quest for a definition of complexity, and make use of the mathematical idea of probability. Suppose we try out the following definition: a complex thing is something whose constituent parts are arranged in a way that is unlikely to have arisen by chance alone. To borrow an analogy from an eminent astronomer, if you take the parts of an airliner and jumble them up at random, the likelihood that you would happen to assemble a working Boeing is vanishingly small. There are billions of possible ways of putting together the bits of an airliner, and only one, or very few of them would actually be an airliner. There are even more ways of putting together the scrambled parts of a human. . . . We were looking for a precise way to express what we mean when we refer to something as complicated. . . . The answer we have arrived at is that complicated things have some quality, specifiable in advance, that is highly unlikely to have been acquired by chance alone.[5]

In other words, as Plantinga well notes, for Dawkins something has complexity when its material parts are arranged in a manner unlikely to have resulted from chance alone. In this definition Dawkins assumes that complexity involves materialism and includes improbability. Cardiff University astronomer Chandra Wickramasinghe drew the Boeing 747 analogy because of his understanding that the "parts" of a simple bacteria (nucleic acids, enzymes, molecules, atoms, etc.) all joined together in a precise sequence. Similarly, the parts in a junkyard are formed into a precise sequence when a typhoon blows through and structures a Boeing 747.

But Plantinga calls our attention to the fact that this 747 analogy only applies to Dawkins's definition of complexity if God is made of material parts. In his definition Dawkins makes the following unwarranted assumptions: (1) God is made of many parts; and (2) these parts were unlikely (improbable) to be assembled to form a precise sequence (or in his words, a "heterogenous" or "many-parted" "structure").

Any of my third-year law students at the University of Virginia would have noted that in his argument Dawkins is assuming what he is attempting to prove, i.e., that only matter/energy exists. He is assuming in his definition that God is a "many-parted structure" and that that structure is improbable. In other words, in his definition he is assuming that God is made of matter and that God's structure is improbable. He then uses that definition as part of his premise from which he draws a materialist conclusion that God does not exist. This is a good example of the logical fallacy known as *circulus in probando* or circular reasoning.

The Dawkins Ultimate 747 gambit analogy and his conclusion fail because by definition God is spiritual and does not have material parts to be arranged like the parts of a 747. Dawkins is conceiving of God as something made of matter. His definition of complexity assumes the truth of a reductionist materialism, but this is only his assumption and not something he can prove. *To reach his desired conclusion Dawkins begins with materialism in order to arrive at materialism. He tries to define God under a materialist definition of complexity that includes improbability in order to arrive at his conclusion.*

Plantinga knows that in classical theology God is a necessary being existing in every possible universe. Under the classical concept of God as such a necessary being, God is simple, not complex, and, if he exists in all possible universes, the probability that he exists is one with the concurrent probability of his nonexistence equal to zero. In other words, rather than being improbable, God's existence has the greatest probability. He notes that Dawkins may not even be aware of the logical problems included in his definition and analogy: "So if Dawkins proposes that God's existence is improbable, he owes us an argument for the conclusion that there is no necessary being with the attributes of God—an argument that doesn't just start from the premise that materialism is true. Neither he nor anyone else has provided even a decent argument along these lines; Dawkins doesn't even seem to be aware that he *needs* an argument of that sort."[6]

Perhaps more importantly, Dawkins fails to address the following questions: If logical thinking is only the result of accidental processes, why is it trustworthy? Is it probable that accidents will accurately describe other previous accidents? If our thinking is merely the result of accidents, why should we consider our thinking true or logical? Isn't it only accidental? How can we trust thought if it is an accident?

Plantinga has well argued that a theist has a basis for believing that his or her thoughts could be reliable. But a naturalist (one who believes that existence is limited to only matter/energy) has no basis for considering thoughts capable of producing true beliefs. The naturalist can think that the neurophysiology underlying belief formation is adaptive but cannot make any assertion concerning whether the beliefs formed are true or not. Given unguided evolution (an atheist must assume that it is unguided) one would have to think that it is unlikely that our thoughts are reliable. But, as Plantinga writes: "It is as likely, given unguided evolution, that we live in a sort of dream world as that we actually know something about ourselves and our world."[7]

In other words, a naturalist cannot be certain that any belief that is a product of her cognitive faculties is true. *And* this would mean all of her beliefs, including her belief in naturalism. Hence, she could not rationally believe in naturalism.

As Plantinga concludes, the conflict then becomes not one between belief in science and belief in God but between belief in science and belief in naturalism. Naturalism is self-defeating in logical thought. But science depends upon the validity of rational, logical thought processes being true to reality (that is why your cell phone works). It may seem amazing to conclude that the real conflict is not between science and theism but between science and naturalism, but naturalism has no way to show the truth of beliefs depending on a merely adaptive process underlying neurophysiology.[8]

Dawkins is at his best when he writes about science. *The God Delusion* contains very little science and fails to provide critical reasoning. Instead, Dawkins resorts to ridicule and mockery. He resorts to pure ridicule in his comments on Professor Antony Flew's recent change of mind from atheism to theism. He would do well to abandon the vitriol and ridicule and read Flew's book, *How to Think Straight: An Introduction to Critical Reasoning*. Dawkins's writing is entertaining because of his rhetoric, but he employs fallacies of circular reasoning in his principal argument for atheism.

THE MYSTERY OF INFORMATION CHALLENGES A STRICT MATERIALISM

INFORMATION MAY BE THE FOUNDATION OF THE PHYSICAL.

I want to discuss the peculiar nature of information, because I think it may represent a profound paradigm shift in mathematics and physics. The new mathematics of information is consistent with the reasons for the existence of God emphasized in this book. These reasons are based on the argument for a necessary being, the unreasonable effectiveness of mathematics, the order and rationality inherent in the universe, the fine-tuning of the universe for the development of conscious life, the evidential force of religious experiences, and the reason there is something rather than nothing.

In this section, I am merely describing certain fascinating and mysterious aspects of information. I believe that we are only touching on the significance of this concept in present academic inquiry. The study of the characteristics of information should become increasingly significant in this century. Many thoughtful physicists consider information to be the underlying foundation for physical things. John Wheeler has said that the universe appears to be more like the expression of an idea than a physical thing.

The study of information results in a new view of nature. Information is not matter or energy. What is information? This may seem like a simple question to answer, but given that no one has defined the term *energy* in a completely satisfactory manner, we should not be surprised to have some difficulty in defining the term *information*. Semantic information is not synonymous with the concept of a fractal or a patterned form. For the purposes of the present discussion, a definition of information as "instructions" or a "message" will suffice.

Information is nonmaterial in the following sense. When I type these letters, the information contained in this message is encoded in matter on my computer screen and compressed. When I print out this message, I print it out encoded in ink and paper. The chemicals in the ink and paper do not determine the message. Assume you are reading a book on cash flow return on investment theory. An observer who is not absorbing the information from the page you are reading cannot measure the information on cash flow return on investment theory. Photons may provide the light source, but the photons are not the information. The information on cash flow is independent of the photons and independent from the substances encoding the information on the paper, and it is independent from the material substances encoding the information in your brain.

Similarly, the information (instructions) in the DNA molecule is independent of the bases of sugars and phosphates that comprise the molecule. If information is independent from the chemicals of matter encoding the information, the information on cash flow did not arise from the chemicals. If I type an email to you, the information I am sending (right or wrong) is not generated by the matter and energy used to convey the message. One has to make a distinction between the message and the medium.

Gregory Chaitin, perhaps the leading mathematician in the field of algorithmic information theory, questions the traditional paradigm that matter is primary and that information is somehow derived from matter or energy. He asks, "What if information is primary, and matter/energy is a secondary phenomenon?" Chaitin notes that identical information can be conveyed without regard to the particular kind of matter employed. Thus, the same information in DNA can be carried in RNA; the same information on a videotape can be conveyed on a DVD; the same information carried in long-term memory can be carried in short term-memory; the same information in nerve impulses can be carried by hormones. The particular kind of matter doesn't, well, doesn't matter. What is important is the information. As Chaitin states, "The same software can run on many machines."[1]

QUANTUM THEORY AS A THEORY OF INFORMATION AND MEASUREMENT CONTAINS ANOTHER MYSTERIOUS ASPECT

OF INFORMATION THAT CHALLENGES A STRICT MATERIALISTIC, DETERMINISTIC WORLDVIEW.

Quantum physics is the most successful theory in the history of science.

I want to consider an area in which the concept of information points away from a strict materialistic reductionist worldview. This section on information is not central to my argument for the existence of God, but I would like to look briefly at an interesting and quite mysterious aspect of information that challenges a worldview of strict materialism: the extremely successful quantum revolution in physics. This revolution began with Max Planck's paper presented in Berlin in 1900 in which he basically proposed that light was not a continuous stream, but small energy packets that he called "quanta." Beginning with this paper, a new theory was developed over the first quarter of the twentieth century by the brilliant work of many of history's most famous scientists, including Louis de Broglie, Albert Einstein, Niels Bohr, Erwin Schrödinger, Werner Heisenberg, Wolfgang Pauli, Eugene Wigner, Paul Dirac, and John von Neumann. Over succeeding years quantum physics became the most successful theory in the history of science. It consistently is verified in experiment and has given us transistors, lasers, semiconductors, PET scans, and a host of useful products that, on balance, have made substantial contributions to contemporary society.

Quantum theory emphasizes a wave function that is purely a mathematical abstract statement of probabilities, a statement of information.

Unlike Newtonian or classical physics that purports to give one certainty and a consequent philosophical concept of determinism, quantum physics presents probabilities. In classical physics an electron was a particle circling around an atom in a predictable orbit. Quantum theory overturned that concept and emphasized an electron "cloud" that gives us only a description of statistical probabilities. This description, known as a wave function, is not something physical; it is purely a mathematical, statistical, abstract statement of probabilities. In other words, it is *information.* As a statement of information a wave function merely gives us probability statistics concerning the characteristics of the electron and its behavior. For example, the wave function would give the probabilities of the electron being in certain locations within the atom. It would not tell us precisely where the electron is but only the probabilities of it being in a certain location.

Quantum mechanics is based on a probability statement of information and a measurement that yields a definite outcome.

Because the wave function is only abstract probability statistics, quantum theory is all about information. Subatomic particles have no precise location until an agent makes an act of measurement. They are not particles in a given position but a cloud of statistical probabilities that only yield a definite outcome when a measurement is made. Consequently, quantum mechanics is based on (1) a statistical probability description that sets forth the terms of hypothetical possibilities and (2) the measurement by an agent or observer whose act of measurement or observation of the probabilities system yields a definite outcome. As strange as it may seem, it is the act of measurement that is required to yield a definite outcome. In the absence of a measurement, there is only an unrealized, abstract description of possible outcomes. It is this weird aspect of quantum physics that caused Niels Bohr to say, "Anyone who is not shocked by quantum theory has not understood it."

Physicist Stephen Barr has given us a useful analogy of how measurement of a probability description produces a definite outcome.

Physicist Stephen Barr has given a very useful analogy to assist us in understanding the workings of quantum mechanics and how measurement/observation relates to the probability description of the wave function to produce a definite outcome. Basically, the analogy, with some modifications, may be described as follows: Suppose you are required to take a calculus exam to complete your college degree. You work hard during the semester, meet with your professor when a particular area is confusing, and study fairly diligently. Let us assume that a month prior to the giving of the exam, one could calculate the probability of your receiving an A on the exam to be 50-50. However, you intensify your studies during the next two weeks, and one might then calculate the probability of your receiving an A on the exam as 75 percent.

If a severe flu virus interrupts your studies during the first few days of the week immediately prior to the exam, one might calculate your probability of receiving an A to have fallen to 65 percent. Fortunately, you bounce back in better health toward the end of the week and now your chance of receiving an A may be calculated to be 80 percent. You finally take the exam. One week after the date of the exam, your professor reads your answers and gives you an A grade. This is the moment when your previously fluctuating probabilities have a definite grade. This is the moment of measurement that yields a definite outcome.

If your professor was called away to give a lecture in the Greek islands before she could grade your exam and her graduate assistant lost your exam paper, your exam would never have been graded. On that particular exam, there would be no definite outcome from the fluctuating probabilities of your receiving an A grade. You would not have an A grade on that exam, because the exam would never be graded and no measurement of your performance would be made. Consequently, a *possible* A grade would never have a definite outcome.

In quantum physics, the probability description of the wave function is said to "collapse" and yield a definite outcome only when a measurement produces a definite outcome. The one who makes the measurement is known as the observer. *It is the observer's measurement or observation that changes the abstract, nonphysical probability description into a definite outcome.*

The observer is essential and must be outside the physical system described in the calculation of probabilities.

A wave function gives a probability description of a physical system. The observer is the one whose measurements transform the hypothetical possibility to a definite outcome. For purposes of this discussion, it is important to understand that the observer must always be outside of the physical system. The observer cannot make the measurement or observation and also be part of the probability description of a physical system. The observer must always be someone outside of the probability description of the wave function.[2]

Barr's example makes it clear that in quantum physics the definite outcome cannot proceed merely from the calculation of probabilities. The observer is essential to produce a real outcome. It is when the observer makes a measurement and *knows* that one hypothetical possibility is an actual fact and that the other possibilities are not actual facts that the possible is turned into an outcome. This process of *knowing* is an act of the intellect; it is an act of the mind. As Barr has written, ". . . quantum theory is based on the existence of 'knowers.'"[3] He maintains that the observer cannot be something physical and follows von Neumann and Wigner's reasoning to demonstrate the logical problem with an observer being comprised of only matter.

To understand why the observer who makes the measurement that collapses the wave function and produces a definite outcome cannot be regarded as something purely physical, I will describe an illustration used by Barr in his description of quantum theory and the mind. Assume that the physical system with which we are concerned is an electron. One could set up a camera to photograph the position of the electron on film. But the camera and the film are made up of atoms. Consequently, one could use the equations of quantum mechanics to describe the possible behavior of the camera and the film. In other words, one could create a more complex abstract statistical wave function that gives a probability description for the film, camera, and electron.

When the camera takes a photograph of the electron, the electron's behavior and the behavior of the camera and film are correlated. But the camera cannot be the observer that produces the definite outcome because the wave function that describes the "metasystem" of the film, camera, and the electron is only made up of probabilities. The camera and film are brought into the probability amplitudes of the wave function description of the whole metasystem. There is no observer outside this larger wave function to collapse it. The collapse of the wave function can only occur outside of the wave function's statistical probabilities. The camera and film cannot become part of the wave function (which remember is simply an abstract informational description of probabilities) and also remain outside of the wave function and perform the role of the observer who makes the measurement and collapses the wave function. As Barr concludes: "*The mathematical descriptions of the physical world given to us by quantum theory presuppose the existence of observers who lie outside those mathematical descriptions.*"[4] (Barr is not arguing that observation creates reality. He describes a wave function as an observer's state of knowledge. He does not argue that the observer creates reality: "the probabilities calculated in quantum mechanics refer to the knowledge of observers, not simply to 'what is going on.'" Reality is not constituted by the measurement, but the collapse of the wave function implies a change in the observer's state of knowledge, not a sudden change in reality.)

Barr's illustration confirms the belief of many physicists that the mind of the knower/observer must to some extent be outside the wave function.

Barr goes on to point out that human observers have hands, eyes, optic nerves, brains, and other relevant matter that are comprised of atoms and subatomic particles. Consequently, nothing prevents the eyes, the optic nerve, and the brain from being drawn mathematically into the larger metawave function description. This presents a problem: The *human observer cannot be completely part of the description of the wave function, because then the behavior of the observer would be also bound up in the mere abstract hypothetical statistical probabilities of the wave function.* Who would remain to "collapse" the wave function and produce a definite outcome? If the observer is completely brought over into a wave function that includes his or her behavior, then the observer could no longer be the one who makes the measurement. Barr, von Neumann, Henry Stapp and many other physicists conclude that it is *mind* that must remain on the observer's side of the boundary line between the system and the observer. The reason for their conclusion is that it is the mind that *knows* the outcome of the measurement. Only when the outcome is known to have happened are the myriad of probabilities reduced by measurement to an outcome of 100 percent probability.[5]

This means that the mind of the observer cannot be reduced to a strict materialistic explanation. The mind and the brain are closely related. We see the results of drugs, surgery, and accidents affecting the mind. However, the mental cannot be reduced completely and only to the material.

I will discuss the concept of an underlying unity that allows for the relationship between the mental and the material. This concept considers them as distinct but corresponding aspects of the same essence. However, my point for the moment is that a mathematician's mind is not reducible to mere equations of matter. The mind may produce the equations but cannot be completely described by them. An algorithm or physical law (equation) cannot describe the mind. It is impossible to bring the complete act of knowing into the mathematics of the wave function. The observer who "knows" by an act of his or her intellect must stay outside of the system to observe the system and make the measurement necessary to produce an outcome.

This concept of the role of the mind in quantum mechanics is quite controversial. As mentioned above, it is not a central part of my rationale for the existence of God, but I want to explore it a bit more, because it cautions against a strict reductionist materialistic view of reality.

Mental processes appear to transcend the purely physical.

Our bodies are intertwined with our mental processes in an essential manner. This is obvious when one considers the result produced when someone receives a blow to the head or when one considers the effect of certain drugs or surgery on one's thoughts. I sometimes use the expression "that's the real me" when I strike a particularly effective golf shot (a rare occurrence). But what is actually the real me? What is the true identity of a person? I don't think that Shakespeare was only a conglomeration of chemical substances, nor do I think that one could reduce Albert Einstein or Niels Bohr to a cluster of chemicals that discover relativity and quantum physics. The ability of mental processes to identify abstract mathematical concepts that match the physical world in a counterintuitive way appears to transcend the purely physical.

Physicist John Polkinghorne believes that the material and mental may be complementary poles of the same substance.

Polkinghorne believes that the material and mental may be complementary poles made of the same substance. But this does not subordinate the mental to the material. The mental is not merely a phenomenon of the physical. Polkinghorne rejects a strict reductionism and sees the mental and material as complementary poles of reality in a manner analogous to the way in which quantum physics demonstrates that light expresses a polar duality in its ability to act as a particle and a wave.[6]

This is consistent with the thought of David Hodgson, a justice on the Supreme Court of New South Wales, who used quantum theory to make a powerful case for the efficacy of the mind in his highly regarded book, *The Mind Matters*. Hodgson credits Leibniz with the insight that the mind and brain are two manifestations or perspectives of a single underlying reality.[7] Many quantum theorists cite with approval Hodgson's outline of a theory of mind based on quantum mechanics. Polkinghorne agrees with him, but he is hesitant to conclude that quantum effects present the whole solution. He also appeals to chaos theory for insights to emphasize the role of local energy exchanges and "active information" to accommodate a distinction between mind and matter.[8]

In addressing the mind-brain dilemma, Polkinghorne explains the concept of his dual aspect monism: "The world is made of one sort of 'stuff,' but of a subtlety that it reduces neither to mere matter nor to pure mind. Our encounter with the material and the mental are to be given equal force in assessing the adequacy of our metaphysical conjectures." He rejects the perspective that the mental is a "mere epiphenomenal froth on the surface of the material."[9]

Polkinghorne carries this concept over into his discussion of the soul. He points out the difficulty of conceiving of a person as only the matter that comprises his or her body, because this matter is constantly changing. There are very few atoms in your body that were part of your physical makeup five years ago. So what is the real you or the real me? Polkinghorne makes a plausible argument that the real person is the information-bearing pattern that provides the continuity in the changing matter of every individual. He considers this consistent with Aristotle's view of the soul as the "form" of the body and quite distinct from Plato's concept of the soul as a separate entity imprisoned in the body. Barr notes that animals and computer programs have information bearing patterns and, along with Aquinas, considers an "active intellect" to be a necessary aspect to a discussion of the soul. I will discuss this concept in a related writing, but for now I want to consider the interesting work of Berkeley's quantum physicist Henry Stapp, who also argues against Kant's overly restrictive epistemology.

Physicist Henry Stapp criticizes Kant's theory of knowledge and views reality as information based.

Henry Stapp is a renowned scientist who worked with Werner Heisenberg, Wolfgang Pauli, and John Wheeler. He is keenly devoted to clarifying the important role of consciousness in quantum physics and the relationship between consciousness and moral philosophy.

Stapp criticizes the outdated concept of science underlying Kant's theory of knowledge and followed by so many philosophers and scientists from the Enlightenment forward. He argues that moral philosophy has to become more aware of the significant changes made by quantum theory's understanding of the nature of reality and its effect on our understanding of the nature of human beings. In his view, contemporary quantum theory can best be understood as describing reality in terms of *information*. Stapp emphasizes the relationship between how a person views consciousness and central moral issues: "What a person values depends, basically, on what he believes himself to be. If he believes that he is an isolated hunk of protoplasm, struggling to survive in a hostile world, or a physical organism constructed by genes to promote their own survival, then his values will tend to be very different from those of a person who regards himself as a being with a mind-like aspect that makes conscious choices that control in part his own future, and are also integral parts of the global process that generates the unfolding of the universe."[10]

Consciousness, free will, and the ability of nonmaterial information-based mental processes to change the physical structure of one's brain have practical effects in the world.

Stapp emphasizes that his point is not a mere philosophical abstract concept but one that has practical effects in the world. He illustrates this by referring to a legal case in which the man who killed San Francisco mayor George Moscone and the city's supervisor Harvey Milk was sentenced to only five years in prison. The reason for the light sentence was that the defendant's consumption of junk food caused his mental derangement. The idea that he was not responsible for his actions became known as the "Twinkie defense." This follows from the view of such philosophers as Daniel Dennett, who claim that consciousness does not actually exist, that the brain's action is chemically determined, and no one makes any decisions by his or her volition. A human being's actions then are merely a mechanical extension of the circumstances preceding those actions. Under this perspective, humans have no control over their thoughts or behavior, and any legal system that is based on the premise that one has responsibility for one's actions is wrong.

Stapp works with UCLA research psychiatrist Jeffrey Schwartz, author with Sharon Begley of *The Mind and the Brain.* Schwartz and Begley convincingly argue against Dennett's position and hold that science demonstrates the existence of mental force that endows humans with free will and the inherent capacity to make moral decisions. In rejecting the idea that a human being is a mere automaton, Schwartz provides significant evidence that a person has the ability to change the physical structure of his or her brain. Persons also have mental volitional power that allows them to make choices and be responsible for their actions. This is consistent with results obtained by Dr. Herbert Benson at Harvard's Mind/Body Institute. When one stops to think about it, it is remarkable that nonmaterial information-based mental processes can change physical matter, including the alteration of neurons. Yet that is the observed result demonstrated by brain scans performed with the newest technologies. A strict materialist view of reality appears completely inadequate when one recalls that information is not matter or energy. Stapp emphasizes the information-based nature of quantum theory and the effectiveness of intentional, conscious thoughts upon one's brain and body.

The central concept is that quantum mechanics describes the ability of a human being to engage in conscious, intentional activity as a "knowledge-seeking and knowledge-using agent." In other words, quantum mechanics requires intentional actions by agents who acquire knowledge. It is an information-based theory that explains the causal effects of one's mental intention upon material, physical systems. One's mental effort can result in changes in the brain that produce actions by one's body (such as the lifting of an arm). Quantum theory transforms the old Newtonian machine concept of a human being into a person with a will and the ability to perform intentional actions. If one regresses to an outdated classical Newtonian physics, one ineluctably will eliminate any effect of a conscious thought upon one's brain or body. Stapp considers such a regression to an outmoded physics to be absurd: "Hence, from a physics point of view, trying to understand the mind-brain connection by going to the classical approximation is absurd: it amounts to trying to understand something in an approximation that eliminates the effect you are trying to study. . . ."[11]

I want to emphasize again that my discussion of quantum physics is not central to my principal argument. However, one cannot ignore the ramifications of contemporary physics. Many persons, including Daniel Dennett and Richard Dawkins, fail to comprehend how significantly quantum mechanics undermines a deterministic worldview. Henry Stapp has been a leader in articulating the effect of quantum physics in changing a Newtonian worldview. He is not an average physicist, but one who is highly regarded in theoretical physics; one who studied under Nobel Laureates Emilio Segre and Owen Chamberlain. He also worked with Wolfgang Pauli and developed his ideas from von Neumann's work on the mathematical foundations of quantum theory. This Berkeley physicist has centered a substantial portion of his work on the quantum measurement problem and the influence of conscious thought.

Stapp holds that it is incorrect to think that science is morally neutral and cannot influence the priorities of our values. He insists that science plays a central role in setting our moral priorities: "For what we value depends on what we believe, and what we believe is strongly influenced by science."[12]

In noting the effect of science upon the church's value system in the Middle Ages, Stapp points out how the inaccurate, outdated Enlightenment "scientific" credo of human beings as "mechanical automata" eroded the basis for moral values in a religious worldview and abolished the concepts of personal responsibility and free will. As I noted, this outmoded "scientific credo" is still embraced by many persons today, despite the advent of contemporary quantum mechanics which completely destroys the Enlightenment empirical base. Newtonian physics were demonstrated to be "profoundly incorrect." The view of reality as a deterministic process was revised by new mathematical rules that have been empirically verified to a remarkable and consistent degree.

The idea that the laws of nature proceeded in a "miniaturized" replication of the observed motion of large visible objects like planets and stars was demonstrated to be an inaccurate view of reality. Newton and Rutherford's view of atomic processes were replaced by a new understanding of quantum physics that included an emphasis on the knowledge of an observer. Stapp notes that the Enlightenment view, based on Newton's physics, was turned "upside down" by the strange characteristics of the new physics that were empirically verified to one part in a hundred million. In his recent book, *Mindful Universe*, he writes:

> Perhaps I should say that they turned right side up what had been upside down. For the word 'science' comes from the Latin word 'scire', 'to know', and what the founders of the new theory claimed, basically is that the proper subject matter of science is not what may or may not be 'out there', unobserved and unknown to human beings. It is rather what we human beings can know, and can do in order to know more. Thus they formulated their new theory, called quantum mechanics, or quantum theory, around the knowledge-acquiring actions of human beings, and the knowledge we acquire by performing these actions, rather than around a conjectured causally sufficient mechanical world. The focus of the theory was shifted from one that basically ignored our knowledge to one that is about our knowledge, and about the effects of the actions that we take to acquire more knowledge upon what we are able to know.
>
> This modified conception differs from the old one in many fascinating ways that continue to absorb the interest of physicists. However, it is the revised understanding of the nature of human beings, and of the causal role of human consciousness in the unfolding of reality, that is, I believe, the most exciting

> thing about the new physics, and probably, in the final analysis, also the most important contribution of science to the well-being of our species. . . . (A)ccording to the new conception, the *physically described world* is built not out of bits of matter, as matter was understood in the nineteenth century, but out of objective *tendencies*—potentialities—for certain discrete, whole *actual events* to occur. Each such event has both a psychologically described aspect, which is essentially an increment in knowledge, and also a physically described aspect, which is an action that *abruptly changes* the mathematically described set of potentialities to one that is concordant with the increase in knowledge. This coordination of the aspects of the theory that are described in physical/mathematical terms with aspects that are described in psychological terms is what makes the theory practically useful. Some empirical predictions have been verified to the incredible accuracy of one part in a hundred million.[13]

The standard interpretation of the quantum world is based in information as the irreducible seed of the universe and all physical existence; such an interpretation is inconsistent with a strict reductionist materialism.

How we regard human nature affects how we treat one another. In his excellent book, *Information*, Hans Christian von Baeyer, Chancellor Professor of Physics at the College of William and Mary, recognizes the information-based foundation of quantum mechanics and emphasizes that the standard interpretation of the quantum world is inconsistent with a strict reductionist materialism.

Information is not matter or energy, and yet when we look at the deep-down reality of nature we may be surprised to discover that the underlying nature of physical reality is nonmaterial information. As von Baeyer notes, a reductionist first reduces solids, liquids, and gases to molecules. Molecules are then reduced to atoms. Atoms are reduced to their components of subatomic particles, including quarks and leptons, which in turn may be reduced to strings. However, when one continues to push down to the deepest reality and asks what lies beneath, the astonishing answer in the standard interpretation of quantum mechanics is that one is left only with an abstract description of *information* in the form of a calculation of probabilities in a wave function. Recalling that the wave function is not a physical reality itself, but only a statistical summary of information, one can understand why physicist John Wheeler has said that the universe and all existence may be founded on an expression of information, an expression of an idea or of wisdom. Even when one attempts to apply a reductionist method and press on to deep-down reality, one finds that the foundation for all energy and matter appears to be an expression of information. This may remind one of the claim that "in the beginning was the Word (*Logos*)."

Information appears to be the irreducible seed from which every particle, every force, and even the fabric of space-time grows. Stapp encourages us to abandon an outdated Enlightenment understanding of knowledge based on Newtonian physics. He wants us to comprehend that quantum physics is clearly pointing in the direction of an informational basis for reality. Quantum theory is the most successful theory in the history of science, and contemporary human thought needs to be brought into the twenty-first century. Stapp wants intelligent humans to understand that materialism as a philosophy is outmoded. He calls for a serious educational effort to update people's understanding of twenty-first century science. Arguing that most human beings continue to view the world with a false materialist mind-set based in seventeenth century science, he calls for an updating of scientific understanding in rational discourse and in college curricula.

Stapp and other highly regarded physicists criticize their colleagues for being content only to apply quantum mechanics without considering its ontological significance. In giving up the traditional scientific quest to comprehend reality, they settle for what works in practice. Of course, what works in practice produces considerable useful technology, but Stapp believes that physicists should also attempt to understand the physical world and frame a statement of the nature of reality and articulate what that nature means for our understanding of the meaning of human beings. He believes that quantum physicists will have a near-unanimous agreement that reality is *informational*, not material, at its core. As he writes: "For the whole language of the quantum physicist, when he is dealing with the meaning of his symbols, is in *terms of information*, which an agent may or may not choose to acquire, and in terms of Yes-or-No answers that constitute *bits of information*. Just getting that one idea across could make a significant inroad into the corruptive materialist outlook that, more than three-quarters of a century after its official demise as a basic truth about nature, still infects so many minds."[14]

Stapp's criticism of the outdated and limited Enlightenment understanding of knowledge is echoed by Peter van Inwagen, professor of philosophy of the University of Notre Dame, who points out that much of current popular thought follows an outmoded eighteenth century Enlightenment "creed." Although the creed is not recited in an official formulation, he believes it can be stated as follows:

> There is no God. There is, in fact, nothing besides the physical cosmos that science investigates. Human beings, since they are part of this cosmos, are physical things and therefore do not survive death. Human beings are, in fact, animals among other animals and differ from other animals only in being more complex. Like other animals, they are a product of uncaring and unconscious physical processes that did not have them, or anything else, in mind. There is, therefore, nothing external to humanity that is capable of conferring meaning or purpose on human existence. In the end, the only evil is pain and the only good is pleasure. The only purpose of morality and politics is the minimization of pain and the maximization of pleasure. . . . Religions invent complicated and arbitrary moral code and fantastic future rewards and punishments in order to consolidate their own power. Fortunately, they are gradually but steadily being exposed as frauds by the progress of science (which was invented by strong-minded progressives), and they will gradually disappear through the agency of scientific education and enlightened journalism.[15]

This "creed" is not only out of date with the science of the twenty-first century; it was even out of step with the science of the nineteenth century. Nevertheless, many uninformed adherents follow it. The creed required a universe with infinite time and space; today we know that the universe is finite. The creed considered the motion of matter to be the source of complexity and consciousness; today science points to a beginning of the universe and an end to its ability to sustain life. Science also points to a fine-tuning in the laws of physics that has not been completely understood by the popular mind. Today we also know that nonmaterial information underlies the quantum events that produce a physical presence. The theist is much more at home in the universe of contemporary science than is an adherent of this Enlightenment creed.[16]

9

THE EXISTENCE OF GOD GIVES AN ABSOLUTE THAT IS CONSISTENT WITH THE REAL EXISTENCE OF RIGHT AND WRONG

THE DISTINCTION BETWEEN GOOD AND EVIL ARGUES FOR THE EXISTENCE OF AN ABSOLUTE.

If God does not exist, there are no absolutes, and without absolutes, as Plato stressed, morals do not exist. Right and wrong then have the same meaninglessness. Dostoevsky wrote that if there is no God, everything is permitted. If God does not exist, evil is not evil and good is not good. Nothing is right, and nothing is wrong. But no one lives as if nothing is right and nothing is wrong. No one regards a torturous murder as the same as a warm embrace. One of the principal reasons people doubt the existence of God is the existence of pain and wrong in the world. But when one sees pain and wrong in the world and distinguishes it from right and wholeness, one presupposes a standard of right and good. Our distinctions between good and evil and between right and wrong are absurd if there is no God. If there is no God, a serial killer and a benevolent charity are ultimately of equal moral value. (Actually there is no moral value if there is no God.)

This inability to distinguish between right and wrong behavior would also apply to societies and nations. If no set of moral ideas was better than any other set of moral ideas, one could not legitimately value Gandhi's behavior over Hitler's behavior. For the ideas espoused by the Nazis to be of less moral value than the ideas espoused by Gandhi, there must be an absolute standard against which these ideas are measured. When one asserts that a certain society's ideas are morally superior to another society's ideas, he or she is asserting that a standard of morality exists that is more fundamental than the moral ideas of a particular society. There is a sense of "righteousness" that pervades all cultures at certain basic levels. Every time we appeal to the world community for the purpose of settling international disputes, we are appealing on the basis of the community's sense of "righteousness."

Emil Brünner, a professor at the University of Zurich and Princeton Seminary, gave the following analysis concerning morality and the existence of God:

> To ask the question, then, "Is there a God," is to fail to be morally serious. One who is morally serious knows that good is not evil, that right and wrong are two different things, that one should seek the right and eschew the wrong. There is a divine order to which one must bow whether one likes to do so or not. . . . If there is no God then it is absurd to trouble oneself about right or wrong. It all comes to the same ultimate chaos. Scoundrel and saint are only phantoms of the imagination. The man who can stop here must probably be left to go his own way.[1]

Some persons refuse to acknowledge a distinction between good and evil. This is always a theoretical, not a practical, position (notice their reaction when someone steals their car). No sane person can fail to notice that evil is not good. One cannot ignore the distinction between good and evil. Everyone has to decide about the reality of good and evil as factors in his or her life. The reality of everyone's ethical obligations means that choices count in deciding between good and evil in one's life.

Although atheists have used the existence of evil as an argument against the existence of God, from one perspective our ability to *know* of the existence of evil is actually an argument *for* the existence of God. For something to be wrong, it must be inconsistent with something that is good. *The very fact that we see and recognize* evil in this world is an indication that we believe that something is wrong. When we call something wrong, we are appealing to a standard of nonwrong. But where does this standard come from? Why do we think that the torture of innocent persons is wrong? If there is no God, we can only say that we don't like the torture of innocent persons. Wrong becomes, then, a matter of taste, not a matter of truth.

If there was not an absolute standard of right and wrong, we would not recognize the existence of evil. We could not call something evil when it is only a matter of taste. If God did not exist, we would have no benchmark for judging something to be evil. But we see evil, and even degrees of evil, so that some evil can be described as horrendous. But what makes it horrendous if nothing is intrinsically wrong? How can we claim that something is horrendous if there is nothing with which to compare it?

Don't we need *a standard of good* to recognize that something is not right? How can a standard of good exist in a universe that is only the result of blind forces with no consciousness? Our recognition of evil and our certainty that horrendous evil exists requires an explanation. The explanation points to the existence of a God who sets an absolute standard of good that allows us to recognize the ills of this world. Without the existence of God, we would not even know that evil exists, because we would not recognize it.

WHY DOES AN OMNIPOTENT, OMNISCIENT GOD ALLOW THE EXISTENCE OF EVIL?

David Hume presented the existence of evil as an argument against the existence of God. Basically his argument is as follows: Why does an omnipotent, omniscient, infinitely good and loving God allow the existence of evil and suffering? If God is all powerful, completely good, why is evil and suffering so traumatically present in existence? This question appears to argue against the existence of God, because if a truly all-powerful and infinitely good God exists, then such a being would not permit evil.

This argument assumes that a good being will always prevent evil. But this assumption is obviously not true in our own experience. Good persons do not always prevent all evil. For example, parents may not allow their children to ride in automobiles, because automobiles have accidents that cause pain and even death. But this prohibition against riding in automobiles, even though it would prevent the children from being involved in an automobile accident, would also preclude the children from riding in a car to receive emergency medical treatment. Perhaps a more plausible assumption than a good being always preventing evil would be that a completely good being will prevent all evil, unless the prevention of that evil precludes a greater good or causes a greater evil.[2]

CAN AN ALL-POWERFUL BEING NECESSARILY DO THE LOGICALLY IMPOSSIBLE AND SIMULTANEOUSLY ALLOW FOR FREE WILL AND NOT ALLOW FOR FREE WILL?

Arguments against the existence of God based on the problem of evil also have the questionable assumption that an all-powerful being can do everything, even things that are logically impossible. But this is also obviously not true. An all-powerful being could not make a circle that is a square or a person that is not a person. Such a being could not give a person free will but completely control the will of that person. Moreover, several things that are good appear to be linked with the existence of evil. We consider physical courage to be a virtue and award medals to honor persons who display courage. In order for this kind of physical courage to exist, physical pain would have to exist.[3] Alvin Plantinga is widely known for his emphasis on the logical requirements of free will in considering the problem of evil. His argument may be summarized as follows:

> God desired to love and be loved by other beings. God created human beings with this in view. To make us capable of such fellowship, God had to give us the freedom to choose, because love, though it does have elements of "compulsion," is meaningful only when it is neither automatic nor coerced. This sort of free will, however, entailed the danger that it would be used *not* to enjoy God's love and to love God in return, but to go one's own way in defiance of both God and one's own best interest.[4]

Even an omnipotent being cannot make an individual who has the capacity of free will always choose to do what is right. One cannot have free will and not have free will. God cannot perform logical impossibilities that are true contradictions. Just as God cannot make himself exist and not exist; he cannot give a person free will and give that person no choices. The theist's view is that God granted humans free will so that they would have the dignity of making authentic choices with real consequences. If God were only to allow good choices, humans would be mere robots involuntarily carrying out God's orders.[5] Does a robot then have the capacity to love?

CHAPTER 9

IF GOD ALWAYS PREVENTED EVIL, GOD WOULD BE INCESSANTLY INTERFERING WITH HUMAN LIVES.

If God were to intervene to prevent any harm from resulting from a bad choice by a human, God would be incessantly interfering with the lives of human beings and defeating any authenticity and integrity in their choices. If we hypothesize that a good God would always prevent any evil, we can imagine a kind of world that would lack any true moral choices. This kind of world would be one in which no one was harmed and no adverse consequences from one's freely made choices would result. God would intervene to prevent any such consequences. In response to David Hume's question of why God could not directly intervene in the workings of nature to prevent any suffering and to maximize human pleasure, British philosopher John Hick allows that God could do this, but questions what that would mean in practice.

If Hume's suggestion were implemented, how would that affect the moral choices of human beings? Hick emphasizes that there would be no adverse effects from wrong or even criminal behavior. If someone acted in an intentionally grossly negligent manner, there would be no harmful results. God would intervene to always prevent any harm of any kind to anyone. If a person attempted to use a machine gun to fire into a crowd of innocent persons, my quick and resourceful golden retriever would catch all of the bullets in his teeth, leaving everyone in the crowd and the dog unharmed. The person attempting to kill with the machine gun would bear no responsibility because there would be no harm and therefore no foul. Deception, fraud, theft, and betrayal would never hurt anyone. If your banker absconded with all of your money, an equivalent sum would suddenly appear in your bank account. Somehow it would not be taken from anyone and would not increase the money in circulation and encourage inflation. If a drunken or malicious driver ran over pedestrians, no one would be injured. If in a fit of rage you jumped off a mile-high cliff, you would merely float to the ground like a feather and land uninjured. One can imagine how Hume's suggestion could work with God constantly intervening to prevent all harm and increase all human pleasure.

After describing a similar scenario for a magical world with the same kind of constant supernatural intervention, Hick notes that in such a world, we would lose the capacity for moral qualities and moral values: "If to act wrongly means, basically, to harm someone, there would no longer be any such thing as morally wrong action. And for the same reason there would no longer be any such thing as morally right action. . . . It would be a world without need for the virtues of self-sacrifice, care for others, devotion to the public good, courage, perseverance, skill, or honesty. It would indeed be a world in which such qualities, having no function to perform, would never come into existence."[6]

Hick goes on to argue that the capacity to love could never develop in such a world in which God intervened to remove all of the consequences of one's action. We may ask why doesn't God prevent evil consequences, but it is difficult to imagine on a practical basis how such a prevention could occur without giving up authentic good.

TO ARGUE THAT THE EXISTENCE OF EVIL IS LOGICALLY INCOMPATIBLE WITH GOD'S EXISTENCE DISREGARDS THE FLAWED, FINITE LIMITS OF HUMAN KNOWLEDGE.

To use the existence of evil as an argument against the existence of God means that we must know that the existence of evil is logically incompatible with God's existence. But if God has good reasons for allowing the existence of evil, because such existence allows for a greater good, the argument fails. For Hume's argument to prevail he must demonstrate that God has no good reason for allowing the evil that exists in the world. No one has ever been able to demonstrate that this is true.

The problem for the person who uses this argument is that he stands in a position in which his perspective and reason is vastly inferior to that of a Supreme Being. The atheist cannot know for certain that allowing the existence of evil does not result in far greater good. To assume that there are no good reasons why God allows evil is to assume that one has the perspective, knowledge, and reasoning capacity equal to that of an all-knowing, omnipotent, infinite being. Human beings are finite. We reason with finite minds. In addition to this finitude, our process of human reason is flawed, defected, and infected with inaccuracies and limits caused by our imperfections. Our thinking is always clouded by emotions, past histories, unverified presuppositions, and influences that distort our thinking whether we know it or not. For example, when accused of misconduct, a frequent human reaction is to justify our actions by pointing the finger at other events or persons who caused our misconduct. Our minds quickly marshall evidence why we are not at fault. The persons we then blame for our misconduct quickly marshal their own evidence why they are not at fault and so on. The processes of the human mind do not result in pure reason. We reason as whole persons, subject to all the imperfections in our being.[7]

Pride in human reason propels us to assume that we are able to understand the reasons for God's action. But human reason is finite and limited. God is infinitely above human reason, and God's goodness is infinitely above human goodness. Our understanding of perfection and good is limited by our lack of experience of a perfect good. Such a perfection does not exist in human experience or thought. We have no analogy to which we can point to demonstrate a being of perfect goodness. We can only guess with a very limited, less-than-infinite power of reason.

With respect to seemingly pointless suffering, we must ask the question: How probable is it that the outweighing good from any given suffering would be apparent to us? If the question that disturbs us arises from the characteristics of God as all-knowing, all-powerful, and all good, we, who are finite in our knowledge, limited in our power, and imperfect in our goodness, may not be able to detect the purposes of God in permitting evil and whether those purposes justify the existence of the evil.[8]

The limited understanding of a human being and the unlimited understanding of the divine may be analogous to the difference in understanding between an amoeba and an infinite, all-knowing God. Infinity has a way of requiring that statement, even though it is clearly beyond our understanding to even grasp a significant portion of the analogy, let alone the reality of the distance between finitude and infinity. How can the finite ever grasp the infinite?

Consequently, we have to acknowledge that appearances can be deceiving; now we see in a glass darkly. Can we leap to conclusions when we cannot understand all of the evidence?[9] Human reason is flawed and limited. The reasoning of an infinite God would vastly exceed the abilities of humans to comprehend the rationale behind all of creation. To assert that we would have made a better world, perhaps, is to claim that we have a greater understanding than the One who creates. In the words of Stephen Evans, professor of philosophy at Baylor University: "One way of looking at some evidential arguments from evil is to see them as making a claim that the world does not look as I myself would expect it to look if it were created by a good God. But what does this mean? Does it mean that if I were God and had created the world, I would have created a different world? Who am I to make such a claim?"[10]

This question is reminiscent of the book of Job, in which out of the whirlwind God asks Job, "Where were you when I laid the foundation of the earth?" Job realizes his human status and responds, "Therefore I have uttered what I did not understand, things too wonderful for me, which I did not know."

Our knowledge is incomplete, and we do not know why God permits the existence of evil. But this does not mean that there are no good reasons or purposes behind God's action or inaction. *Only if we assert that we would know if God had good reasons for allowing evil do we face an issue that is incompatible with the existence of an omniscient, omnipotent, completely good God.* As Evans notes: "Suppose it is true that I do not know why God allows evil. What follows? It does not follow that God has no good reason for allowing evil unless I am willing to claim that the following principle is true: If God had a good reason for allowing evil, I would know what that reason is. (But) . . . we have no reason to think this principle is true; in fact, we have good reason to think it is false."[11]

Our inability to see any apparent good is exactly what we should expect if an infinite, all-knowing, all-powerful, good God exists. Only if we look at God as limited by our anthropomorphic understanding is the problem of evil insurmountable. Only if our concept of God is limited to a mere "superman" who is always saving the day for us are we entitled to believe that we would know the good that results from suffering. But the universe is too vast and complex for such a concept of God to be rational; God is infinitely above our understanding. He is beyond our ken.

MUCH SUFFERING APPEARS TO BE FOR NO GOOD REASON.

Nevertheless, we see many events of what appear to be pointless suffering. I do not want to minimize the reality of pain. There appears to be no good reason why so much suffering was caused by the tsunami disaster in the Indian Ocean. Hundreds of thousands of people died, many were injured, whole villages were destroyed. It is very difficult to see how this disaster had any good purpose. The tsunami appears to have no good reason why it was allowed to occur.

We know so much horrendous suffering that does not *appear* to serve any good. What is the apparent good in a fawn caught in a forest fire, burned, and dying a slow, agonizing death over several days? Isn't the suffering of the fawn apparently for no good reason? We can think of many events in which the existence of suffering seems pointless, such as the Lisbon earthquake on November 1, 1755, where, similar to the recent tsunami, a prolonged earthquake in the ocean sent a massive wave devastating the capital of the Portuguese empire. The destruction that followed the quake had a profound effect on Voltaire, who then wrote his satirical book, *Candide*, against Leibniz's philosophical argument that this was the best of all possible worlds. It was difficult for Voltaire, just as it is difficult for us today with respect to the tsunami, to find some outweighing good for the disaster. I do not minimize the issue of suffering; there is real pain in this world. One cannot ignore or make trivial the deep suffering and travail in existence.

Perhaps, in our final human logical analysis, following the principles of imperfect, human logic, we encounter a stalemate: The atheist cannot demonstrate that no good comes out of suffering, and the theist cannot demonstrate that good always comes out of suffering. The demonstration of either position may simply be beyond human capacities.

ONE MUST REFRAME HUME'S QUESTION WITH A CONSIDERATION OF THE TOTALITY OF EVIDENCE FOR THE EXISTENCE OF GOD.

I will reframe Hume's question and merely inquire whether the existence of so much evil makes it *improbable* for a good God to exist. This inquiry requires that we consider the *totality of evidence* for the existence of God. If all one considers is the problem of evil, then we are not addressing Hume's reframed question with all of the information necessary to make a judgment on the probability of the existence of God, given the existence of the evil in the world. We must look at all the information available to us and put that information into our answer.

When we look at the areas previously discussed concerning the existence of God and the evidence from beauty and mathematical beauty, the full stage of evidence, even including the problem of evil, suggests that not only does a good God exist but also that this God is working in a purposeful direction to bring about a plan for our good.

The world has many pleasures and many beauties. We have the joy of love, human intimacy, and creativity. Most importantly we have the joy and knowledge that comes from an intimate fellowship with the Wholly Other God. Christians affirm that God is completely light with no darkness in him. This affirmation claims that God is perfect love and infinitely greater than any being of which we can rationally conceive. The good that comes to us in an encounter in which we are surrounded and embraced by this Being overwhelms any earthly ill. The experience of divine love can engulf the struggles and pain of this world.

AN IMPERFECT WORLD ALLOWS THE DEVELOPMENT OF GREATER CHARACTER AND GROWTH IN VALUES OF INTEGRITY, LOVE, COMPASSION, COURAGE, TRUTH, AND SELF-GIVING.

Each of the three monotheistic faiths of Islam, Judaism, and Christianity assert that the universe is moving toward an ultimate fulfillment that will clarify the true nature of reality. They all look to the future for the explanation of the present and the past. According to these faiths, this future will mean a peaceful and wonderful existence in a relationship with God, unmarred by human conflict.[12]

Hick believes that in raising the problem of evil as an argument against the existence of God, Hume confuses his concept of what the world should be with God's purpose in creating the world. In Hume's view the world should be a paradise made for the pleasure and happiness of its inhabitants. Hick argues that the world is not to be a hedonistic paradise in which God's human pets are given immediate pleasure, but a world in which humankind is allowed to develop greater character and grow in greater values, such as integrity, love, compassion, humor, courage, truth, and self-giving. Hume seems to base his ideal on human pleasure as the ultimate good and perhaps as the real purpose of human existence.

Certainly, as parents we do not want our children to seek only pleasure but to develop in character and in ethical virtue, to become persons of eternal worth. So the question to ask is not is this the most hedonistically pleasurable world, but rather is this the kind of world in which human beings can foster the development of valuable characteristics and make choices that allow them to participate in a divine plan that will only have its fulfillment in the future and beyond time. On a practical level, our response to evil matters greatly. When a reporter questioned Mother Teresa and asked where God was when an abandoned baby died in Calcutta, she responded by saying, "God is there, suffering with that baby. The question really is, *where are you?*"[13] Albert

Einstein made a similar point when he noted: "The world is too dangerous to live in—not because of people who do evil, but because of people who sit and let it happen."

The Christian position is that the chief end of man is to know and glorify God and enjoy him forever. The chief end of man is not his eternal pleasure or his constant happiness. The joy that comes from a knowledge of God is a by-product of that knowledge. Humans were not created for the purpose of pleasure and happiness. The Christian view on the reason for the creation of humans is the knowledge of God and an eternal fulfillment lived in a loving relationship with God. Evils may prevent human happiness in this world, but they may end up producing a deeper relationship with the God, who, according to Christian scripture, loves us with an unlimited, infinite love that is to be expressed in an everlasting relationship of complete goodness.

FOR CHRISTIANS THE PROBLEM OF EVIL IS ADDRESSED BY A GOD WHO PARTICIPATES IN HUMAN SUFFERING.

Christians believe that the divine plan is focused on the God-man born in poverty at the beginning of the first century. The problem of evil is addressed for the Christian by the life, crucifixion, and resurrection of Jesus of Nazareth. Although I will not explain the earliest evidence concerning Jesus fully here, there is strong support for believing that, almost contemporaneous with the event of the crucifixion, he was worshiped as God in human form. If the Incarnation, crucifixion, and resurrection, as proclaimed by the early church, are true, then God is not remote from human suffering but is a crucified God, who is working in history to fulfill his purposes. If Jesus is the Incarnation of God, then we have a God who participates in human suffering.

If Jürgen Moltmann is right in his book, *The Crucified God*, God himself hung on the gallows, taking into himself the pain and sin of the world, the events of Auschwitz, and all other grisly misdeeds against humankind. If the Incarnation is correct, then the God behind the vast expansions of space and the complexity of the smallest cell did not stand removed from the problem of evil but addressed it by sharing in human suffering and enduring agonizing pain.

If Jesus of Nazareth was fully divine and fully human, then God has suffered along with humankind. This is the conclusion reached by Martin

Luther and many contemporary theologians. In summarizing Luther's view, Moltmann notes that the person of Christ is determined by the divine person, and this divine person is not a mere bystander but one who participates and shares human suffering: "Therefore the divine person also suffers and dies in the suffering and death of Christ. So he (Luther) can say, '*Vere dicitur: Iste homo creavit mundum et Deus iste passu, mortuus, sepultus. . . .*'"[14] This thought echoes the chorus in the hymn "And Can It Be That I Should Gain?": "Amazing love! How can it be that Thou my God shouldst die for me!"

This is a difficult concept, for how can a necessary being die? Moltmann addresses this in again quoting Luther: "In his nature God cannot die. But now that God and man are united in one person, when the man dies, that is rightly called the death of God, for he is one thing or one person with God."[15] In other words, God was in Christ, nailed to a cross, and, in Dorothy Sayers's words, experienced "the worst horrors of pain and humiliation, defeat, despair, and death."[16]

Brutal, physical suffering is clear to us when we see the pain of God on the cross. Some believe that God expressed His love in this way and provided atonement for all of the evils and wrongs of humankind in a physical way because it was something every one of us could understand. The Christian faith also believes that He suffered in nonphysical ways that were far greater in pain. According to the Christian faith, all the wrongs of the world were focused in that event. An old English hymn captures this concept: "I may not know; I cannot tell what pains He had to bear. But I believe it was for me He hung and suffered there."[17]

The knowledge of God in the Christian faith is ultimately based on our conviction that He is the flogged and crucified God who suffers with us and leads us to a better existence. In this faith one can say, "Even though he slay me yet shall I trust him."

10

EVIDENTIAL FORCE OF RELIGIOUS EXPERIENCE

If God is a Person, God can be Known to Only a Very Limited Extent by Abstract Reasoning and is More Fully Known by Personal Acquaintance in an I–Thou Relationship with the Wholly Other

GOD CANNOT BE KNOWN BY ONLY OBJECTIVE, NEUTRAL MEANS BECAUSE GOD IS ABOVE ALL CATEGORIES AND HAS PERSONHOOD.

Swiss theologian Emil Brünner understood that one could never really objectively analyze the question of God's existence. Brünner held that we cannot examine God as if God were a part of the universe, because God is not part of the universe and is not subject to traditional human methods of analytical examination. The answer to the question of God's existence can never be known in a merely objective, neutral manner. We cannot examine God as if God were something that can be placed in a neat category. By definition God is infinitely above all categories, including the categories of our human reason.

Sören Kierkegaard, a nineteenth century Copenhagen philosopher, preceded Brünner in grasping this concept and maintained that because our reason is flawed with pride, we cannot see its limits clearly until we encounter the divine who cannot be just a vastly superior caricature of a human person, but a person beyond, above, and behind all that exists. Such an encounter is necessary, because, assuming that God is a person, a person's knowledge of another person is not first and foremost an intellectual activity, but an activity integrated with the quality of one's character and affected by one's experience. Kierkegaard used the Danish word *kendskab* to describe this kind of knowledge by personal acquaintance.

Is Kierkegaard's assumption that God is a person justifiable? Most humans consider themselves persons, but many of us assume that although we have personhood, the "thing" behind all of existence does not have personhood but has a lower form of existence. We consider persons to have a higher form of existence than mere things, but many of us relegate the source of the universe and all its components to a status below personhood, a status of "thinghood." As noted in chapter 2, Russian philosopher Nicholas Berdyaev called this truncation of the personhood of the divine a "thingification" or *Verdinglichung* of the divine dimension and considered it a source of the degradation of humankind. Despite Berdyaev's thoughtful argument, a common, contemporary materialist perspective is that there is an unconscious principle or law acting as the source of the universe and the source of human existence.

Given the power, precision, and rational order in our universe, isn't it more likely that whatever is behind the universe is conscious and has a higher form of existence than human existence? After all, humans are conscious but lack the ability to generate a universe finely tuned to allow for the development and existence of conscious inhabitants. Why do we assume that an unconscious law can do so? Why should we hold the *presupposition* that a nonpersonal law gives rise to persons and consciousness? As William Temple wrote: "For no law, apart from a Lawgiver, is a proper object of reverence. It is mere brute fact; and every living thing, still more every person exercising intelligent choice, is its superior. The reverence of persons can be appropriately given only to that which itself is at least personal."[1]

Many persons with strict materialistic worldviews simply assume that the unconscious laws of physics are the means by which a higher form of existence, i.e., conscious personhood, comes to be. This assumption appears frequently to have another leap of faith underlying it that endows these laws with their own peculiar "personhood." For example, this endowment is implied in what we do semantically when we refer to "Nature" as if nature were a person who makes conscious choices and "decides" to move in one direction or another. Purely physical processes are described with characteristics of a mind that "knows" how to act to bring about certain complex results. Other than the spelling of the words, what is the difference in these descriptions between "God" and "Nature"? If nature is endowed with the characteristics of knowledge, choice, and power, how does "Nature" differ from "God"? When a materialist states that "Nature" chooses to act in a certain way and causes life or other complex phenomena to be in a certain way, isn't he giving the attributes of personhood and consciousness to something impersonal and unconscious? I am not denying that the laws of physics have certain limited self-organizational powers. Rather, I am questioning whether a materialist worldview can be consistent and coherent when it ascribes attributes of consciousness, choice, and knowledge to purely physical processes.

As noted above in the section on quantum physics, I question the reduction of the life of humankind to complex containers of chemicals with energy-generating electrical impulses resulting in a mind with a conscious admiration for the equations of the laws of physics. Unconscious, impersonal laws of physics seem rather inept compared to the abilities of human persons to think and relate to one another. I can see that humankind also rises to the level of personhood capable of virtuous acts of love. If human beings are essentially physical, psychosomatic beings, they are also persons capable of beautiful, marvelous, and even courageous, heroic actions. And if this is true of human beings, a plausible position is that this may also be true of the source of the universe and humanity.

The reduction of God to a mere principle or source of laws is another one of the absurd remnants left to contemporary society by the philosophy of Immanuel Kant. His argument for the existence of a moral imperative reduced the concept of a personal God to a mere formula for ethics. In his *Metaphysics of Morals* Kant made the moral law the object of his religious faith. Kant ignored the personhood of God so that his religion became a mere legalistic moralism with God relegated to an ultimate Legislator, not a person worthy of participating in communication with human beings.

Consequently, one of the questionable legacies of Kant's eighteenth-century philosophy is a contemporary concept of respect for the moral law and no devotion to the person who inspires the law. Kant's deist concept of God precluded the personality of God as one with whom humans can converse and interact. As noted above, in some sense, this God has a lesser form of existence than you and I if we consider ourselves persons. We at least act as if we are persons and have a tendency to acknowledge our friends as persons. If one follows Kant's logic and perceives God only as a divine Legislator, then one assumes a greater status than God, because one considers himself or herself to be a person and acts in a manner consistent with that belief. John Baillie, formerly a professor at Edinburgh University, disagreed with Kant and held that the source behind the universe and the development of human consciousness was more likely to be a person. In commenting on Kant's reduction of religion to a mere legalistic moralism without worship or communion with a person, Baillie held that it is precisely the ability to *converse* with God that bestows personhood on humankind: "It is no mere formula with which the sons (and daughters) of men have ever found themselves faced as they approached life's most solemn issues, but a Reality of an altogether more intimate and personal kind."[2]

The hypothesis that the source of the universe is a person with whom we can interact is consistent with the perception of humans as personalities with whom we converse. It seems rationally plausible that a person is behind the existence of persons rather than an impersonal law acting as the foundation for personhood. In noting that Kant erred in his comprehension of the obligations of humankind when he viewed the obligations as a mere law detached from any person who places the obligations upon humankind, Baillie wrote:

> We, on the other hand, have argued that the Source of the obligation is Himself directly revealed to us and that it is in this vision of His glory and His holiness that our sense of obligation is born. It is *His* perfection that rebukes us; it is *His* love that constrains us. Hence it is no mere law that is revealed to us, but a living Person, and what we call the moral law is but an abstraction which our limited and limiting minds make from the concreteness of the living Glory that is revealed.[3]

A rational discussion of religious faith is necessarily combined with a discussion concerning the means of encountering the divine. Evidence from religious experience can never be understood outside of a transforming relationship with the God who makes himself known to us in personal experience. This was a flaw in Freud's reasoning that religious experience was an illusion. He did not have that experience and consequently did not have the understanding or knowledge given by such an experience. Consequently, he could only consider it an illusion; he lacked the understanding or knowledge given by an encounter with the divine.

We can never draw close to God in a merely objective, neutral manner. Our understanding depends in large measure on our relationship to God, our trust in him, and our willingness to allow him to transform our character. Pure reason has its limits, and one of these limits is the inability of our finite minds to grasp even a portion of the infinite without having our minds transformed, renewed, and remolded by God's action within our own consciousness. As illustrations of the kind of transforming friendship or encounter with the divine that allows us to understand the evidence in a new light, I set forth a series of testimonies from the lives of persons who relate similar experiences of an awakening and a new understanding that accompanied their encounter with God.

The similarity of their experiences is some evidence of the repair of flawed human reason to know the divine who ultimately is above and beyond reason. In countless instances throughout history, persons claim to have encountered God and experienced the removal of opaque scales that previously clouded their vision and understanding. I do not mean this in a literal sense, but the experience is quite common and the description consistent. The encounter often produces joy, a new capacity to love, and a clarified understanding of an infinitely loving deity.

Oxford chemist and philosopher Michael Polanyi emphasized the "skill of religious knowing."[4] For him religious knowledge is a product of worship. One knows God by participation in worship, including the singing of hymns, prayers, the Eucharist and, in a broader context, the admiration of the beauty of the universe. The encounter with God that produces religious knowing may not be confined to a single event, even though a dramatic single event may radically transform a person such as the slave trader John Newton, who aided William Wilberforce in his political victory over the British slave trade.[5] However, we also have the example of the transformation of Oxford professor Basil Mitchell, who gradually developed an increased capacity for religious knowing through his participation in Anglican worship. Some persons come to faith gradually while others have a more profound, radical, single event whereby they are overwhelmed by the presence of divine love. Polanyi held that religious knowing, in all events, requires participation in some form of worship; it cannot occur by mere objective analysis or observation alone.

When one realizes the vastness and complexity of the universe, its laws, and the remarkable nature of life and consciousness, it should not come as a surprise that the source of such vastness and complexity should be a Being with a mind that is beyond human reason. If, however, humans are able to commune with such a Being, then the transformation of character that may follow from such a communion may open our minds to understand in a way that is superior to a finite and necessarily flawed capacity for mere human rational inquiry. Perhaps because our reason is flawed with pride, we cannot see its limits clearly until we are in communion with a God whose consciousness knows no limits and who understands all things. Existential theologians have held that a strictly empirical attempt to understand God will naturally fail, as will any purely rational attempt to approach the divine without first encountering, trusting, and committing oneself to a transforming relationship with the divine. In this respect, the argument for the existence of God is not first and foremost an intellectual activity, but an activity integrated with the quality of one's character. Jewish philosopher Emmanuel Levinas argues that by looking into the face of the Other we begin to be transformed and gain an understanding of ourselves.[6]

KIERKEGAARD USED THE DANISH WORD *KENDSKAB* TO MEAN THE KIND OF KNOWLEDGE THAT COMES FROM PERSONAL ACQUAINTANCE.

The discussion above concerning whether or not our definition of God includes personhood is important, because when we attempt to have knowledge of a person's existence, we have to consider *how* we know the person. A strictly empirical attempt to understand or know another person will fail. This is because a person's knowledge of another person is not an intellectual activity. We can have a knowledge based on abstract reasoning about a person, but a deeper form of knowledge of a person is derived from *personal acquaintance*. This personal knowledge is much more informative.

Sören Kierkegaard used the Danish word *videnskab* to describe knowledge based on abstract propositions and the word *kendskab* to mean the kind of knowledge that comes from personal acquaintance. The distinction between the two kinds of knowledge can be illustrated in the example of a young man who hears about a wonderful woman who is joining him and his companions on a trip. As he thinks about what she might be like, he uses abstract concepts to try to imagine her. When he meets her, however, and falls in love with her, his knowledge of her is not derived from abstract thought but from personal acquaintance.

Kierkegaard maintained that this was also true of the knowledge of God. When one encounters and grasps a glimpse of an infinite loving God, one knows by personal acquaintance. For Kierkegaard this *kendskab* gives rise to a deep trust that transcends human reason and opens one's mind to truth. Deep belief and transformation flow from this kind of knowledge.

One's ability to know reality results from an encounter with the divine. Human pride and selfishness hinder one's ability to see one's limitations. By encountering God and knowing God's concern and compassion for all humans, a person's pride and egoism are diminished so that he can see truth. For Kierkegaard our knowledge of the divine depends upon our encounter with God's personhood, which is one of infinite and unlimited love. Once one moves toward God, one becomes more open to the magnitude and reality of his beauty, power, and love. A natural response is a "passion of trust" that transforms one's being and gives one an ability to see truths that otherwise may appear vague and absurd.[7]

Kierkegaard's emphasis is on a faith in God resulting from a transforming encounter with the divine that increases one's spiritual capacity. He regards faith as a matter of a long-term passion. Rational arguments for God's existence provide some evidence that points to God's presence, but the ability to recognize the presence of God depends on the development of one's spiritual abilities. This is required because God is a spiritual being. As Kierkegaard held, "like can only be known by like." Knowledge of God can then only come from a true personal acquaintance with God, not from a "neutral," purely objective approach. Evidence for God's existence can only be recognized well when one has developed the spiritual capacity to see reality through the eyes of faith. To develop such a capacity one may need to step forward in trust as one attempts to commune with God.

For Kierkegaard, the evidence for God's existence springs from a relationship of personal acquaintance with the divine. Kierkegaard compared such a relationship with the interaction of two human lovers. As Stephen Evans notes:

> He (Kierkegaard) often illustrates faith by comparing it to love, not the momentary passion of someone who is infatuated, but the developed,

> "formed" disposition of the true lover. One of the characteristics of a person who genuinely loves another is a heightened sensitivity, an ability to recognize the good qualities of the loved one. In an analogous way, a person of faith, a kind of lover of God who has developed the capacity to trust God, has a heightened capacity to see God's presence. Just as a lover knows how to interpret the behaviour of the beloved, so the person of faith knows how to interpret the handiwork of God seen about us.[8]

Kierkegaard is often referred to as the father of existentialism. This may not be a totally accurate description because existentialism is mainly concerned with an analysis of the existence of human beings. Kierkegaard was more concerned with the relationship between humans and God, whom he saw as a "Wholly Other" being.[9] Kierkegaard held that the knowledge of God was not something that could exclude the character of the person claiming such knowledge. In other words, the knowledge of God could not be separated from the kind of person the knower is to become. This theory of knowledge is not an epistemology that only centers on objective knowledge, such as one may have about the laws of physics. To have the kind of existential knowledge of God described by Kierkegaard, a person must decide to become a person of spiritual conviction. The kind of knowledge with which Kierkegaard is concerned is not derived from the mere transmission of information. In this sense it is not mere objective knowledge but relates to the character of the subject or human being who is the knower. Kierkegaard, in essence, is describing the kind of knowledge that came to Augustine in a garden during his conversion experience. Augustine had objective knowledge about God and about the doctrines of the Christian faith, but his knowledge did not affect him until he made his choice in the garden. In more modern times, Mortimer Adler gave his account of his transformation over a long period of time from a person with considerable understanding of the intellectual arguments for the existence of God to a person who was transformed by his experience of God in 1984.

MARTIN BUBER EMPHASIZED THAT THE PERSONHOOD OF GOD MEANS THAT WE CAN ONLY HAVE KNOWLEDGE OF GOD IN AN I-THOU RELATIONSHIP WITH GOD'S

PERSON, NOT IN AN INVESTIGATION OF GOD AS AN OBJECT OR A THING.

Martin Buber was a Jewish philosopher who was profoundly influenced by Kierkegaard. Buber brought additional insight into Kierkegaard's emphasis on the importance of a person's actions, commitments, and spiritual development in his or her quest for knowledge in the publication of his widely read book on epistemology, originally translated from the German as *I–Thou* (*Ich und Du*). Buber disagreed with Kant and held that empiricism, knowledge gained only through the five senses alone, is a theory of knowledge that is too limited to take into account the profound variety and depth of our ability to gain knowledge through relationships. If God is a person, then knowledge of God requires that we respond to the divine being as a person, not as an object or a thing. Buber agrees with Brünner in holding that God cannot be known through a merely objective, neutral inquiry. In Buber's words, if our relation to God remains only in the realm of an "I-It" (*Ich-Es*) objectivity, we can never have significant knowledge of God.

Of course, we can know something about God by abstract thought, but God cannot be analyzed as a thing. Agreeing with Kierkegaard, Buber asserts that God is a person and cannot be encountered only as an object of investigation. In Buber's definition of the "I–Thou" relationship, one becomes totally involved and committed in the relationship with God and in that relationship gains a knowledge that is denied to the person seeking only an "I-It" relationship. In other words, one can only have access to God in an encounter with God that involves a dialogue with God and a commitment of one's being to the relationship.

Buber's position may be illustrated by reference to the music of Bach. His music can be studied objectively in the sense of our deciphering the notes, bars, and verses, but we can also encounter and experience the music as we listen to it as it is played by a great symphony orchestra and as it pervades our being. Our knowledge of the music is no longer just an objective, analytical exercise, but an experience of beauty and power. Similarly, we can know many things about God and analyze the universe for signals of a transcendent being, but it is in the encounter with the divine person that we experience and know the Thou. Buber held that this encounter involved sacrifice and risk. For Buber, the person in search of the knowledge of God must sacrifice, take risks, and search with one's whole being. In Buber's words, "whoever commits himself may not hold back part of himself."[10] Realizing the inadequacy of words to describe the I–Thou encounter, Buber emphasizes that such an encounter can only take place in activity, not in a reserved holding back of one's self. This is true in the encounter with the divine, and for Buber, this kind of encounter can also take place with other persons and with great works of art.[11]

More specifically, Buber insists that the knowledge of God requires *activity and mission*. This may not be what we want to hear when we would prefer only a mystical "I–Thou" encounter that would enhance our own sense of well being. But Buber believes that a person's *calling* and *mission* are inextricably linked to the ability to know God. To remain in an encounter with the divine, one cannot fall back into only contemplating the divine being. For Buber, any encounter that elucidates the knowledge of God cannot be limited to a passive contemplation of God. If one attempts to limit his activity to only an experience of God, he will lose the experience, and any knowledge of God will fall back into a mere "I-It" analytical relationship. The encounter with God is a calling to not merely attend to God but to take His life into the world and act in the world motivated by a deep love of God and of humanity: "When you are sent forth, God remains presence for you; whoever walks in his mission always has God before him: the more faithful the fulfillment, the stronger and more constant the nearness."[12]

If we attempt to only search for God as a thing to be experienced, we will never succeed in our attempt to gain the knowledge of God. This is why an investigation into the question of God's existence cannot be done by purely logical, scientific, and historical means. Although, given the unity of truth, these means are useful; any epistemology that limits knowledge to these means will be inadequate and defective. God is not an It, but the eternal Thou who calls us into action, commitment, risk, and sacrifice for the sake of the world.

FOR RUDOLF OTTO THE HOLY WHOLLY OTHER GOD IS NOT AN IDEA, NOT A CONCEPT THAT CAN BE DESCRIBED

CHAPTER 10

BY LANGUAGE; LANGUAGE CAN NEVER CAPTURE THE EXPERIENCE OF THE PERSON OF GOD.

Kierkegaard's understanding of *kendskab* and Buber's *I–Thou* epistemology have much in common with the thinking of the twentieth century German philosopher, Rudolf Otto. For Otto, God is *sui generic*, a uniquely *Wholly Other.* Any attempt to describe an encounter with God in words will lose the essence of the encounter. Consequently, a strictly empirical theory of knowledge or a strictly empirical attempt to understand God will naturally fail, as will any purely rational attempt to approach the divine in a neutral, objective manner.

In 1917 Otto published his major work *Das Heilige*, which was translated into English under the title *The Idea of the Holy*. The English wording is not a direct translation, which may be unfortunate, because a major point of Otto's book was that *the holy is not an idea*, not a concept that can be communicated by means of rational language. Otto argued persuasively that a naturalistic science could never explain or comprehend spiritual experience. Although many philosophers believed that Immanuel Kant had successfully collapsed the theistic arguments, Otto saw in Kant's writing a way prepared by Kant to see the experience of sublimity and beauty as nonrational symbols of supersensible purpose in the universe. Following in the footsteps of Friedrich Schleiermacher (1768–1834), Otto looked upon religion as a unique experience that was part of the realm of nonrational feeling or *Gefühl*, an affection felt at a primal level. This was the realm of the uncanny, the realm of reverence and a sense of awe, a sense of the awful, mysterious, and tremendous. Otto made new words to describe this feeling of a presence that is Wholly Other. He used the term *numinous* to designate the unique holiness of the divine.

He argued that the presence of the *numinous* was experienced as the *mysterium tremendum.* In his view religious experience is a legitimate, unique dimension of human experience. His writing should not be interpreted as a defense of an irrational approach to religious experience but as a rational inquiry into the suprarational characteristics of an encounter with the divine Wholly Other.

The experience of the *numinous* is not subject to description in language. Once one attempts to describe the experience, the experience is gone. It cannot be communicated by means of a definition. Yet something objective and external to one's self is present as an active, living, and willing of the *numen*, which cannot be contained in strict, rational definitions or concepts.

The *mysterium* is the symbol of the Wholly Other that is utterly beyond human comprehension but nevertheless overpowers and awes a person with a fascinating charm. The awful aspect of the *numinous* he named the *tremendum*. The quality of fascination was an extension of the *tremendum* and was part of extraordinarily intense encounters with the awe-inspiring character of the transcendent, such as in profound conversion experiences. In these experiences there is not only a feeling of dread but also, much more powerfully, an intense affection and fascination that embodies the mystical movement. This kind of experience is beyond adequate human conceptualization. Otto uses the example of music as a more mundane experience but one that illustrates a nonrational feeling that is a valid mode of experiencing reality.[13]

It is important to note that Otto's word *Heilige* cannot be only an uncanny eeriness. To stop only with the concept of the mysterium tremendum and dissociate the *numinous* from the moral conscious is a great error. Reverence does not flow merely from the "otherness" encountered. John Baillie emphasized the need to remember that the Wholly Other is *holy* and that only a holy Wholly Other can be the subject of human reverence. There is a grave mistake in the attempts to draw near something mysterious in New Age and other religious movements that may not include a sense of holiness in the encounter. In warning against the dissociation of holiness from the search for an encounter with a mysterium tremendum, Baillie saw that the attitude of reverence was part of the essence of religion that could not be reduced to a mere feeling of the presence of something mysterious.[14]

In the presence of the *numinous* one feels the need for atonement and experiences the grace of the Wholly Other. Otto's work emphasized the *sui generic*, unique status of religious experience as a powerful dimension of human experience. Otto was familiar with many religions, but in his emphasis on the Christian faith he attempted to answer the question of how a person can come to experience in Christ "holiness made manifest": "Whoever can thus immerse himself in contemplation (of Jesus's message and life, death and resurrection as a whole) and open his whole mind resolutely to a pure impression of all this combined will surely find growing in him, obedient to an inward standard that defies expression, the pure feeling of 'recognition of holiness', the 'intuition of the eternal in the temporal.'"[15]

According to Otto, in the encounter with the *numinous* one comprehends that one's fulfillment is to be found in a union with the holy Wholly Other. Augustine, the fourth century Bishop of Hippo, finally realized this truth and wrote: "O Lord, thou hast made us for thyself, and our hearts are restless until they rest in thee."

GABRIEL MARCEL EMPHASIZED THE NECESSITY OF MYSTERY AND PARTICIPATORY KNOWLEDGE.

Gabriel Marcel (1889–1973) taught and wrote philosophy in Paris, Montpellier, and Sens. His main vocation was as a drama critic and a playwright. He was part of a distinguished group of philosophers and writers who met in Paris at his residence on Friday evenings to discuss philosophical and literary themes. Emmanuel Levinas, Paul Ricoeur, and Jean-Paul Sartre were among those who gathered with him to share their ideas and exchange perspectives. Sartre described Marcel as a Christian existentialist. Marcel was keen to avoid the elaborate and often vague expressions of contemporary philosophy and attempted to express his thoughts in ordinary language, such as his concept that we live in a "broken world" (*le monde cassé*).

The fact that one may question the logical proofs for God's existence or nonexistence does not mean that God's existence cannot be known. Rather, lack of a compelling proof merely implies that the path by which a person knows of God's existence is not the path of abstract reasoning. One can regard Gabriel Marcel's writings as an attempt to describe the efficacy of one's discovery of the constant presence of the divine.[16] Marcel's philosophy emphasized the need for participation and engagement. Detached, abstract thought was not as efficacious as the "immediacy of participation." Consequently, detachment led to regarding another person (human or God) as an object. Such a perspective, argued Marcel, had the deleterious effect of turning the detached observer also into an object. Marcel distinguished between problems and mystery. He regarded problems as abstract, detached rational concepts that merely require solutions. He was far more interested in encountering a mystery, which does not have a "solution" but invites participation. For Marcel, *knowledge depends upon participation.*

In Marcel's view arguments for the existence of God can only be confirmatory; they can only serve to verify what one has learned from another approach than pure reason. Marcel believed that there are logically valid arguments for the existence of God but that there are several reasons why one will not see their validity. One reason that the argument for God's existence may not convince a particular person is that he or she may be a person with a predetermined, willful position to resist the persuasiveness of the argument. Marcel thought that another reason one may have a predisposition not to believe in God could be one's aversion to having any limitations placed on his own being, so that one *wills* that God not exist to remain independent of God. Marcel notes the irrefutable nature of the arguments for God's existence but blames the disintegration of humans in a broken world as the reason for the inability of persons to see the validity of the arguments: ". . . the relative ineffectiveness on the apologetic level at least of so-called rational theology. . . . In the final analysis, it is because the unity of man has been shattered, because his world is broken—that we confront this scandal of proofs which are logically irrefutable but which in fact exhibit a lack of any persuasive power."[17]

Thus, in contemporary society the will not to see the validity of the arguments is in essence a will that God not exist. Coming up against this will, the arguments for God's existence are completely inefficacious. As Clyde Pax writes: "When, as appears to be the case in some quarters today, the will not to believe is, in fact, also a will that God should not be, the proofs become totally ineffective."[18]

Rather than beginning with rational proofs for the existence of God, Marcel believed that a more meaningful approach would be to begin with the historic evidence that many persons of keen intelligence have claimed to have encountered God and committed their lives to living in a transforming relationship with God. The rational proofs can only be supplemental confirmations of what these persons have been given in another fashion than mere abstract thought.

Following Marcel's emphasis on witnesses, I will now turn to the testimony of nine persons who I will call to the witness stand to describe the knowledge they derived from their experiences of God.

11

RECORDED EXPERIENCES OF ENCOUNTERS WITH THE DIVINE BEAR WITNESS TO A WAY OF KNOWING THAT INCLUDES KIERKEGAARD'S *KENDSKAB*, BUBER'S *I–THOU*, OTTO'S *WHOLLY OTHER*, AND MARCEL'S *MYSTERY*

In the pages that follow I call nine persons to the witness stand who claim to have experienced the kind of knowledge that is derived from an encounter with the *Wholly Other.* This knowledge includes the personal acquaintance of Kierkegaard's *kendskab*, Buber's *I–Thou*, and Marcel's emphasis on *mystery* and *participatory knowledge.* The encounters (whether sudden or taking place gradually from time to time) led to powerful, beautiful changes in the hearts, minds, and lives of the persons gaining this knowledge. The similarity in their experiences constitutes some evidence to the effect that though human reasoning is flawed, we have some ability to know the Wholly Other Person who is above and beyond reason. Through *kendskab, I–Thou*, *Wholly Other*, and *participatory* experiences these persons testify to a transformation in their worldviews and in their abilities to interpret and live in closer communication with the underlying reality of existence. Although one can choose to discredit their stories, their testimony is that a new kind of personal knowledge of God produced joy, a new capacity to love, and an undescribable understanding of God's existence. Their narratives indicate that it is ultimately by the renewing of our minds that we can gain the capacity or skill to know more of God, and in knowing more of God, to better understand ourselves and others.

AUGUSTINE EXPERIENCED A LIFE-TRANSFORMING CONVERSION IN A GARDEN IN MILAN.

Aurelius Augustinus was born in 354 AD in Tagaste in the Roman province of Numidia (currently Algeria). His family sacrificed most of their finances to send him to school in New Carthage so that he might receive an education that would allow him to serve in the government. At about the age of nineteen he read Cicero's *Hortensius,* a treatise now lost except for some fragments. Cicero's writing gave him a passion for philosophy.

Although his mother, Monica, was a committed Christian, in his early life Augustine considered Christianity too mystical and nonrational. He became intrigued by the Manicheans, who believed in two eternal principles: Light and Darkness. Essentially, this was a belief in good and evil as universal principles eternally fighting for control of the universe. Manicheans held that the human soul was comprised of particles of Light that were locked in a material body that was seen as part of the Darkness of matter. The goal of life in this gnosticlike religion was to free the Light from the prison of the body so that it could reunite with the larger Light from which the particles of Light comprising the soul originally came.

Augustine had an inquisitive mind, and when he determined that the Manicheans could not supply him with rational answers concerning a sufficient explanation of the cosmos and the origin of evil, he looked in other directions. In Rome he considered academic skepticism, and then under the influence of Bishop Ambrose of Milan, he studied Plotinus, who had engaged in a Neoplatonist search for a mystical union with the divine by means of abstract thought. All during Augustine's searches down many intellectual blind alleys and cul-de-sacs, his saintly mother continued to pray for him and his conversion to Christianity.

Finally, in 386 AD when he was thirty-one and a professor of rhetoric at Milan, a distraught Augustine heard a child's voice as he was lamenting in a garden. He described his conversion experience in some detail in his *Confessions,* one of the most widely read narratives of transformation in Christian literature. After his conversion, he left his teaching position, returned to Tagaste, became a priest and then the Bishop of Hippo. He never married but engaged in an extremely active and productive life, performing the considerable duties of a bishop and writing a staggering volume of letters, sermons, and books. The following is a modern translation of his description of his conversion experience in a garden in Milan:

CHAPTER 11

There was a garden next to our lodging, which we had free use of since the owner of the house lived elsewhere. One day during this period of my spiritual turmoil, I made my way into the garden accompanied by Alipius. I felt I had arrived at a crisis. My voice was strained and strange, my face flushed, and tears were beginning to wet my cheeks. . . .

I now could see that everything came down to a problem of the will. We can do nothing unless we will it, from raising a hand to setting out on a journey over land and sea. We must have the will to do it, a determined and strong will, not a halfhearted, ambiguous, indecisive one. . . .

So I sat there in the garden, in a private world of my own. . . . I kept saying to myself, "Come on, let it happen now, let it happen *now*," and as I spoke I almost resolved to do it. But I did not. Yet I did not slide back into my old nature either. It was as though I stood outside myself and watched the struggle. I was hanging there suspended between dying to death and living to life. I was surprised how powerful was the restraint of my old evil habits and how subtly they tugged at me, holding me back. . . .

I flung myself to the ground under a fig tree and wept bitterly, a "sacrifice acceptable to You, O Lord." I cried out loud, in some such words as these: "How long, Lord? How long? Will you be angry with me forever? Do not remember my former sins." It was indeed those former sins and their present power that seemed to be holding me back. So I went on praying. "How long, Lord? Tomorrow and tomorrow? Why not now? Why not at this moment make an end of my uncleanness?" Then, as I prayed, I heard a voice, like a little boy or girl in a nearby house, repeating some words by heart in a singsong manner. "Take it up and read it. Take it up and read it."

I was arrested by the sound. I had never heard those words used in a children's game. My bitterness and tears stopped. I got up, convinced that the message was from heaven and that it was telling me to read from the first chapter I should find on opening my book of Paul's writings. I remembered how Anthony had been told—in a rather similar way, by a passage in the Gospels that was apparently meant for him at one point in his life—"Go, sell all you have, and give to the poor, and you shall have treasure in heaven. And come, and follow me."

So I went back to the table where Alipius was sitting and picked up the book of Paul's writings which I had left there. I took it quickly in my hand, opened it, and read silently from the chapter that my eyes first lighted on. "Not in orgies and drunkenness, not in promiscuity and lust, not in anger or jealousy: but put on the Lord Jesus Christ, and make no provision for the flesh and its desires."

I needed to read no further. Instantly, as I reached the end of the sentence all the darkness of my former doubts was dispelled, as if a clear and

> insistent light had flooded my heart. I must turn from the old; I must put on the new, and I must do it now.
>
> I shut the book, though marking the page, and told Alipius in a quiet and calm voice exactly what had happened. In his turn, he told me what had been going on in his own heart, which I knew nothing about. He then asked if he could see the passage I had read—but he read on a little further to some words I had not known were there. "Now him who is weak in the faith take with you." He applied this to himself, he told me, and at once without any hesitation, he joined me in my newfound purpose and commitment. Immediately we went into the house to find my mother and tell her what had happened. Needless to say, she was overjoyed. As she said, the Lord is "able to do more abundantly than we either ask or think." She said that because she had limited her prayers to my conversion. But so deeply had God worked in me that I had instantly forsaken all human ambitions, even the desire for a wife, and had decided to dedicate myself to that very rule of life which the Lord had shown my mother many years before that I should accept, an acceptance which even she had scarcely the faith to believe would ever actually happen.[1]

Augustine never looked back. He returned to North Africa, became a bishop, founded the Augustinian order, and wrote some of the most significant theology in the history of the Church. His postconversion life is a testament to the fulfillment of Allport's definition of a mature religious sentiment. In addition to his brilliant theological writings, his life produced a steady capacity for joyful love, service, and self-giving to the people of North Africa.

Given my discussion above concerning contingent and necessary beings, it is interesting to note that Augustine described a person's pride as the major impediment in establishing a belief in God. Pride in his sense of the term became an obstacle to the fulfillment of a person's purpose. Pride was manifest in the attempt by a contingent being to set himself up as the center of the world in his desire to be as God. It was "a movement whereby a creature (that is, an essentially dependent being whose principle existence lies not in itself but in another) tries to set-up on its own, to exist for itself. . . . From the moment a creature becomes aware of God as God and of itself as self, the terrible alternative of choosing God or self for the centre is opened to it."[2]

In regarding pride as the main obstacle for belief, Augustine preceded many thoughtful philosophers and theologians, including Kierkegaard, in emphasizing the centrality of this attitude as an impediment to belief.

CHAPTER 11

BLAISE PASCAL TESTIFIED TO A POWERFUL ENCOUNTER WITH THE PRESENCE OF A PERSONAL GOD.

Blaise Pascal was a genius in mathematics and science in the seventeenth century, but he was also profound and rigorous in philosophy, literature, and theology. Born in Clermont in central France in 1623, he moved with his father and two sisters to Paris when he was seven years old. His mother had died when he was only three, and his father was a government official working in the area of tax assessment and collection. One of Pascal's earlier inventions was a calculating machine built to assist his father in his work. This machine is the direct ancestor of contemporary computers. He was a committed Catholic who became associated with the Jansenist movement, moving to their monastery at Port-Royal, France, near Paris. This monastery was also a school for the education of the most promising young minds in France. Jansenism was similar in some ways to Puritanism, but with a deep Catholic emphasis on relating religious understanding to divine grace and spirituality.

The defining moment in Pascal's life came when an overwhelming experience of God invaded his inmost being and became an ecstatic encounter with the presence of the God of Abraham, Isaac, and Jacob, rather than the God of the philosophers. This experience occurred on November 23, 1654, when he was reading the seventeenth chapter of the gospel of John. The experience became the basis for his devotion to philosophy and spiritual contemplation. He continued with his scientific and research activities, but he was always mindful of this overwhelming encounter with the presence of God. Pascal recorded this experience in his own hand in a document known as *The Memorial*, which was sewn into the lining of his coat and found by a servant after his death. Evidently, Pascal had so treasured the experience that he had kept his reminder preserved in the lining of his coat and always transferred it whenever he replaced his coat by again sewing the document into the lining.

THE MEMORIAL

In the year of Grace, 1654,

On Monday, 23rd of November, Feast of St. Clement, Pope and Martyr, and others in the Martyrology, Vigil of Saint Chrysogonus, Martyr, and others from about half past ten in the evening until about half past twelve,

FIRE

God of Abraham, God of Isaac, God of Jacob, not of the philosophers and scholars (Ex. 3:6; Matt. 22:32).

Certitude. Certitude. Feeling. Joy. Peace.

God of Jesus Christ

Deum meum et Deum vestrum ("My God and your God," John 20:17).

Forgetfulness of the world and of everything except God.

He is to be found only by the ways taught in the Gospel.

Greatness of the Human soul.

"Righteous Father, the world hath not known Thee, but I have known Thee" (John 17:25).

Joy, joy, joy, tears of joy.

I have separated myself from Him.

Derelinqueruni me fontem aquae vivae ("They have forsaken me,

the fountain of living waters," Jer. 2:13).

"My God, wilt Thou leave me?" (Matt. 27:46).

Let me not be separated from Him eternally.

"This is the eternal life, that they might know Thee, the only true God, and the one whom Thou has sent, Jesus Christ" (John 17:3).

Jesus Christ.

Jesus Christ.

I have separated myself from Him; I have fled from Him, denied Him, crucified Him.

Let me never be separated from Him.

We keep hold of Him only by the way taught in the Gospel.

Renunciation, total and sweet,

Total submission to Jesus Christ and to my director.

Eternally in joy for a day's training on earth.

Non obliviscar sermones tuos ("I will not forget Thy words," Ps. 118:16). *Amen.*[3]

Pascal's ecstatic conversion experience increased his understanding that the goals people seek in their lives cannot bring authentic happiness. For Pascal, real understanding is gained through religious experience, as indicated in his famous statement: "The heart has its reasons that reason knows not of." It is in the presence of God that knowledge of reality breaks through and points us to the way for happiness. Most of our time, unfortunately, is spent in avoiding the presence of God by giving our attention to diversions and distractions that only assist us in evading the reality that provides an answer to the human predicament. Our involvement with diversions prevents us from seeing the beauty and meaning of reality.

This experience gave Pascal a new level of knowledge, a new way of knowing, that came from a relationship with God as a personal being, not as an abstract concept. Pascal now realized that reason alone was not sufficient to gain access to all that one can know. God is not merely an abstract inference at the end of a logical argument, but a person with whom one may enter into a transforming friendship. On November 23, 1654, Pascal entered into a new level of existence, one that gave him peace, joy, and certitude.[4]

LEO TOLSTOY FOUND MEANING IN UNITY WITH THE INFINITE GOD.

Leo Tolstoy is considered by many to be the greatest novelist of the nineteenth century. He was born in 1828 into an aristocratic Russian family at their estate ("Yasnaya Polyana"), which is now a museum near Tula. Count Tolstoy became an orphan when his mother died before he was two years old, and his father died when he was only eight. He was raised by a grandmother and his aunts and was privately tutored before attending Kazan University, where he studied law and languages. Tolstoy was not a great student and left school without graduation. After a time of army service in the Caucasus he married Sofia Andreevna Bers in 1862 and started a family that grew to thirteen children. He led a profligate and promiscuous life and between the years of 1862 and 1869 wrote two of the nineteenth century's most outstanding works, *War and Peace* (1863–1869) and *Anna Karenina* (1873–1878). In the late 1870s he had a spiritual crisis that culminated in his conversion in 1879. He was convinced of the doctrine of Christian love and the necessity to resist evil. His conversion is described in his *Confession* (1879), written when he was fifty-one years old. After his conversion he spent the rest of his life in practicing and propagating his faith, emphasizing nonviolence and the merits of a simple life. He renounced his inherited title, declared his post-1880 writings to be public property, and gave the title of his estate to his wife and children. From then on he would only allow himself to be known as Leo Nikolayevich Tolstoy, not Count Tolstoy. This caused further discord with his wife. In 1910 Tolstoy set out from his home with his daughter, Alexandra, became ill, and died at the house of the railroad stationmaster at Astapovo.

Beginning in his youth, Tolstoy sought to understand the meaning of life. His search intensified in the 1870s with an examination of great philosophical and religious writings from antiquity to his own time in the nineteenth century. He became intrigued and impressed with the way of life of believers in the working population of Russia. In examining the Christian faith, he defined authentic belief as "a relationship established with God, in conformity with reason and contemporary knowledge, and which alone pushes humanity forward to its destined aim."[5]

During his conversion process as he struggled with the intellectual arguments for and against the existence of God, Tolstoy's mood ebbed and flowed between joy and despair. He was revived by the arguments that indicated God's existence and then discouraged by counterarguments that questioned that existence. In his work entitled *Confession*, he described the process by which he resolved this struggle between discouragement and revival:

> Having understood this, I realized that it was impossible to search for an answer to my questions in rational knowledge; that the answer given by rational knowledge simply suggests that the answer can only be obtained by stating the question in another way, by introducing the question of the relation of the finite to the infinite. I realized that no matter how irrational and distorted the answers given by faith might be, they had the advantage of introducing to every answer a relationship between the finite and the infinite, without which there can be no solution. Whichever way I put the question: how am I to live? the answer is always: according to God's law. . . . Or, to the question: what meaning is there that is not destroyed by death? The answer is: unity with the infinite, God, heaven.
>
> Thus in addition to rational knowledge which I had hitherto thought to be the only knowledge, I was inevitably led to acknowledge that there does exist another kind of knowledge—an irrational one—possessed by humanity as a whole: faith, which affords the possibility of living. Faith remained as irrational to me as before, but I could not fail to recognize that it alone provides mankind with the answers to the question of life, and consequently with the possibility of life. . . .
>
> * * *
>
> I did not think so at the time but the germs of these thoughts were already within me. I realized that: (1) Despite our intelligence the contentions of Schopenhauer, Solomon and myself were foolish: we considered life to be evil and nevertheless continued to live. This was apparent stupidity because, if life is meaningless and I am so fond of reason, then I must destroy life so that no one can deny it. (2) All our arguments went round in a vicious circle, like a wheel that is not attached to the carriage. However much, and however well, we deliberated, we could find no answer to the question be-

cause 0 will always equal 0, and therefore, our method must be mistaken. (3) I began to realize that the most profound wisdom of man is preserved in the answers given by faith, and that I did not have the right to negate them on grounds of reason and, above all, that it is these answers alone that can reply to the question of life. . . .

I can remember once in early spring I found myself alone in the woods. I was listening and concentrating my thoughts on the one thing I had been continuously thinking about over the last three years. Again I was searching for God.

"Fine then," I said to myself, "so there is no God, other than something I imagine and the only reality is my own life. There is no God and no miracle can prove that there is because it would only be part of my imagination, and would be irrational."

"But what about my concept of God, of He whom I seek?" I asked myself, "Where does this concept come from?" Once again, confronted with these thoughts, joyous waves of life surged up within me. Everything around me came to life and took on meaning. But my joy did not last long. My mind continued its work. "A concept of God is not God," I told myself. "A concept of God is something within me that I can either evoke or not evoke. It is not this that I am seeking. I am seeking that, without which there cannot be life." Once again everything within and around me began to die, and again I wanted to kill myself.

But then I stopped and looked at myself and at what was going on inside me. I recalled the hundreds of occasions when life had died within me only to be reborn. I remembered that I only lived during those times when I believed in God. Then, as now, I said to myself: I have only to believe in God in order to live. I have only to disbelieve in Him, or to forget Him, in order to die. What are these deaths and rebirths? It is clear that I do not live when I lose belief in God's existence, and I should have killed myself long ago, were it not for a dim hope of finding Him. I live truly only when I am conscious of Him and seek Him. What then is it you are seeking? A voice exclaimed inside me. There He is! He, without whom it is impossible to live. To know God and to live are one and the same thing. God is life.

"Live in search of God and there will be no life without God!" And more powerfully than ever before everything within and around me came to light, and the light has not deserted me since.[6]

Tolstoy recognized that God is life, and God's presence can become a habitual one, which requires only our attention to give us a more permanent peace and joy. With this realization the cycle of misery and elation ceased, and the light that shone on him never left him again. Since God seeks us first, we do not need to rely on arguments for God's existence; knowledge of God is possible through conscious *interaction* with God.[7]

FYODOR DOSTOEVSKY'S RELIGIOUS EXPERIENCE PROVIDED THE CENTRAL FOCUS FOR HIS THOUGHT.

Fyodor Dostoevsky (1821–81) lived his early life in Moscow, where his alcoholic father worked as a medical surgeon in the military. His mother died from tuberculosis when he was sixteen years old. He was then enrolled at the Military Engineering Academy in St. Petersburg. His father died two years after his mother and may have been murdered by peasants in his employ. In 1842 Fyodor became a lieutenant in the Russian military and began to write, translating some of Balzac's writings into Russian. He published his first short novel in 1845 entitled *Poor Folk*. This work was very well received in Russian literary circles, and Dostoevsky's reputation began to spread.

In 1849, however, he was arrested for participating in a political entity known as the Petrashevsky Circle. He was sentenced to death along with other members of the Circle and had the frightening experience of facing a firing squad. As he stood in front of the firing squad a messenger arrived with the message that the czar had commuted his death sentence to a sentence of four years in exile and hard labor. Upon his release in 1854 he was required to serve an additional five years in the military. Dostoevsky appears to have experienced profound insights into the value of religious experience and gained a broad understanding of human psychology during his time in prison and the military. One influence was the New Testament. As he was going to prison, a woman put a New Testament into his hand. This book changed Dostoevsky's life. Ernest Gordon wrote about the effect of the New Testament on Dostoevsky:

> On his way to prison a woman thrust a New Testament into his hand. This provided him with the means of entering into and dwelling in the passion and exaltation of Jesus. Suffering had become a way of the cross for him even after his return from Siberian exile. His lot was one of sickness, poverty, debts, and overwork. The fruits of his suffering, however, are his literary achievements.[8]

One cannot even begin to comprehend Dostoevsky's thought without understanding that so much of it is grounded in and derived from his religious experience and persuasion. He believed that a man who was not in communion with God was lost. He saw the Enlightenment and its promulgation of secularism as a distortion of reality. From his perspective, Kant and other Enlightenment philosophers had removed a personal God from man's existence.

Dostoevsky shares much in common with Kierkegaard and from one perspective can be described as a Christian existentialist. Perhaps more than any other writer, Dostoevsky struggled with the problem of evil and sin. He came to recognize sin as a core flaw in the human predicament. Dostoevsky spent much of his life working in an atmosphere of doubt. Like Augustine, Dostoevsky was for many years in search of a fulfilling philosophy.[9]

Dostoevsky saw the fallacy in attempting to build a utopia based on a human ideology. Malcolm Muggeridge later took up his banner on this theme. Both men claimed that although politics and government are important areas of Christian concern, one can never substitute a political philosophy for the Christian faith. The Christian scriptures are not intended and can never be a *Magna Charta* or road map for a political philosophy leading to utopia. They were never intended to serve in that capacity. Every attempt to build a utopia based on scripture has failed. Such an attempt reflects an Enlightenment, Euclidean thought process that can never realize its goals. Romantic visions of a utopia built on a scriptural political philosophy are fantasies. The nature of sin in the human predicament prevents the realization of such a vision. Of course, this does not mean that there are no right or just laws or principles for government, but utopia is unattainable and the Kingdom of God can never be a human construct.[10]

Dostoevsky emphasized the human will and the freedom to choose over and above reason. He respected reason but saw it as incomplete and unable to satisfy all the capacities for life. As far as he was concerned, Enlightenment philosophy was based on a mistaken perspective of man as a machine without free will. Dostoevsky refused to reduce human beings to merely rational creatures and believed in the power of human choices. In this regard, he could well serve as a model for the moral philosophical position of quantum physicist Henry Stapp that I described above. Consistent with Stapp's current position, Dostoevsky considered the power to choose as the most precious aspect of human nature. For Dostoevsky, free will preserved humankind's integrity as persons.[11]

Dostoevsky respected reason but emphasized its limits. His views found fertile ground in the mind of Nicholas Berdyaev (1874–1948), an exiled Russian who lived in Paris as an existentialist contemporary of Jean-Paul Sartre. Berdyaev credited Dostoevsky with playing a crucial role in the development of his Christian spiritual life. Berdyaev shared much in common with Sartre, as both men saw *the human predicament as the desire of finite humans to be God.*[12] Berdyaev's philosophy emphasized freedom and criticized the Kantian "objectivization" of knowledge. Much of his philosophy was derived from Dostoevsky's writings, but for Berdyaev the most profound influence was spiritual.[13] It was in reading the passage on the *Legend of the Grand Inquisitor* that Berdyaev had a transforming encounter with the divine. In the Foreword to his book, *Dostoevsky*, Berdyaev described the effect of his reading this passage from Dostoevsky's greatest novel, *The Brothers Karamazov*:

> Dostoevsky has played a decisive part in my spiritual life. While I was still a youth a slip from him, so to say, was grafted upon me. He stirred and lifted up my soul more than any other writer or philosopher has done, and for me people are always divided into "dostoievskyites" and those to whom his spirit is foreign. It is undoubtedly due to his "cursed questioning" that philosophical problems were present to my consciousness at so early an age, and some new aspects of him is revealed to me every time I read him. The *Legend of the Grand Inquisitor*, in particular, made such an impression on my young mind that when I turned to Jesus Christ for the first time I saw him under the appearance that he bears in the Legend.
>
> At the base of my notion of the world as I see it there has always lain the idea of liberty, and in this fundamental intuition of liberty, I found Dostoevsky as it were on his own special ground.[14]

Dostoevsky is always writing about himself, his experiences, and the persons who influenced his life. In this sense his writing is always autobiographical. Long before modern psychology theory and long before the advent of quantum mechanics, he understood the power of the human will and refused to see man as only a rational and not a spiritual creature. I recommend that anyone unfamiliar with Dostoevsky's writing read his *Legend of the Grand Inquisitor*. The speaker in the passage is Ivan Karamazov, who believes in the existence of God but will not recognize God. He is a Euclidean rationalist and refuses to accept the Gospel, *because he does not like it.* For my present purposes, I will quote from two Dostoevsky writings, one a private letter and the other a passage from *The Brothers Karamazov*. In a private letter to the woman who had placed a copy of the New Testament into his hands as he went in chains to Siberia, Dostoevsky wrote:

> I am a child of unbelief and doubt even now and (as I well know) I shall be to the grave. What fearful suffering this desire to believe has caused me and still causes me as it increases in strength in my soul as the contrary proofs multiply! However, God sends me at other times many minutes during which I am entirely at peace . . . and during such minutes I have composed for myself a confession of faith . . . this is it: to believe that there is nothing

> more beautiful, more profound, more sympathetic, more reasonable, more manly and perfect than Christ, and not only nothing like Him exists but I say to myself with jealous love, that it even cannot exist. And even more: if someone were to prove to me that Christ is not the truth, I would rather remain with Christ than with the truth.[15]

This testimony of Dostoevsky summarizes his sentiments as he experienced a spiritual transformation in a prison in Siberia. Because Russian authorities did not separate political prisoners from thieves, murderers, and the most degraded criminals, Dostoevsky's transformation took place in an ambience of brutality, including torture. His response was not one of retribution but of redemption, humility, and love. Dostoevsky so experienced the love of God that it was this encounter with the all-embracing love of the divine that bowled him over and formed a new character deep within him.

One can see the emphasis on love in his religious thought in *The Brothers Karamazov*, for, as noted, he is always writing experientially about himself. In the following passage, Father Zosima, an Elder in a local monastery, gives the following exhortation to his fellow monks:

> They have science, and in science only that which is subject to the senses. But the spiritual world, the higher half of man's being, is altogether rejected, banished with a sort of triumph, even with hatred. The world has proclaimed freedom, especially of late, but what do we see in this freedom of theirs: only slavery and suicide! . . .
>
> But God will save Russia, for though the simple man is depraved, and can no longer refrain from rank sin, still he knows that his rank sin is cursed by God and that he does badly in sinning. So our people still believe tirelessly in truth, acknowledge God, weep tenderly. Not so their betters. These, following science, want to make a just order for themselves by reason alone, but without Christ now, not as before, and they have already proclaimed that there is no crime, there is no sin. And in their own terms, that is correct: for if you have no God, what crime is there to speak of? . . .
>
> Young man, do not forget to pray. Each time you pray, if you do so sincerely, there will be the flash of a new feeling in it, and a new thought as well, one you did not know before, which will give you fresh courage; and you will understand that prayer is education. Remember also: every day and whenever you can, repeat within yourself: "Lord, have mercy upon all who come before you today.". . .
>
> Brothers, do not be afraid of men's sin, love man also in his sin, for this likeness of God's love is the height of love on earth. Love all of God's creation, both the whole of it and every grain of sand. Love every leaf, every

> ray of God's light. Love animals, love plants, love each thing. If you love each thing, you will perceive the mystery of God in things. Once you have perceived it, you will begin tirelessly to perceive more and more of it every day. And you will come at least to love the whole world with an entire, universal love. . . . Love children especially, for they, too, are sinless, like angels, and live to bring us to tenderness and the purification of our hearts and as a sort of example for us. Woe to him who offends a child. I was taught to love little children by Father Anfim: during our wanderings, this dear and silent man used to spend the little half-kopecks given us as alms on gingerbreads and candies, and hand them out to them. He could not pass by children without his soul being shaken: such is the man.
>
> One may stand perplexed before some thought, especially seeing men's sin, asking oneself: "Shall I take it by force, or by humble love?" Always resolve to take it by humble love. If you so resolve once and for all, you will be able to overcome the whole world. A loving humility is a terrible power, the most powerful of all, nothing compares with it. Keep company with yourself and look to yourself every day and hour, every minute, that your image be ever gracious.[16]

All through his life Dostoevsky sought after God. He had a keen understanding of the problem of evil but also a grateful heart for his freedom of choice. He exercised that freedom by attempting to draw close to God, and, even in his doubts, he testified that God had drawn close to him.

CLARE BOOTHE LUCE HAD A PROFOUND EXPERIENCE OF THE *NUMINOUS* ON AN AMERICAN BEACH.

Clare Boothe Luce was born in 1903 in New York City. Her father was a business executive and a musician, and her mother was a dancer. After a failed marriage, she started her writing career as a caption writer at *Vogue* magazine and then became an editorial assistant at *Vanity Fair*, eventually rising to the position of managing editor. Resigning from that position to pursue a career as a playwright, she wrote many successful plays, including *Abide with Me* (1935), *The Women* (1936), *Kiss the Boys Goodbye* (1938), and *Margin for Error* (1939). In 1935 she married Harry Luce, the publisher and founder of *Time* magazine.

Clare Boothe Luce was elected to Congress in 1942 and reelected in 1944, representing the Fourth District of Connecticut. On January 11, 1944, her daughter Ann, a senior at Stanford University, was killed in a car accident. She was overwhelmed at this loss, retired from Congress, and returned to writing plays. She campaigned for Dwight Eisenhower in 1952 and was appointed ambassador to Italy. She was very effective and was responsible for settling a dispute between Italy and Yugoslavia concerning the territory around and including the city of Trieste. Because of a serious case of paint poisoning, she had to resign her post in 1956. After recovering, she continued to write, travel, and remained active with the Republican Party. In 1981, she was appointed to the President's Foreign Intelligence Advisory Board. In 1983, she was awarded the Presidential Medal of Freedom. She died of a brain tumor at age 84 in her Watergate apartment.

She was a dynamic person with a sense of her place in the world. In her writings she described an early mystical experience, which she remembered as she made a decision to be confirmed in the Catholic Church. Although her reasons for joining the church principally had an intellectual basis, she recognized that the prior encounter with what Otto called the *numinous* played an important role. In her words:

> Let me give one example from my own experience of the honest difficulty in revealing all that seems important to a conversion.
>
> It is an experience which occurred when I was perhaps sixteen or seventeen years old. I no longer remember where it took place, except that it was a summer day on an American beach. I seem to remember that it was early morning, and that I must have been standing on the sand for some time alone, for even now I distinctly remember that this experience was preceded by a sensation of utter aloneness. Not loneliness, but a sort of intense solitariness.
>
> I remember that it was a cool, clean, fresh, calm, blue, radiant day, and that I stood by the shore, my feet not in the waves. And now—as then—I find it difficult to explain what did happen. I expect that the easiest thing is to say that suddenly **SOMETHING WAS**. My whole soul was cleft clean by it, as a silk veil slit by a shining sword. And I *knew*. I do not know now what I knew. I remember, I didn't know even then. That is, I didn't *know* with any "faculty." It was not in my mind or heart or blood stream. But whatever it was I knew it, it was something that made **ENORMOUS SENSE**. And it was final. And yet that word could not be used, for it meant *end*, and there was no end to *this* finality. Then joy abounded in all of me. Or rather, I abounded in joy. I seemed to have no nature, and yet my whole nature was adrift in this immense joy, as a speck of dust is seen to dance in a great golden shaft of sunlight.
>
> I don't know how long this experience lasted. It was, I should think, closer to a second than to an hour—though it might have been either. The memory of it possessed me for several months afterward. At first I marveled at it. Then I reveled in it. Then it began to obsess me and I tried to put it in

some category of previous experience. I remember, I concluded that on that certain day the beauty of nature must have concorded with some unexpected flush of tremendous physical well being. . . . Gradually I forgot it.

The memory of it never returned to me until one day several years after my conversion, during the first minute of the liturgy of the Mass, where the server says: "*Ad Deum qui laetificat juventutem meum. . . .*"

My childhood had been an unusually unhappy and bitter one. I had brooded about it increasingly as I grew older. Indeed until the very day of my conversion, it was a source of deep *melancholy* and resentment.

"Unless the cup is clean, whatever you pour into it turns sour," said Plato. A conversion cleans the heart of much of its bitterness. Afterward I seldom remembered my marred childhood, except at one strange moment: at the very beginning of the Mass, during the prayers at the foot of the altar. The priest says: "I will go in unto the altar of God." And generally a small altar boy responds in a clear, shy, thin, little voice: "Unto God who giveth joy to my youth." This phrase, unhappily, always awakened faint echoes of bitter youth, and I would think: *Why* didn't God give joy to *my* youth! Why was joy withheld from *my* innocence?

One day, long months after I had been a convert, as these words were said, the bitterness did not come. Instead there suddenly flooded into my mind the experience of which I speak, and my heart was gently suffused after an afterglow of that incredible joy.

Then I knew that this strange occurrence had had an enormous part in my conversion, although I had *seemed* to forget it completely. Long ago, in its tremendous purity and simplicity, and now, in its far fainter evocation, I knew it had been, somehow, the most real experience of my whole life.

But how exactly did this affect my conversion? Why had I forgotten it? Why had I remembered it? God only knows. And what use is it to recount it to anyone interested in "Why I Became a Catholic?"

I mention it here partly to elucidate the real difficulty of "telling all," and partly lest anyone think the convert is not aware of the mysterious movements of his own soul, and that much of a conversion may take place on subconscious levels.[17]

Clare Booth Luce's mystical experience influenced her decision to join the Catholic Church. She then turned her formidable intellect toward the study of theology and philosophy and maintained an evangelical disposition to inform others of the benefits of her faith. When I was a White House Fellow, several fellows and I had lunch with her in her Watergate apartment. She had a delightful enthusiasm that bore witness to the presence of God in her life. Three decades later my colleagues still discuss the attractiveness of her spirited joy.

CHAPTER 11

MALCOLM MUGGERIDGE FOUND HIS LIFE'S PURPOSE IN KNOWING AND LOVING GOD.

Malcolm Muggeridge was born on March 24, 1903, as Thomas Malcolm Muggeridge. His first name was in honor of Thomas Carlyle, whom his father, H. T. Muggeridge, admired. Malcolm's father, a one-time Member of Parliament and a Labor councilor in South London, was enamored with Carlyle's attacks on materialism. Young Malcolm studied science at Cambridge University, graduated in 1924, and took up a teaching position in India. In 1927 he returned to England and married Kitty Dobbs. After a brief stint teaching in England, Kitty and Malcolm moved to Egypt where he had another teaching position. In Egypt he met Arthur Ransome, who helped him secure a position as a journalist for the *Manchester Guardian.*

In 1932 Malcolm and Kitty moved to Moscow, where he was a correspondent. When they made the move they believed in the virtues of the Soviet Union, but upon witnessing the famine in the Ukraine and the inefficacy and corruption of the government, he became discontented with communism and questioned socialism. Gradually he moved substantially to the right on the political spectrum. From the 1930s through the 1970s he became a major force in journalism and in television, working on assignments in Washington, Tokyo, Berlin, and New York and meeting the political leaders of his day. From 1953 to 1957 he served as editor of *Punch* magazine. He served as a BBC interviewer and correspondent and was known for his sharp, sarcastic, and irreverent wit.

In 1968 he met Mother Teresa and brought her worldwide recognition with the publication of his book about her work in India, entitled *Something Beautiful for God.* It was through his relationship with her that he began to move in a more rapid and steady pace toward an acceptance of the Christian faith. Muggeridge shared Gabriel Marcel's belief that the heart of reality is a mystery, that the mind was "sort of a cul-de-sac," and that one could only grasp reality through faith.

Muggeridge's writings on his faith and his search for God are voluminous. The following excerpt will give the reader some of the wisdom his seeking produced, together with some of the advice with which he encouraged his fellow seekers.

> . . . The hope is simply that, by identifying ourselves with the Incarnate God, by absorbing ourselves in His teaching, by living out the drama of his life with Him including especially the Passion, that powerhouse of love and creativity,

> by living with and in Him we are suddenly caught up in the glory of God's love flooding the universe: every colour brighter, every meaning clearer, every shape more shapely, every note more musical, every true word written and spoken more explicit. Above all, every human face, all human companionship, each and every human encounter, a family affair, of brothers and sisters, with all the categories, beautiful or plain, clever or slow-witted, sophisticated or simple, utterly irrelevant. And any who might be hobbling along with limbs and minds awry, any who might be afflicted, particularly dear and cherished. . . . All, irradiated with this same new glory. . . . It is then that Christ's hand reaches out, sure and firm; that his words bring their inexpressible comforts; that His light shines brightest, abolishing the darkness for ever, so that, finding in everything only deception and nothingness, the soul is constrained to have recourse to God himself and to rest content.[18]

Muggeridge lived a full and adventurous life. He interviewed and knew the great leaders of his time and often exposed them to sardonic analysis. He came to believe that the pursuit of power, wealth, fame, or even happiness was a preposterous waste of one's life. He understood the buffoonery involved in what he called "the worldwide soap opera going on from century to century." But he would not allow himself to become only a cynic or a hedonist. Instead, he marvelled at the Incarnation and the transformation that results from taking God's action seriously. He summed up his perspective in the following quotation from his book, *A Twentieth Century Testimony*:

> When I look back on my life nowadays, which I sometimes do, what strikes me most forcibly about it is that what seemed at the time most significant and seductive, seems now most futile and absurd. For instance, success in all of its various guises; being known and being praised; ostensible pleasures, like acquiring money or seducing women, or traveling, going to and fro in the world and up and down in it like Satan, exploring and experiencing whatever Vanity Fair has to offer.
>
> In retrospect all these exercises in self-gratification seem pure fantasy, what Pascal called "licking the earth." They are diversions designed to distract our attention from the true purpose of our existence in this world, which is, quite simply, to look for God, and in looking, to find Him, and, having found Him, to love Him, thereby establishing a harmonious relationship with His purposes for His creation.[19]

Muggeridge concluded that our purpose in life is to know God. If we know him, we will love him, because His character is such that it satisfies the deepest longings of the human heart.

SIMONE WEIL HAD AN UNEXPECTED MYSTICAL ENCOUNTER WITH THE DIVINE THAT TRANSFORMED HER LIFE.

Simone Weil (1909–43) was born into a Jewish family in Paris on February 3, 1909. Her father was a doctor, and the family was completely agnostic. Her extraordinary intellectual abilities were apparent at an early age when she studied at the Lycée Henri IV. She then studied at the École Normale Supérieure between 1928–31 and received a degree in philosophy when she was twenty-two. She taught philosophy at a number of schools and participated in a labor movement that emphasized the production capabilities of small groups of workers. In 1932–33 she visited Germany and wrote ten articles indicating the dangers that were mounting, partly because of the conditions of workers. In 1934–35 she took a leave of absence from her position as an instructor in philosophy and worked as a common laborer in the Renault auto factory. The work in the factory gave her an understanding of the degrading aspects of affliction, as she saw not only the physical pain of the workers but also their destruction as persons. An attack of pleurisy forced her to end her factory experience.

She then went to Spain to participate in the anarchist movement of the Spanish Civil War. She was wounded in an accident and recuperated in a field hospital. After her experience in Spain, her parents took her to Portugal, where she had three surprising religious experiences that changed her life and thought. She was not in search of God when this happened, as she later wrote:

> I may say that never at any moment in my life have I "sought for God." For this reason, which is probably too subjective, I do not like this expression and it strikes me as false. As soon as I reached adolescence, I saw the problem of God as a problem the data of which could not be obtained here below, and I decided that the only way of being sure not to reach a wrong solution, which seemed to me the greatest possible evil, was to leave it alone. So I left it alone. I neither affirmed nor denied anything. It seemed to me useless to solve this problem, for I thought that, being in this world, our business was to adopt the best attitude with regard to the problems of this world, and that such an attitude did not depend upon the solution of the problem of God.[20]

Her early writings confirm that she was not attempting to move toward the divine. There is no sense of a pursuit of anyone or anything beyond this world. She later saw her lack of interest in spiritual matters as evidence that she had not manufactured her experience of God. The most profound of these experiences occurred when she was at the abbey of Solesmes where a young English Catholic had told her about the seventeenth-century British poets who had written metaphysical poems. She read a poem by George Herbert, entitled, "Love (III)" and committed it to memory. From the age of fourteen she had continually suffered from severe migraine headaches. The headaches never left her, but in moments of intense pain, she would recite Herbert's poem, which, without her realizing it, had the virtue of a prayer. The poem is worth quoting, because its imagery is essential to her thought.

> Love bade me welcome: yet my soul drew back,
> Guiltie of lust and sinne.
> But quick-ey'd Love, observing me grow slack
> From my first entrance in,
> Drew nearer to me, sweetly questioning,
> If I lack'd anything.
> A guest, I answer'd, worthy to be here:
> Love said, You shall be he.
> I the unkinde, ungrateful? Ah my deare,
> I cannot look on thee.
> Love took my hand, and smiling did reply,
> Who made the eyes but I?
> Truth Lord, but I have marr'd them: let shame
> Go where it doth deserve.
> And know you not, sayes Love, who bore the blame?
> My deare, then I will serve.
> You must sit down, sayes Love, and taste my meat:
> So I did sit and eat.

In 1938 she spent ten days at Solesmes, and while in the abbey church she had an unexpected mystical encounter that had a lasting effect on her life. In a letter to her friend, Father Perrin, she describes her experience at Solesmes:

> There was a young English Catholic there from whom I gained my first idea of the supernatural power of the sacraments because of the truly angelic radiance with which he seemed to be clothed after going to communion . . . he told me of the existence of those English poets of the seventeenth century who are named metaphysical. In reading them later on, I discovered the poem which I read you what is unfortunately a very inadequate trans-

> lation. It is called "Love." I learned it by heart. Often, at the culminating point of a violent headache, I make myself say it over, concentrating all my attention upon it and clinging with all my soul to the tenderness it enshrines. I used to think I was merely reciting it as a beautiful poem, but without knowing it the recitation had the virtue of a prayer. It was during one of these recitations that, as I told you, Christ himself came down and took possession of me.
>
> In my arguments about the insolubility of the problem of God I had never foreseen the possibility of that, of a real contact, person to person, here below, between a human being and God. I had vaguely heard tell of things of this kind, but I had never believed in them. In the *Fioretti* the accounts of apparitions rather put me off if anything, like the miracles in the Gospel. Moreover, in this sudden possession of me by Christ, neither my sense nor my imagination had any part; I only felt in the midst of my suffering the presence of a love, like that which one can read in the smile on a beloved face.
>
> I had never read any mystical works because I had never felt any call to read them. In reading as in other things I have always striven to practice obedience. There is nothing more favorable to intellectual progress, for as far as possible, I only read what I am hungry for at the moment when I have an appetite for it, and then I do not read, I *eat*. God in his mercy had prevented me from reading the mystics, so that it should be evident to me that I had not invented this absolutely unexpected contact.[21]

Even after this profound experience, she did not pray for more than five years. She then began to recite the Lord's Prayer on a daily basis with an intense concentration, memorizing the prayer word for word in Greek. To her surprise this exercise had a deep effect on her sense of the presence of God:

> The infinite sweetness of this Greek text so took hold of me that for several days I could not stop myself from saying it over all the time. A week afterward I began the vine harvest. I recited the Father in Greek every day before work, and I repeated it very often in the vineyard.
>
> Since that time I have made a practice of saying it through once each morning with absolute attention. If during the recitation my attention wanders or goes to sleep, in the minutest degree, I begin again until I have once succeeded in going through it with absolutely pure attention. Sometimes it comes about that I say it again out of sheer pleasure, but I only do it if I really feel the impulse.
>
> The effect of this practice is extraordinary and surprises me every time, for, although I experience it each day, it exceeds my expectation at each repetition.
>
> At times the very first words tear my thoughts from my body and transport it to a place outside space wither there is neither perspective nor point

> of view. The infinity of the ordinary expanses of perception is replaced by infinity to the second or sometimes the third degree. At the same time, filling every page of this infinity of infinity, there is silence, a silence which is not an absence of sound but which is the object of a positive sensation, more positive than that of sound. Noises, if there are any, only reach me after crossing this silence.
>
> Sometimes, also, during this recitation or at other moments, Christ is present with me in person, but his presence is infinitely more real, more moving, more clear than on that first occasion when he took possession of me.[22]

Even though her experience of God was powerful and real, Weil understood that her encounter with the presence of Christ should not be regarded in isolation but should be coupled with an intellectual process of searching for the divine truth. She avoided the mistake sometimes found in philosophies of religion where one only centers their search for God on the experience of God and does not also attempt to understand the Christian doctrines that can illuminate the experience.[23] In Weil's words:

> If I light an electric torch at night, I don't judge its power by looking at the bulb. . . . The brightness of a source of light is appreciated by the illumination it projects upon non-luminous objects. . . . The value of a religious or, more generally, a spiritual way of life is appreciated by the amount of illumination thrown upon the things of the world.[24]

Diogenes Allen stressed Weil's view of the role of intellectual understanding in the nonrational experience of the divine. He noted that she had a keen sense of the role of the mind in understanding the truth of a Christian vision. Weil's mystical experience was not divorced from her intellect; rather, her intellectual understanding was enhanced and confirmed by her mystical experiences:

> It is important that Christianity make intellectual sense so that emotions are not the only basis for being a Christian. But if such understanding is all that Christianity has to offer, then it is merely an intellectual option. Christianity's appeal to the understanding has to be balanced by a reaching out to God in prayer. However natural it is to seek to enlarge our understanding of God through our mind, Christianity is not merely an intellectual option.[25]

In 1940 Weil moved to Marseilles with her parents to avoid the Nazi occupation of Paris. In Marseilles she met Father Perrin, in whom she found a friend who encouraged her in her practice of the presence of God. In her letter of May 15, 1942, to Father Perrin, she noted the power that derives from a close friendship with one who is also a friend of God:

> But the greatest blessing you have brought me is of another order. In gaining my friendship by your charity (which I have never met anything to equal), you have provided me with a source of the most compelling and pure inspiration that is to be found among human things. For nothing among human things has such power to keep our gaze fixed ever more intensely upon God, than friendship for the friends of God.[26]

After a brief stay in New York between June and November of 1942, she was commissioned to undertake a study on behalf of the French provisional government in London. This study, published as *L'Enracinement* (*The Need for Roots*), set forth religious and social principles for building a Christian French nation. In this work, Weil emphasized the need for freedom of thought, including religious thought. Weil was motivated by her conviction that government should not oppressively separate the secular and the religious. She emphasized the rights and duties of the State and the individual in society. Committed to participating in the hardships of those suffering the Nazi occupation in France, she declined supplemental food and, already in a state of poor health, only consumed the same rations that were allowed to her fellow French citizens in France. Her health worsened, and she died in Kent on August 29, 1943, at the age of thirty-four.

BASIL MITCHELL HAD A GRADUAL BUT PROFOUND SPIRITUAL AWAKENING.

Basil Mitchell, formerly the Nolloth Professor of the Philosophy of the Christian Religion at Oxford University's Oriel College, was born in Bath, Somerset, in 1917 and spent his early years in Southampton, England. He was raised in a family that was heavily influenced by the Sufi movement. His mother suffered from a severe form of rheumatoid arthritis, became bed-ridden, and, in the absence of help from standard medical practices, turned toward the Sufis, who held a regular worship service in Southampton. These services involved readings from sacred texts of many religions, including Jewish, Christian, Hindu, Buddhist, Islam, and Zoroastrian.[27] By

1935, when Mitchell enrolled as an undergraduate at Oxford, he was deeply influenced by Sufism.

He was visiting Sufi friends with his mother in Rotterdam in 1938 when the Munich crisis developed, culminating in Chamberlain's weak response to Hitler's demands on Czechoslovakia. This political situation created an inner turmoil in Mitchell. He had strong inclinations toward pacifism but thought that Chamberlain's action was disgraceful and that the United Kingdom should have gone to war to protect Czechoslovakia. He had received a scholarship at Oxford that would allow him to study Indian philosophy under a renowned Indian professor and was torn between enlisting in the military and doing his work at the university. At the beginning of 1940 he registered as a conscientious objector and assumed that he would be drafted to serve as an aide in the ambulance sector of the armed forces. When Hitler's tanks moved through France in May 1940, his personal crisis became more acute. His Sufi advisers pointed to the Bhagavad Gita for the answer to his dilemma whether to fight or remain a pacifist. Mitchell read this work in Sanskrit and discovered to his dismay that it was not helpful. The section of the Gita upon which he centered was the indecision of an Arjuna, a member of the warrior caste known as Ksatriya, who was confronted with an army advancing against him. The Gita's answer was that as a warrior Ksatriya had a duty to fight, not because of right or wrong, but simply as a duty. Mitchell discovered that he could not accept this rationale:

> I found that I just could not view the matter in these terms. Not only was the concept of duty deriving from one's social status totally irrelevant to my situation, but the underlying philosophy was one I could not accept. I felt profoundly that what was at stake in Europe was (when all the necessary qualifications had been made) a fight of good against evil and that the outcome was of momentous importance.
>
> From that time on, although I did not clearly perceive it, the Sufi influence began to lose its hold on me. I had been compelled to deny, under the pressure of practical decision, that the same truth was to be found in all religions. The Gita, impressive though it was, represented a view of the world and of our place in it that was not only different from but incompatible with any that I could bring myself to believe or live by.[28]

Mitchell received a letter of advice from a woman and fellow student with whom he had a fine "marriage of true minds." This letter appears to have had a significant influence on his spiritual perspective. He then enlisted in the Royal Navy and served as a sailor for the next six years. While on the battleship *Queen Elizabeth*, he met Launcelot Fleming, a chaplain in the Church of England with a rare ability of spiritual discernment. The Anglican services on board the ship had a profound effect on Mitchell. He was impressed with the timeless language of the Book of Common Prayer and was moved by the prayers in that book, particularly the one that was written for the Fleet, considering it a splendid and memorable summation of all that a sailor asks of God.

When he returned to complete his studies at Oxford in 1946, Mitchell was no longer interested in the study of Sanskrit, Indian philosophy, or research into the Vedanta. He perceived the essential differences between the worldviews represented by the Vedanta and the worldview of the Christian faith. Consequently, he made a shift to a tutorial fellowship in philosophy at Keble College within Oxford University in 1947. Now he felt truly at home, and the influence of the prayers and services he had experienced in the navy blossomed into a full and powerful faith. He understood the reason for his movement away from Sufism to the Christian faith and described it in the following terms:

> What had increasingly led me to be dissatisfied with the essentially monistic philosophy of my Sufi mentors was its failure, as I now saw it, to attach enduring importance to individual persons; to the institutions that molded them and enabled them to flourish; to the historical processes that had formed them; and to the natural world that nourished them. My native cast of thought was idealistic, and, left to myself, I was liable to rest satisfied with abstractions. But I had been compelled by circumstances to attend to particulars—in the Navy to the needs of particular individuals acting out a particular role in a particular historical situation through involvement in a particular institution; and, in my personal life, in responding to the demands of a person of very acute observation who had a sharp sense of truth in respect of feelings and their expression. Hence what had initially, in my Sufi days, repelled me in Christianity—its insistence upon the embodiment of the divine in a particular figure who had entered the world at a particular time and place—now seemed to me congruous with what I had learned about the nature and development of human beings. The destiny of individual souls was such that it could be realized only in a community, both in this life and beyond, a community in which they could be known and loved. The ultimate love that expressed and reflected the love of God in Christ was of worth in itself and unaffected by change.[29]

Mitchell's experience with the Book of Common Prayer was such that he was not aware of the effect that the prayers in the book were having on him, but when he returned to Oxford, he realized that he had been pursuing a protracted path toward the Anglican faith. He found that his spiritual and intellectual development grew ensembled as he became a committed Anglican:

> I became a regular churchgoer, and my intellectual and spiritual lives became increasingly intertwined. I underwent a process that in theological writing is often supposed not to happen, in which my attempts, philosophically, to achieve a coherent view of the world went hand in hand with my efforts to live a Christian life. I went to church and said my prayers because to do those things followed from what I was coming to believe about the nature of God, humankind and the world.[30]

Austin Farrer's Bampton Lectures at Oxford in 1948 also influenced Mitchell, presenting him with a Christian mystical vision that enhanced his understanding of the ordered nature of reality, the importance of history, and the significance of the loves and lives of individual persons. These lectures gave him an understanding of divine knowledge that emphasized the abiding presence of God and the unlimited nature of the human personality.[31] His experience in the navy caused Mitchell to realize the importance of events in history. Events in time and space were not considered significant in the Sufi mystical philosophy to which he was attached in his youth. His experience of the necessity of love, which involved valuing individuals, presented him with a metaphysical question inquiring into how one increases his or her capacity to love and the issue of what kind of love is required of us. Mitchell found the answer to this question in the literature he had come to know in his service in the Royal Navy:

> It was in answering this question that a metaphysic must be judged, and I found an answer, once again in the Book of Common Prayer. This time the answer was in the General Thanksgiving: "We bless thee for our creation, preservation, and all the blessings of this life; but above all, for thine inestimable love in the redemption of the world by our Lord Jesus Christ; for the means of grace and for the hope of glory." Men and women are to be loved as those whom God has loved—created, redeemed and destined to eternal life. They are to be loved by us with that same love, and it is through grace that in spite of our weakness and our limitations, we are able to love and be loved in that way.[32]

CHAPTER 11

MORTIMER ADLER ALSO HAD A GRADUAL SPIRITUAL AWAKENING, CULMINATING IN A LIFE-CHANGING MYSTICAL ENCOUNTER.

Adler's intellectual investigation into the existence of God gave him a rational basis for faith.

Mortimer Adler, a professor at Columbia University and at the University of Chicago, was one of the most prolific philosophical writers of the twentieth century, publishing more than fifty books, serving as chair of the board of editors of the Encyclopedia Britannica, and an active participant in the Aspen Institute. He was born into a Jewish family with an orthodox Jewish father but was uninterested in worship and regarded his study of philosophical arguments concerning God's existence as an objective, analytical exercise, similar to the study of mathematics. At the age of twenty he began teaching seminars at Columbia University on the great books of Western civilization with Mark Van Doren. He became fascinated with the writings of Thomas Aquinas but considered himself a pagan.

Adler knew that a merely objective inquiry into the arguments for the existence of God would not result in belief. In describing this understanding, he referred to his communications with Clare Boothe Luce, and his response to her was that he had a dead, purely objective faith in God, even though he was convinced that he could construct a rational argument for God's existence beyond a reasonable doubt.

> When Clare Boothe Luce, who had herself then recently converted to Roman Catholicism, made a strenuous effort to convert me, I explained to her the difference between dead and living faith—faith without hope and charity and faith that is enriched by the other two theological virtues, hope and charity. I told Clare that simply being able to understand Thomist theology was what Aquinas called dead faith. It was not enough to carry one into a Christian life.[33]

Adler later believed that his writing of his book, *How to Think About God*, in 1979 was an important advance toward his becoming a committed Christian. In this book he set forth what was for him the culmination of decades of thought and analysis concerning a satisfactory argument for the existence of God. He considered his argument valid "beyond a reasonable doubt (not with certitude beyond the shadow of a doubt)."

After his conversion by a leap of faith made in March 1984, which is described below, he published *Truth in Religion: The Plurality of Religions and the Unity of Truth* (1990). In this book he held that the unity of truth requires that any religion with factual truth claims for its beliefs must be consistent with other truths that are known in philosophy, history, and science. If various religions claimed truths that were in conflict with each other, not all their claims could be true. Accordingly, a polytheistic religion and a monotheistic religion could not both be true. Similarly, a theistic religion and a nontheistic religion could not both be true. The question then that confronts us is: Which of the world religions has the best claim to being true? Knowing the tendency in contemporary culture to regard all religions equally, Adler pressed the rationality of this question:

> In the concluding chapter of *Truth in Religion*, I enumerated the consideration that individuals should have in mind when trying to answer this question for themselves. If the religions of Far Eastern origins do not claim to be supernatural knowledge, based on divine revelation, then they are theoretical or moral philosophies masquerading as religions. Even as counterfeit religions, if they are polytheistic or nontheistic, then their philosophical doctrines come into conflict with the truths of philosophical theology (e.g., physics, mathematics and metaphysics), and must be rejected. That leaves the three monotheistic and revealed religions of Western origin: Judaism, Christianity and Islam. These conflict with one another in their truth claims. If one has a better claim to being true, the others may partially share in that truth. Each is compatible with the truths affirmed in philosophical theology, but all three may not be equally compatible with the established truths of empirical science and history.[34]

Adler went on to describe four considerations that must be considered in determining which of the three religions had the best claim to being true. These considerations concerned missionary efforts, perspectives on immortality, views on the immanence and the transcendence of God, and the extent to which God's revelation involves mysteries or articles of faith beyond a human's ability to know.

Adler believed that these additional considerations pointed to Christianity as the religion with the best claim to truth. Part of his reasoning for this conclusion was that only in the Christian faith is God considered to be both transcendent and immanent. In reflecting upon why he held this position, Adler commented:

If I have not been a sinless Christian, I have at least been a thoughtful one. I have pondered the mysteries that in the concluding pages of *Truth in Religion* I said were some of the things to be considered in deciding where greater truth was to be found among the three monotheistic religions of Western origin. For both Judaism and Islam the God believed in is entirely transcendent—outside the cosmos as its creator and governor. Only for Christianity is God both transcendent and immanent—at once the eternal Creator of the cosmos and the earthly redeemer of humankind, as well as its indwelling spirit, omnipresent as well as omnipotent. This is, of course, the mystery of the Trinity—the one God, of which there are three persons or aspects, the one God who is both in Heaven and on earth.[35]

Adler's leap of faith came from a mystical encounter.

Adler believed that even the most rational argument for the existence of God could not compel a person to believe in God. He held that a person must make a leap of faith from the purely intellectual to a relationship with God. The God of the philosophers is an idol. The God of the true theist is a God who communicates and encounters the theist. In this sense, Adler appears to share something in common with the existential theologians and the recent postmodern writings of philosophers such as Jean-Luc Marion, also of the University of Chicago (and the University of Paris). Adler was not thinking about a leap of faith when in 1984 his world changed and he began a transforming friendship with God. Here is his story in his words:

In March of 1984, after a trip to Mexico in February, I felt ill, probably from a virus that I picked up there. The illness was protracted. I was in the hospital for five weeks and then in bed at home for several months or more. Though I underwent all the diagnostic tests and procedures that the physicians could think of, the illness was never adequately diagnosed; and the cure, when it finally came, involved numerous antibiotics and two blood transfusions that brought my red corpuscle count back to normal.

During this long stay in the hospital I suffered a mild depression, and often when Caroline visited me I would, unaccountably, burst into tears. Father Howell, the rector of St. Chrysostom's Church, also visited me, and once when he prayed for my recovery, I choked up and wept. The only prayer that I knew word for word was the Pater Noster. On that day and in the days after it, I found myself repeating the Lord's Prayer, again and again, and meaning every word of it. Quite suddenly, when I was awake one night, a light dawned on me, and I realized what had happened without my recognizing it clearly when it first happened.

I had been seriously praying to God. But had I not said at the end of *How to Think About God* that no one who understood the God of the philosophers as well as I thought I did would worship that God or pray to him? Only if, by the gift of grace, one made the leap of faith across the chasm to the God of religious Jews and Christians would one engage in worship and prayer, believing in a morally good, loving, just and merciful God.

Here after many years of affirming God's existence and trying to give adequate reasons for that affirmation, I found myself believing in God and praying to him. I rang for the night nurse and asked for paper and pen, and with great difficulty—for I was at that time not very mobile in bed—I managed to sit up and scrawl a letter to Father Howell. Caroline transcribed the letter for me the next day and then typed it out before sending it to Father Howell. It was dated April 1, 1984.

In the letter I told Father Howell of the conflicts and difficulties in my life and thought that had been obstacles to my becoming a Christian. I told him that when he prayed for me at my bedside, I wept and was convulsed. With no audible voice accessible to me, I was saying voicelessly to myself, "Dear God, yes, I do believe, not just in the God my reason so stoutly affirms, but the God to whom Father Howell is now praying, and on whose grace and love I now joyfully rely."

I went on by saying that "Caroline, I know, will receive this news with as much joy as you. She and I have talked about how our Christian marriage would end up. It has been a good marriage, but would not have been fulfilled without the step I am now prepared to take." I ended the letter by asking Father Howell to pay me a visit after I returned home.

He did and, on April 21 (1984), I was baptized a Christian by Father Howell in the presence of Caroline. A year later, at Father Howell's request, I took the pulpit at St. Chrysostom's Church and gave an account of my conversion to the congregation, of which I had been a nonbelieving member for many years.

In that brief address, I reminded them that two years earlier I had given three Lenten talks about the substance of my book, *How to Think About God,* which had just been published. I reminded them especially about what I had to say concerning the leap of faith—that no one in his right senses would pray to the God affirmed in philosophical theology, but only to a God believed in and worshiped for his love and care, his grace and providence. I told the congregation of Father Howell's visit to me in the hospital and how at last I had been moved to prayer, which I recognized as an act of faith on my part, a living faith with hope and charity to complete it. I said that I still had residual difficulties—things that I still do not understand, and may never fully understand. But these, I said, do not matter. I ended by quoting Mark 9:23–24, where Jesus says to the father whose child is ill: "All things

> are possible to him who believes"; to which the father replies: "O Lord, I do believe, help thou my unbelief."
>
> I do not foresee future progress in our scientific knowledge that will require any advances in philosophical theology. I feel secure in my rational affirmation of God's existence and of my understanding of the chasm between that philosophical conclusion and belief in God. I thank God for the leap of faith that enabled me to cross that chasm.[36]

After his leap of faith Adler went on to explore many aspects of Christian theology. He brought the same brilliant analytical ability to theology that he had employed all of his life in his philosophical writings. Many of his thoughts on theology from the later years of his long life are described in his autobiography, *A Second Look in the Rearview Mirror*, a book I encourage everyone to read. It represents an honest discussion of his attempt to live a life of natural piety.

12

THESE NINE WITNESSES TESTIFY TO ANOTHER WAY OF KNOWING THAT IS COMPATIBLE WITH THE EMPIRICAL AND THE METAPHYSICAL RATIONAL WAYS OF KNOWING, BUT IS BEYOND THE DESCRIBABLE AND REQUIRES PERSONAL PARTICIPATION, COMMITMENT, AND PERSONAL TRANSFORMATION

These nine witnesses all testify to the way of knowledge resulting from an encounter with the Wholly Other. Their descriptions indicate the personal nature of their encounter and a knowledge derived from personal acquaintance (*kendskab*). In each person's testimony one hears of an increased understanding, a clearer vision of reality, and a transformation in their lives. One recurrent theme in their lives is an increased capacity to understand their own place in existence, coupled with a more profound joy and an increased capacity to love. One may choose to think their experiences are illusions, but if they claim another valid way of knowing derived from these experiences, can we reject their testimony simply because we have not experienced a similar knowledge derived from personal acquaintance?

If we have not experienced such a way of knowing, how can we know that this way of knowledge is not real? We may choose to side with Freud and call their experiences illusions, but we should also understand that Freud had not experienced a *kendskab*, participatory knowledge of the divine. If one has not experienced this way of knowledge, how does one know that it is an invalid way of knowing? We may choose to revert to a Kantian empiricism requiring input from our five senses, but that choice reflects a leap of faith and the adoption of what may be an overly restrictive worldview.

The knowledge from personal acquaintance does not mean that one cannot come to terms with God's existence through a more intellectual route. Antony Flew claims that his conversion to theism was done through reason. Jacques Maritain argued that all forms of knowledge, including empirical, metaphysical, and mystical are valid. Nor does one have to make an approach to God by way of one specific encounter. A participating knowledge in the love of God may develop over a long period of time on a substantial journey through the course of one's life. Michael Polanyi held that one can increase one's skill of "religious knowing" by participating in worship (e.g., participation in hymns, prayers, or the Eucharist).

The kind of knowledge or understanding described by these nine witnesses is not the kind of understanding derived from an empirical or scientific investigation but is more closely analogous to an understanding derived from the arts in which music, paintings, poetry, and fiction can enrich us in ways beyond an objective description. Consider the difficulty in describing the experience of listening to Pavarotti.

Participatory knowledge is not opposed to reason. Reason serves as a confirmation of participatory knowledge in many respects. Participatory knowledge is not irrational. Participatory knowledge should be consistent with what we know to be true in all areas of rational disciplines. But this knowledge by participation is not confined to an inference drawn from a premise. It requires more than mere reason; it requires a commitment and a transformation of the knower, not a mere rational argument. A mere intellectual analysis will not bring participatory knowledge. One cannot know love intellectually. To gain this way of knowing, one must be willing to act and step forward into a process of transformation. The path to participatory knowledge is through the forest of interior change. Such a path is more demanding than a detached, objective analysis of a syllogism.

For a person participating in a religious experience, an indescribable cogency may vividly connect the experience to what the person knows to be true. Although the experience is not subject to empirical investigation, there is a knowledge of truth that has its own indescribable explanatory power. This may be quite dramatic as in some of the conversion experiences described by our witnesses or it may be only a glimpse that serves as an intimation of a more comprehensive reality full of love and beauty. But this reality is not experienced in a detached methodology. The person engaged in a spiritual practice is not objective but is an acting subject who participates from a perspective of personal transformation. Rudolf Otto held that the experience of the Wholly Other cannot be described but is nevertheless known powerfully by the participant. Clare Boothe Luce wrote as well as anyone of her enormous sense of another reality of beauty and truth, but she warned that she could not capture her participation in words alone. William Wordsworth used poetry to attempt to convey a sense of his experience.

> And I have felt
> A presence that disturbs me with the joy
> Of elevated thoughts; a sense sublime
> Of something far more deeply interfused
> Whose dwelling is the light of setting suns,
> And the round ocean, and the living air
> And the blue sky, and in the mind of man.
> A motion and a spirit, that impels
> All thinking things, all objects of thought,
> And rolls through all things. Therefore am
> I still
> A lover of the meadows and the woods,
> And mountains; and of all that we behold
> From this green earth; of all the mighty world.[1]

Clare Boothe Luce's and William Wordsworth's experiences in all likelihood involved changes in their brains. A scientific explanation of the chemistry of the brain, however, does not deny the possibility of a true transcendent reality that may produce intimations of overwhelmingly love, beauty, and purpose. Intimations of a transcendent reality may correlate with physical events, but that does not mean that the transcendent reality is dependent upon the physical. More importantly, the glimpse of a transcendent reality appears to require a trust and a receptivity to an inner transformation. One may not be able to approach the transcendent as a scientific investigator with no personal stake in the question of the experience on one's life.

This is the subjectivity that Kierkegaard held to be required in gaining a knowledge of transcendence. A person brings the integrity of a desire for inner transformation to the experience. In the personal involvement of a spiritual practice this integrity may be tested, and the fruits of the transformation bear their own witness to the veracity of the intimations. Ultimately, this may involve participation in a community given to spiritual practices. These practices, in turn, must remain connected with what one knows to be true in other areas of knowledge, including the quantitative and the empirical aspects of the physical world. One cannot be connected with an ultimate truth and follow a path that denies the other aspects of truth verified in other disciplines. My friend Jim Houston describes untethered spiritual practices as "California Cotton Candies" that may contain very little real substance.

For most persons transformation is not merely a one-time event but a process encouraged by involvement in a community of persons engaged in spiritual practices. Reason should not be abandoned in this community involvement. One needs to evaluate the moral nature of the community, particularly the capacity to love generated by the practices or worship patterns of the community. Our discussion of the boundaries of right and wrong is relevant in considering the value of a participatory transformational knowledge engaged in community. The moral content is important and should reflect what we know to be in harmony with our moral reflections. The spiritual practices of the community should increase one's ability to love. Authentic love in turn should bear the fruit of joy, peace, patience, kindness, goodness, and self-control.

Involvement in a community does not mean that one is never gaining knowledge in solitude. Solitude is a necessary complement of community participation. One who is in community must also take time to be in solitude.[2] One cannot grow in the knowledge (and love) of God by frenetic participation in a constant flow of group meetings. The knowledge of God requires solitude, reflection, and personal communion with the divine.

13

CONCLUDING REFLECTIONS AND SUMMARY

Theism Requires a Leap of Faith, but it is a Leap into the Light, not into the Dark; Theism Explains more than Atheism, which also Requires a Leap of Faith

Earlier in this book I noted that everyone makes a leap of faith in accepting presuppositions that comprise a worldview, and every worldview has inevitable uncertainties. We know that this universe will end its ability to sustain life. In a search for ultimate meaning one cannot limit a theory of knowledge to only that which can be empirically verified. Reason can take us only so far. There are other ways of knowing, including credible religious knowledge by personal acquaintance. In examining the question of God's existence, one may rationally conclude that God is a personal God who can only be known in reality as a person, not as an inference. Reason and faith are both required as a basis of knowledge. They are complementary. Reason without faith experience is dead. Experience without reason can be fantasy.

Given the recent discoveries in science and philosophy, it is remarkable that Hume and Kant still influence the question of God's existence. Kant based his theory of knowledge on a Euclidean geometry and a Newtonian view of the universe, which in today's science has been modified by Einstein's theory of relativity, non-Euclidean geometry, and quantum physics. His theory of knowledge is too restrictive and does not include all that we can know or detect.

Because Kant's theory is discredited by contemporary science and mathematics, one can use reason to address basic metaphysical questions, such as the following: Why is there something rather than nothing? Why does that something have the particular members and order that it has? Why does this particular kind of universe exist? Why does the universe have an inherent order that makes it intelligible? Einstein marveled at the intelligibility of the universe. He knew that science could not even begin if the world was not intelligible. As he noted, "Let us concede that behind any major scientific work is a conviction akin to religious belief, that the world is intelligible."[1] If one stops and thinks about it, the intelligibility of the universe is rather astonishing. After all, it could be simply a chaos and not a rational universe with inherently mathematical principles.

My argument is not limited to a discussion of the relationships among the contingent components of the universe but considers the existence of a radically contingent universe and why it has the particular components that make up such a universe. Because the question addressed in the argument relates to the universe as a whole and not only the relationships among its constituent components, the question falls outside the capacity of science. This does not mean that we have nothing to learn about the existence of the universe from science, but ultimately science by its nature is restricted to a discussion of the relationships among the members of the universe and does not address the question why there is something rather than nothing, or, in the case of the universe (entire cosmos), why the universe exists.

If one closes one's heart and mind to the possibility of God's existence, he or she is not likely to be convinced even by strong evidence. The Enlightenment residue in contemporary culture approaches the question of the possibility of God's existence as if it were a closed, rather than an open, question. Actually, contemporary science and contemporary philosophy indicate that the question is not only open but also that the evidence available points to the existence of God.

Assuming the question of God's existence to be an open question, the argument I consider is not an argument that fills a gap in our present knowledge. On the contrary, this argument looks to God as the ground for the existence of the universe and its particular component constituents. It is an argument that considers the universe as a whole and is outside the capacity of science, even though various aspects of science have some relevance to the question. The essence of my thought in this regard is not limited to the relationship among the constituents of the universe but also emphasizes the question raised by the intelligible nature of the universe and the reason for the existence of this particular universe with its particular constituents.

The contingent nature of the components of the universe and of the universe itself raises the question whether the universe and its particular components are *intended.* This is different from the question of whether or not they are *designed.* Design is a concept that applies to watches, machines, and other human creations. Intention is a concept that is outside the scope of Darwinian theory, evolution, and other aspects of the examination of the relationship among constituent components of the universe. These theories attempt to describe the order of these relationships *but do not address the question of whether or not there is intention underlying the ground of the universe and its constituents.*[2]

Many scholars have not realized that Hume and Kant's arguments have failed and that, with respect to the cosmological argument for the existence of God, misinterpreted the concept of a necessary being. Hume held that this term meant a being that necessarily exists. But the argument I set forth uses the term *necessary being* in another sense. In this sense the term means a being whose existence is independent of anything. It does not imply that this being exists necessarily. It means that a "necessary being" does not depend on anything else. This is the precise emphasis of Thomas Aquinas's use of this term. Kant and Hume misinterpreted Aquinas in his use of "necessary being."

Hume's criticism of the argument for a necessary being was based on the self-contradiction that applies when one attempts to say that a being who exists necessarily does not exist. Aquinas, however, did not think of a necessary being as a *logically* necessary being or one that necessarily exists. Rather, Aquinas thought of a necessary being as one who does not have a beginning or an end and is not dependent on anything else for its existence. Hume's criticism is not effective against Aquinas's interpretation of the term because Aquinas is not positing a logically necessary being but an independent and infinite, noncontingent being. If such a being exists, of course, it is not a being who could not have existed. One must make the distinction between logical necessity (e.g., a questionable attempt to define a necessary being into existence) and conditional necessity. Conditional necessity follows from the premises of the cosmological argument I have set forth. The conclusion of a necessary being is necessitated by the premises and conditions contained in the argument.

Kant objected to the cosmological argument because he thought it was based on the ontological argument. He held that propositions must contain a subject *and* a characterizing predicate. For Kant, existence was not a property or characteristic and thus not a real predicate so the proposition set forth in the ontological argument could not be applied validly to a being. But in the argument set forth in this book I use the term *necessary being* to mean a being without beginning and end. In Kant's terminology these characteristics are a real predicate in a valid proposition.

The universe as a whole depends upon something else for its continuing existence. Its existence is not indefeasible. It is not necessary, but dependent. Because the universe is only a possible universe, it is not necessary, but radically contingent.

Moreover, our existence and the existence of all humans and any other contingent components of the universe cannot be explained by examining the relationship among contingent components. We do not know the reason why there are these particular components rather than nothing at all. This "why" question is not addressed by merely postulating an infinite succession of dependent, contingent things.

Assume that there exists an infinite series of rabbits. In the whole collection of rabbits, each rabbit's existence depends upon another rabbit that generated it. Each rabbit is contingent on a previous rabbit. But the fact that each rabbit's existence depends upon another rabbit does not explain why there have been any rabbits rather than no rabbits at all. Why does this infinite collection of rabbits have its particular members? It is not a sufficient answer to say that this collection always had rabbits. This is true for all the contingent (dependent) beings or things in an infinite succession in our universe. We still have to ask the legitimate question of why these members (rather than no members) exist. Nor does an explanation of the existence of each rabbit in terms of another rabbit explain the entire collection of rabbits. As philosopher William Rowe writes: "When the existence of each member of a collection is explained by reference to some other member *of that very same collection* then it does not follow that the collection itself has an explanation. For it is one thing for there to be an explanation of the existence of each dependent being and quite another thing for there to be an explanation of why there are dependent beings at all."[3]

This argument is not defeated by Kant's objection, sometimes known as the fallacy of composition, to the effect that one cannot ascribe a property of a member of a group or collection as a characteristic of the whole of the collection. Diogenes Allen described this fallacy, giving the example that one cannot infer from the fact that if every component part of a given machine has a light weight that the whole machine has a light weight. Consequently, Kant would argue that the fact that every component of the universe has a reason for its existence does not mean that the universe as a whole has a reason for its existence.

Yet Kant misses the concept of radical contingency and fails to see the application of the argument to the universe as a whole.[4] The contingency of the universe as a whole concrete entity is a radical, not a superficial contingency. As discussed above, the components of the universe have only superficial contingency. But a radical contingency means that the universe's existence is dependent to the extent that the removal of a sustaining cause of its existence would result in its annihilation (reduction to absolute nothingness).

Contemporary physics supports this understanding of the treatment of the universe as a concrete entity. The expansion of the universe, the general theory of relativity, and the intelligibility of the universe that allows for its study are all reasons for the legitimacy of the questions: Why does the universe exist? Why is there something rather than nothing?

One often hears the question: If God caused contingent beings, who or what caused God? The fallacy in this question is regarding God as another member of an infinite series of contingent beings. Theology has traditionally held that God is not part of the universe. God is not another member of the universe. God is not one who stands in a similar relation to the members or components of the universe in a manner similar to other members or components. God's relationship to the members or components of the universe differs from their relationship to each other.

When one realizes that God is not a part of the universe, not another member of the universe that can be examined objectively as all other members of the universe, one can see why God can never be the object of a scientific, empirical observation. God is not just another member in a continuous succession of finite contingent beings or things. God does not have the causal relationship with the universe that contingent successive things have with each other. God is not the last member in a long succession of contingent things or beings and not subject to scientific study that only applies to the relationships among members or components of the universe. Science relies on sense experience and examines relationships among the members of the universe. The concept of God as an uncaused being is outside this membership and transcends time.[5]

The argument that God must have a cause is a fallacious argument raised from the anthropomorphic perspective of a divine being subject to time. Anything subject to time would have a beginning. If something has a beginning, it has a cause. But a divine being need not be confined to time and thus not need a beginning. A divine being outside of time and not considered part of the universe would have no beginning and no end.

The existence of God is a rational and consistent explanation of a necessary cause of a radically contingent universe. God's existence is consistent with the requirements of something existing necessarily for anything to exist at all. With a rational, plausible argument for the existence of God as the preservative cause of the continuing existence of the universe, we can follow the lead of Adler and consider plausible reasons why the universe had a beginning. The Second Law of Thermodynamics requires that disorder in the universe tends toward a maximum. The universe could not be dissipating from infinity or it would have run down by now. Consequently, the universe had a beginning that had to be highly ordered. One could hypothesize that the universe came about through a series of endless past contingent events that stretch backward through infinity, but such a series may not be possible in reality. Recent proofs imply that any universe (or multiverse) with an average positive expansion rate had to have a cosmic beginning. Our universe had a beginning and requires a cause of its coming to be, regardless of any possible "pre" Planck time quantum physical description.

The laws of physics are not good candidates for a necessary being because they do not explain: (1) why there is a physical universe to describe, (2) why the physical world is rationally transparent to us, and (3) why the particle astrophysics of the universe are so finely tuned to allow for life. Nor do the laws of physics exist prior to Planck time. The existence of God, however, explains all of these issues and many more.

The recent discoveries of modern science concerning the rationality, order, and fine-tuning in the universe caused the famous British atheistic philosopher Antony Flew to reverse his position on atheism. These discoveries are consistent with the astonishing intelligibility of the physical world and are consistent with a rational argument for God's existence. Flew stressed that his belief in God was a journey of reason; he attempted to follow the evidence wherever it led him. He states his conclusion:

> I now believe that the universe was brought into existence by an infinite intelligence. I believe that this universe's intricate laws manifest what scientists have called the Mind of God. I believe that life and reproduction originate in a divine Source.
>
> Why do I believe this, given that I expounded and defended atheism for more than a half century? The short answer is this: this is the world picture, as I see it, that has emerged from modern science. Science spotlights three dimensions of nature that point to God. The first is the fact that nature obeys laws. The second is the dimension of life, of intelligently organized and purpose-driven beings, which arose from matter. The third is the very existence of nature. But it is not science alone that has guided me. I have also been helped by a renewed study of the classical philosophical arguments.[6]

The existence of God is also consistent with the underlying foundation of information as the basis for physical existence. Because statistical information in a wave function is neither matter nor energy, quantum theory challenges a strict materialistic, deterministic worldview. Quantum mechanics is based in information as the immaterial irreducible seed of the universe and all physical existence.

Mental processes appear to transcend the purely physical, even though our thoughts are clearly influenced by the physical brain. Perhaps Polkinghorne is correct in viewing the material and the mental as complementary poles of the same substance. This is consistent with the Judeo-Christian view of the soul. Physicist Henry Stapp and psychiatrist Jeffrey Schwartz have demonstrated that consciousness, free will, and nonmaterial information-based mental processes have the ability to change the physical structure of a person's brain (e.g., increasing the number and efficacy of the dendrites in one's brain). Their perspective has practical effects for moral philosophy and for our judicial system.

Our ability to recognize evil and good and distinguish between them argues for the existence of God. If God does not exist, evil is not evil and good is not good. If no set of moral values were better than any other set of moral ideas, one could not legitimately value Gandhi over Hitler. Even an all-powerful being cannot do the logically impossible and simultaneously allow for free will and not allow for free will. Our human comprehension is flawed and finite; there may be reasons for suffering that are not apparent to us. One must consider the totality of the evidence for the existence of God. For Christians, God participates in human suffering as the crucified God who understands, cares, and suffers with us to bring about a more perfect existence.

I discussed the need to complement intellectual thought with faith and reviewed the testimony concerning a personal knowledge of the divine given by nine witnesses. Christianity and Judaism are not built on natural theology. The argument concerning the question of why there is something rather than nothing and the question of intelligibility is not the foundation for the Jewish and Christian faiths. In these faiths, the question of the sustaining cause of the universe is not the primary issue. The ground of faith is a relationship with God. The concepts of natural theology may sometimes be consistent with that ground, but not precede it.

Following Marcel and Kierkegaard one may argue that the most powerful form of knowledge is not empirical, but an encounter or personal acquaintance with the divine. God cannot be known by only objective means. God is not an object but is above all categories and has personhood. Consequently, the knowledge of God is ultimately a personal knowledge. According to Buber, this knowledge requires commitment, action, and mission. Otto and Levinas hold that God can never be reduced to an idea or a concept that one can describe by language. Language can never capture relationships between persons, let alone capture the experience of the person of God.

The fact that one may question the logical proofs for God's existence or nonexistence does not mean that God's existence cannot be known. One can discover the constant presence of the divine by participating and engaging in an encounter with the mystery of God. But this requires that one be willing to see the validity of God's presence. We live in a broken world that for some may serve as a reason for them to will not to believe. Yet the history of many persons of keen intelligence who have claimed to encounter God and had their lives transformed by a continual communion with God is significant as evidence. There is evidential force to the recorded experiences of persons who describe an encounter with the Wholly Other. These experiences often share many characteristics in common such as joy, an increased capacity to love, a turn from self-centered concerns, and a deep sense of meaning and purpose. Far more than any intellectual arguments, these experiences give certainty to those who claim to have encountered the living God. If we are open to them, we all receive what Peter Berger calls "signals of transcendence," whether in worship services or in ordinary daily events. Sometimes the presence of the divine breaks through in a powerful manner and completely alters a person's worldview.

The testimonies I have discussed above are evidence that one should not quickly dismiss. We can follow Freud and look upon them as neurotic fantasies, but the men and women described above were not neurotics. On the contrary, their religious experiences appear to have transformed their lives and made them more mature persons. In Allport's terms they became more integrated as the result of their mature religious sentiments.

In summary, the argument for the existence of God explains more than does the argument for theism. The leap of faith toward theism is a leap of faith into the light, rather than into the dark.[7] This is true because the argument for theism is much more comprehensive in its ability to explain everything that we observe and that we know than is the argument for atheism.

The existence of God explains why there is something rather than nothing; it explains the intelligibility and order in the universe; it explains the continuing existence of the universe; it explains the beginning of the universe; it explains the inherently mathematical nature of the universe; it explains the existence of the laws of nature; it explains the beauty in the universe and the relationship between mathematical beauty and truth; it explains the existence of information; it explains the existence of free will and the ability to recognize good and evil; it explains religious experience; it explains the fine-tuning in the astrophysics of the universe that allows for conscious life; and it explains why thoughts have the capacity to produce true beliefs.

Atheism lacks an adequate, coherent explanation for any of these things. To take a leap in the direction of materialist atheism requires an enormous faith that may have more to do with one's will than we can understand. The desire to be as God (*eritus sicut dei*), to focus on one's self as equal with the divine, and to put one's pride and own interests at the center of one's life, prior to the interests of any other superior being, may have more to do with our reflections and decisions about the existence of God than may be consciously apparent to us. Many persons throughout history have claimed that, after struggling with their own wills and their own desires, they finally found joy in the presence of

God. I know of no valid evidence to deny their claims. The existence of God appears to be a rational, plausible belief. I have known many persons who claim to be involved in a friendship with God, a friendship that increases their capacity for love and joy. Their claims ring true, because their lives demonstrate a peaceful focus on the welfare of all persons. Of course, this is not always true for all who claim to know God and no human being lives to the highest of standards, but perhaps the authenticity of one's claim may be related to the quality of one's love, joy, sacrifice, and mercy.

AFTERWORD

Armand Nicholi, Harvard Medical School, author of *The Question of God*

Everyone possesses a worldview—a philosophy of life. We begin the process of embracing a worldview early in childhood. In *A Case for the Existence of God*, Dean L. Overman clearly explains the importance of understanding our worldview and the presuppositions that form the basis of that worldview.

A few years after birth, we begin to think about our existence on this planet and to form our philosophy of life. We make one of two basic assumptions: we view the universe as a result of random events and life on this planet as a matter of chance, or we assume some kind of Intelligence beyond the universe Who gives the universe order and life meaning. Our worldview informs our personal, social, and political lives. It influences how we perceive ourselves, how we relate to others, how we adjust to adversity, and what we understand to be our purpose in life. Our worldview helps determine our values, our ethics, and our capacity for happiness—and tells more about us, perhaps, than any other aspect of our personal history. Even Sigmund Freud, who argued strongly against the existence of God, also argued strongly that we should be free to question whether or not God exists. He writes, "The actual question raised is whether there is a divine spirit and a revelation by it, and the matter is certainly not decided by saying the question cannot be asked."

Dean Overman helps the reader comprehend the importance of understanding our personal worldview, the presuppositions upon which it is based, and the many factors that influenced these presuppositions.

Readers will find the book to be a window into their lives and thus difficult to put down.

THE NEW MATHEMATICS OF ALGORITHMIC INFORMATION THEORY IS RELEVANT TO THEORIES CONCERNING THE FORMATION OF THE FIRST LIVING MATTER

THE NATURE OF INFORMATION AND THE SOURCE OF BIOLOGICAL INFORMATION (INSTRUCTIONS) CONSTITUTE THE CENTRAL DISTINCTION BETWEEN LIVING AND NONLIVING MATTER.

For many years scientists thought that there were two fundamentals: matter and energy. Einstein discovered that matter and energy were actually one fundamental: matter/energy. With Claude Shannon's seminal work on information theory and the subsequent discovery of the workings of the DNA molecule, we then discovered that there are still two fundamentals in nature: matter/energy and information.

What is the source of information (instructions) in animate matter? What is the source of the instructions we find in the DNA that exists in all living things? This question is central to an understanding of life, *because biological information is the central distinction between living and nonliving matter*. This distinction can be seen in the difference between the carbon in a pencil and the carbon in one's body. The carbon in the pencil does not act pursuant to any instructions, whereas the carbon in one's body acts pursuant to the instructions contained in the DNA molecules of the human organism.

Currently, self-organization theories fail to explain the initial generation of information in the very first living matter (protobiont), because they describe the formation of order, not complexity as defined by information theory.

I have never regarded an evolutionary process of development as contradictory to my faith. Although the question of the origin of life is not central to my argument, I write this appendix to describe the relevance of a relatively new branch of mathematics known as algorithmic information theory as it applies to the question of life's origin and specifically to the origin of information (instructions) in living matter. I am merely pointing out how mathematics calls into question some of the current origin-of-life research and paradigms. Self-organization appears in the universe, so I have never held that it is impossible. My point is that all current scenarios fail and that algorithmic information theory strongly indicates that the process for the origin of life (first living cell) may be unknowable. Algorithmic information theory imposes real limits on the amount of information that can be derived from physical laws. It is important to understand the implications of Gregory Chaitin and Andrei Kolmorgov's mathematics in searching for the source of living matter.

The enormous information in living matter involves irregular, flexible patterns, while inanimate matter never rises above simple, repeating patterns in its information content. A quartz crystal, for example, has simple order and replicates, but it has very little information content and is not alive. By contrast, DNA exists in all living matter and contains a vast amount of information that allows organisms to replicate and maintain themselves, that is, to live. The DNA for even the smallest single-celled bacterium contains over 4 million instructions. These instructions are encoded in DNA's four "bases"—the rungs of the famous double helix ladder of DNA that are denoted A, G, C, T. The bases act like a four-letter alphabet for the genetic process. The process, like the English language, consists of a code. Acting like sentences, DNA instructions pass on the information needed to form a protein or some other necessity that the living organism needs in order to replicate or maintain itself.

The current problem with self-organization theorists is that the mechanisms they claim could create life lack any plausible method of generating the sort of information DNA contains. A new scenario may appear in the future, but present scenarios only describe the formation of *order*, not complex *information*. Self-organization theorists like to use the term *complexity* in their work, but all they mean by it is highly organized, intricate patterns, which is not a definition capable of distinguishing quartz crystals from rhododendrons or amoebae.

The cause of irregular, almost random sequences in a code required to transmit the significant amount of information (instructions) required for life cannot be derived from the laws of physics.

Current self-organization scenarios claim that the laws of physics (and the laws of chemistry they produce) caused the formation of living matter. But this idea faces a grave obstacle—the simple mathematical fact that the genetic information contained in even the smallest living organism is much larger than the information content derivable from the laws of physics. Where did the greater information content of life come from? Theorists of self-organization have not addressed this fundamental difficulty.

Even if we ignore this fundamental mathematical fact, there is also the problem that the laws of physics only produce regular patterns. DNA—life—requires an irregular pattern to transmit information through the genetic code. To use an analogy to the code in our written English language, if I type the letters "ABC" repeatedly for 1,000 pages, I would have a highly ordered, regular, predictable pattern such as a law of nature would produce. But I would have conveyed very little information. The *Oxford History of the American People*, on the other hand, has an irregular pattern in its alphabet letters, and it conveys a large amount of information. Similarly, DNA varies its letters A, C, T, G in order to transmit the genetic code.

Flexibility and the lack of a regular, predictable pattern in DNA argue against the existence of an inherent law that controls the operation of DNA. A physical law produces a regular, predictable pattern, such as the law of gravity produced in the ordered vortex of water in a bathtub when the drain plug is pulled. If DNA were caused by such a law, it would have a simple, repeating sequence (like ABCABC) without much information. And DNA would not be capable of transmitting millions of instructions, as it does in even the simplest living organism.

The Oxford chemist Michael Polanyi recognized this in the mid-twentieth century. Just as the information contained in a poem is not determined by the chemicals in the pen used to write the poem, so the information in the genetic code, although encoded in a four-letter alphabet, is not determined by the chemical elements of that alphabet.

Presently, *no one has any plausible idea concerning the source of biological information. Most proposed scenarios focus on chance, the laws of physics and chemistry, or a combination of these factors.* But these candidates are lacking in their ability. Meaningful information such as the kind existing in biological molecules does not exist inside the atoms of nonliving matter and cannot be explained by chemical bonding affinities.

For example, sodium and chlorine can combine to make salt. The "knowledge" for sodium chloride is already in the sodium and chlorine. When nitrogen, carbon, and hydrogen combine with an energy input, amino acids (the building blocks of protein) may result, but not molecules rich in information; the "knowledge" of how to make information-rich molecules is not contained in the mechanism that enables nitrogen, carbon, and hydrogen to bond.

Something else is going on that traditional views of nature and nature's laws cannot explain. The laws of chemistry and physics, as we shall demonstrate, cannot be the source of meaningful biological information. Nevertheless, once upon a time, meaningful biological information did not exist. From the fossil records we know that it appeared at least 3.85 billion years ago. Where did it come from?

To clarify the difficulty in looking to a law of physics or chemistry as the source of the information in living matter, we turn to a discussion of the concept of the algorithm as it applies to information theory.

Algorithmic information theory demonstrates that randomness and uncertainty are required to generate complex information; the order produced by the laws of physics is too simple to transmit the amount of information content required for life.

An algorithm is a finite procedure, written in symbols, by which a desired result can be achieved in computable operations. It is a compact formula for solving a problem with a finite series of steps. In the creation of software for a computer, an algorithm is the expression on paper of the proposed computational process.

Rational fractions can be described by an infinite sequence of decimal digits. The computer program for calculating these sequences is a very short algorithm. For example, if we divide 17 by 39, we produce the repeating, infinite sequence: .435897435897435897. This sequence has an orderly pattern from which the rest of the sequence can be predicted. This orderliness allows us to write an algorithm of a short length that will produce the infinite sequence. Such an algorithm may be expressed, "Write 0.435897, and repeat indefinitely." This algorithm is a finite sequence that contains all of the information in the infinite sequence.

"Randomness" and "entropy" are important concepts in information theory. They do not carry the same general meaning in information theory as we use in everyday language. We commonly picture randomness, quite literally, as the paint drippings on a canvas by Jackson Pollock. Entropy is fundamentally a measure of how well a collection of objects fills the places it can access. In the case of the paint in a Pollock painting (or the toys in a child's bedroom), it may not matter if one constrains what is accessible to the whole space or just a corner. There is no information content in either case. It does matter, in contrast, if you are talking about the letters in the alphabet. If you are constrained to a few letters, you have lower entropy than if you were allowed to "access" more of them. You need letters, however, to make more words, so more information requires high entropy. Of course, a larger collection of letters can still give mere gibberish and hence corresponds to our common understanding of randomness. Entropy does not enable us to distinguish between a collection of "random" letters and those that could be rearranged to create a portion of *The Great Gatsby*. Entropy is thus not a sufficient, but it is a necessary, condition for information to exist.

Chaitin and Kolmogorov consider randomness to be a lack of structure. Their concept of randomness is closely related to our common picture of randomness, but it is different in that they are using a logical rather than a statistical concept. Lack of structure is central to their definition of randomness, not physical unpredictability (as in physics). Something is random in algorithmic information theory when it cannot be compressed into a short description (i.e., no concise theory or axiom can produce it). One measures the randomness and complexity of a sequence by counting the number of bits in a computer program that will produce the sequence. Something is random if the smallest algorithm that will produce the sequence is the same size (in bits) as the sequence itself.

In other words, in algorithmic information theory, entropy measures the randomness in a sequence by the length (in bits) of the shortest algorithm that will generate the sequence. In the example of the division of 17 by 39 given above, the length of the algorithm would obviously be much shorter than the length of the infinite sequence. The measure of the amount of randomness in the infinite sequence depends upon the length of the shortest algorithm that will produce the sequence. Similarly, the randomness of a long finite sequence that may be generated by a much shorter algorithm is measured by the shorter length of the algorithm.

When a very long sequence may be expressed by a much shorter sequence in an algorithm, the sequence is an orderly sequence and not a random sequence. An orderly, patterned sequence is a sequence that can be generated by a short algorithm.

In a recent article entitled "The Limits of Reason," published in the March 2006 issue of *Scientific American*, Gregory Chaitin, the cofounder with Andrei N. Kolmogorov of the new branch of mathematics known as algorithmic information theory, defines the precise approach to complexity based on algorithmic information as follows:

> Today the notions of complexity and simplicity are put in precise quantitative terms by a modern branch of mathematics called algorithmic information theory. Ordinary information theory quantifies information by asking how many bits are needed to encode the information. For example, it takes one bit to encode a single yes/no answer. Algorithmic information, in contrast, is defined by asking what size computer program is necessary to generate the data. The minimum number of bits needed to store the program is called the algorithmic information content of the data. Thus, the infinite sequence of numbers 1, 2, 3, . . . has very little algorithmic information; a very short computer program can generate those numbers . . . just the length of the program in bits counts.
>
> To take another example, the number pi, 3.14159 . . . , also has only a little algorithmic information content, because a relatively short algorithm can be programmed into a computer to compute digit after digit. In contrast, a random number with a mere million digits, say 1.341285 . . . 64, has a much larger amount of algorithmic information. Because the number lacks a defining pattern, the shortest program for outputting it will be about as long as the number itself.
>
> No smaller program can calculate that sequence of digits. In other words, such digit streams are incompressible, they have no redundancy; the best that one can do is transmit them directly. They are called irreducible or algorithmically random.[1]

As discussed above, Chaitin defines the complexity of a sequence as the entropy that measures the randomness of the shortest algorithm needed to generate the sequence. Complexity is a scale with orderliness at one end and randomness at the other. When we speak of the amount of complexity in a sequence, we are speaking about the amount of its randomness. As part of my work as a Templeton Scholar at Oxford, I wrote an article with Dr. Hubert Yockey published in *The Princeton Theological Review*, entitled "Information, Algorithms and the Origin of Life."[2] Yockey is the author of the leading text in the field concerning the application of algorithmic information theory to the origin of life.[3]

In our Princeton article Yockey created the following useful table comparing complexity and randomness. One can see that orderliness is juxtaposed to randomness. Again, highly ordered sequences are not sufficiently complex (random) to allow for high information content. To generate the amount of information found in the smallest living organism's genetic code, we must use an irregular, aperiodic, almost random sequence:

Information Content Is a Measure of Complexity

Less Complexity	*More Complexity*
1. Certainty	1. Uncertainty
2. Orderliness	2. Randomness
3. Low Communication Entropy	3. High Communication Entropy
4. Low Number of Allowed Messages or Sequences	4. High Number of Allowed Messages or Sequences
5. Small Information Content	5. High Information Content

Imagine a "source of information" producing the following sequence:

101101101101101101101101101101101101101101101

This string of numbers is a binary sequence with a simple repeating pattern. Because it can be constructed by a simple algorithm or formula, it has a very low information content. The entire information content in this sequence could be given by the simple instructions, "Write 101 fifteen times." The information of the patterned sequence can be compressed into a compact formula or algorithm. The regular pattern of the sequence allows the long string of ones and zeros to be compacted into a simple basic command. If the string of zeros and ones was random with no pattern at all, we would not be able to find a shortened description of it. No compact equation could generate this string as the product of a simple process of computation.

Why the transmission of a significant amount of information requires an irregular, almost random, sequence in a code.

To understand why living matter involves irregular sequences to transmit information, we shall look at the sequence of letters in a message written in the English language and then compare that sequence with a sequence of letters containing a written message in the genetic code. To transmit information in a code, one must use an irregular, aperiodic, and almost random sequence. This is particularly true when one is transmitting large amounts of information or instructions like the amount of information content we see in all living matter's DNA. These instructions tell the organism and, in a human being, the twenty-five chemical elements making up the organism, how to process energy, maintain itself, and replicate. *In other words, the instructions tell chemical elements how to live.*

One may think of the genetic-code process in DNA as similar to the production of a novel. The DNA instructions (information) act like sentences. These instructions, like all information or messages, are not made of matter or energy. They are nonmaterial and cannot be reduced to a physical or chemical property. The genetic code may be compared to the English language as a code using letters of the Roman alphabet. The instructions in DNA that exist in all living matter are written in the genetic code using the letters A (for adenine), G (for guanine), C (for cytosine) and T (for thymine). The rungs of the nitrogen bases of the double helix DNA molecule are pairs of either adenine and thymine (A-T) or cytosine with guanine (C-G). The instructions in DNA are written in the genetic code and carried in sequences of codons.[4]

When one examines a portion of a novel containing information written in the English language, he or she can readily see that *to convey information the letters cannot appear in a highly ordered pattern.* For example, TTTTOOOORRRR is a highly ordered sequence of letters but does not contain information and does not transmit any instructions in the English language. When we look at the irregular, aperiodic, almost random sequences of letters required to transmit significant information in the novel *The Great Gatsby*, we cannot see a repeating pattern in the sequence of letters. This is one reason why a novel could not be produced by a computer algorithm. Novels containing thousands or millions of bits of information cannot be written by means of a computer algorithm. The simplest living organism, a single-celled bacterium, contains an enormous amount of information in its DNA instructions. A computer algorithm could not produce the irregular, random, complex sequences that are necessary to convey such a significant amount of information. Notice the absence of a regular pattern or highly ordered sequence in the letters of the following paragraphs from *The Great Gatsby*:

> Most of the big shore places were closed now and there were hardly any lights except the shadowy, moving glow of a ferryboat across the Sound. And as the moon rose higher the inessential houses began to melt away until gradually I became aware of the old island here that flowered once for Dutch sailors' eyes—a fresh, green breast of the new world. Its vanished trees, the trees that had made way for Gatsby's house, had once pandered in whispers to the last and greatest of all human dreams; for a transitory enchanted moment man must have held his breath in the presence of this continent, compelled into an aesthetic contemplation he neither understood nor desired, face to face for the last time in history with something commensurate to his capacity for wonder.
>
> And as I sat there, brooding on the old unknown world, I thought of Gatsby's wonder when he first picked out the green light at the end of Daisy's dock. He had come a long way to this blue lawn and his dream must have seemed so close that he could hardly fail to grasp it. He did not know that it was already behind him, somewhere back in that vast obscurity beyond the city, where the dark fields of the republic rolled on under the night.
>
> Gatsby believed in the green light, the orgastic future that year by year recedes before us. It eluded us then, but that's no matter—tomorrow we will run faster, stretch out our arms further. . . . And one fine morning—
>
> So we beat on, boats against the current, borne back ceaselessly into the past.[5]

Note that the lettering is not highly ordered; no regular pattern of letters form in this passage, which transmits to the reader considerable information. The first paragraph starts with an "M" then an "o" then an "s" then a "t" then another "o." But the sequence of letters, disregarding its meaning, is almost random. As noted in Yockey's table given above, randomness is correlated with complexity. Almost random sequences are required to carry significant amounts of information.

This is also true in the sequences of letters in the genetic message. When we look at a section of a genome, designated "chromosome 1," we see the following irregular, aperiodic sequence of letters that also is not highly ordered but is almost random and yet carries instructions necessary for an organism to process energy, replicate, and maintain itself.

taaacttcatggcataaccttgccaaagtatactaagaataaccctgacacaaagctctttttcagcaa
catgccatgaaagaaagaagacaaggggtgatctccactctctaagtgaaccactaaacccaccaaa
gaagaaacgagggaaatagaaagaggacccttgcctgagataatggatctgtatgtatgagtagta
gaaccctgctcaaagtacaaggaagggaaaaaaaagttagtttatttggaattttggacattaagagtctt
tattgttcattttcttttaactcacatgaatggcttatcacttcaattaataaatatttcatttcttttcaa
catattcatgaaacaaatctgaaatgaacagtgcaacatgtgaatgtttagaacattataaaattaaaca
caaaatctgtctggcaatcttcctagcatcttaggaaaaaagttgacaaaatttcaagcagca
gaagggggcagtaaaactcaacagaaagctctggaagatttttaagattcttccttattttcttttcatgtag
attatttcccaacaaatttcagacgctaatagaaattttgtacaacagatccatatatttgcctaaaata
gacacagaaacattgaatatatgcaaacatgagagctataagttttacatgatcaaaccttttttttatg
gtacacaatagtcacagtacttttccatataaaacaggtttagtggtcttaatttagtttggcacatttaat
acactcccatgaccagcatcccaaatgtacctatccgttttattttattgtctcagaattgtcagttatttaat
aaattatgtaactttttttccttatgctcagatttgcacttctttctaaaactctgcccatccttaaagtccca
gattctccttgaacttttttttttgactttccaagtacatggaactcttcactctatcctgctatataagt
gacagaatttccactatgggatagatggagttcaattcctttgagtttaaaataatctaaatataattattc
cttatgccctgtttttccctcacttttgtatccaaatctctttcagacaacagaacaattaatgtctgataagg
aagacaatgatgatcacttcaaaatgaattcaggattgtaatgtaaaattttagtactctctcacagtatg
gattctaacatggcttctaacccaaactaacattagtagctctaactataaacttcaaatttcagtagatg
caacctactcctttaaaatgaaacagaagattgaaattattaaattatcaaaaagaaaatgatc
cacgctcttagttgaaatttcatgtaagattccatgcaataaataggagtgccataaatggaatgatgaaa
tatgactagaggaggagaaaggcttcctagatgagatggaattttagtcatccgtgtctcatgaa
gaatcagatgtgtacactaagcaaaacagttaaaaaaaaaaacctccaagtgagtctcttatt
tattttttcttataagacttctacaaattgaggtacctggtgtagttttatttcaggttttatgctgtcattttc
ctgtaatgctaaggacttaggacataactgaattttctattttccacttcttttctggtgtgtgtgtatatatat
atgtatatatacacacacacatatacatatatatatttttttagtatctcaccctcacatgctcctccctgag
cactacccatgatagatgttaaacaaaagcaaagatgaaattccaactgtcaaaatctcccttccatc
taattaattcctcatccaactatgttccaaaacgagaatagaaaattagccccaataagcccaggcaact
gaaaagtaaatgctatgttgtactttgatccatggtcacaactcataatcttggaaaagtggacagaaaag
acaaaagagtgaactttaaactcgaatttattttaccagtatctcctatgaagggctagtaac
caaaataatccacgcatcagggagagaaatgccttaaggcatacgttttggacatttagcgtccctg
caaattctggccatcgccgcttcctttgtccatcagaaggcaggaaactttatattggtgacccgtg
gagctcacattaactatttacagggtaactgcttaggaccagtattatgaggagaatttacctttcccgcct

ctctttccaagaaacaaggagggggtgaaggtacggagaacagtatttcttctgttgaaagcaacttagc
tacaaagataaattacagctatgtacactgaaggtagctatttcattccacaaaataagagttttt
taaaagctatgtatgtatgtgctgcatatagagcagatatacagcctattaagcgtcgtcactaaa
cataaaacatgtcagcctttcttaaccttactcgccc

A computer algorithm that is a short compact formula could not be written to produce the significant amount of instructions or information contained in the quotation from *The Great Gatsby* or the information contained in the genetic letters on chromosome 1. The length of the algorithm would of necessity be almost equal to the length of the entire sequence. The information could not be compacted into a formula.

Now here is the point to which algorithmic information theory leads: As noted above, *the laws of physics are basically compact formulas, the millions of instructions (information) contained in the smallest living organism's DNA requires sequences that are too random and contain too much information to be derived from compact formulas.* The laws of physics by definition are compact formulas and simply do not contain enough information to generate the irregular, aperiodic, almost random sequences that are required in order to transmit the necessary instructions for life. This information, consequently, could not be derived from the laws of physics or chemistry (which are derived from the laws of physics). Again, the central distinction between living and nonliving matter is the information content that exists in all living matter and is found in DNA. As Hubert Yockey and I pointed out in our article in *The Princeton Theological Review,* those who look to the laws of physics as an explanation for life's origin are looking through the wrong end of the telescope.

The information content in the laws of physics and chemistry is inadequate to generate sufficient information-rich sequences.

By definition, a law of nature is a relatively short algorithm. These laws are simple, compressed formulas with low information content. A physical law is a method of compacting data into a simple algorithm. Because the laws of physics and chemistry can be so compacted, algorithmic information theory tells us that they do not have sufficient information content to generate an information-rich sequence.

Life requires much more information than contained in these laws. The genetic information contained in even the smallest living organism is much larger than the information content found in the laws of physics and chemistry. (Chaitin has programmed the laws of physics and determined that their information content is very small.) Theoretical physicist Paul Davies agrees with this position, as he writes in *The Fifth Miracle*:

> The heart of my objection is this: The laws of physics that operate between atoms and molecules are, almost by definition, simple and general. We would not expect them alone to lead inexorably to something both highly complex and highly specific . . . genomes are more or less random sequences of base pairs, and that this very randomness is essential if they are to play the role of evolvable, information-rich molecules. But this fact flatly contradicts the claim that genes can be generated by a simple, predictable, lawlike process . . . a law is a way to compress data algorithmically, to boil down apparent complexity to a simple formula or procedure. Conversely, no simple law can generate, alone, a random information-rich macromolecule to order. A law of nature of the sort that we know and love will not create biological information or indeed any information at all. Ordinary laws just transform input data into output data. They can shuffle information about but they can't create it. The laws of physics, which determine what atoms react with what, and how, are algorithmically very simple; they themselves contain relatively little information. Consequently they cannot on their own be responsible for creating informational macromolecules. *Contrary to the oft-repeated claim, then, life cannot be "written into" the laws of physics—at least, not into anything like the laws of physics that we know at present. . . . Once this essential point is grasped, the real problem of biogenesis is clear.* Since the heady successes of molecular biology, most investigators have sought the secret of life in the physics and chemistry of molecules. *But they will look in vain for conventional physics and chemistry to explain life*, for that is a classic case of confusing the medium with the message. The secret of life lies, not in its chemical basis, but in the logical and informational rules it exploits. Life succeeds precisely because it *evades* chemical imperatives.[6]

Because Chaitin's algorithmic information theory indicates that algorithms cannot generate novel sequences of information, contemporary mathematics calls into question theories of abiogenesis in the problem of the origination of information (instructions) in the first living matter. Algorithms have limits to the amount of information they can generate. When one uses the precise definition of complexity employed in the mathematics of information theory, one can see the distinction between the generation of order (e.g., fractals) and the generation of complexity. Complexity depends upon a structure's information content, which is the minimum number of instructions necessary to specify the structure. Complexity in the mathematics of algorithmic information theory is not found in the generation of highly ordered fractals.

The sequences necessary to transmit the semantic information found in living matter cannot be generated by an algorithm dramatically shorter than the sequence itself. One needs to distinguish between highly ordered sequences that can be generated by a short algorithm and the complexity found in semantic sequences (e.g., sequences found in the DNA of every living organism).

Oxford mathematician John Lennox notes the limits to mathematical reduction required by Gödel's incompleteness theorem. Lennox notes that Gödel held that the complexity of living matter had to be present either in inorganic material or in the laws of physics. Because inorganic matter contains no information (except for a very restricted low level in crystals), Gödel doubted the current biological paradigm and believed that mathematics would disprove it. Lennox points out that Chaitin's algorithmic information theory dramatically calls into question the ability of the physical laws to produce the novel semantic information sequences required for matter to be considered living.[7]

All the examples given by self-organization theorists fail to produce the language (semantic) structures required for life. They focus on the order in crystals or honeycombs, but that kind of order is irrelevant (and in certain respects the opposite of what is required). Fractals are fun but too highly ordered to produce language (semantic) information found in a code. Biologists in general have not understood the implications of algorithmic information theory. They need to address the issues raised by this new branch of mathematics and examine the speculations in the current biological paradigm.[8]

The unknowable: Information's mystery is not a proof for God's existence, but God's existence is consistent with the mystery.

One must be careful in drawing broad metaphysical inferences from the conclusion that I have reached. Perhaps the most that can be said is that the origin of life may be unknowable in principle. Our knowledge has limits.

The existence of a genome and the genetic code divides living organisms from nonliving matter. There is nothing in the physico-chemical world that remotely resembles reactions being determined by a sequence in a code.

Although some are optimistic that life may be made in the laboratory, it may well be that scientists will come closer and closer to the riddle of how life emerged on Earth. But because of the limitations of human reasoning, like Zeno's arrow, they may never achieve a complete solution. Even if life is created in a laboratory, one may only face the question: Is this how God did it or was it done another way? The creation of life in a laboratory would not in any way be dispositive of the question of God's existence.

The mystery of information does not mean that God did it—does not prove the existence of God—but it is consistent with the existence of God. The existence of God is a plausible explanation for the mystery of information generation.[9]

I want to reiterate that the question of information generation is a mystery. Perhaps an adequate self-organization scenario may be forthcoming. I indicated this in my previous book. As I wrote previously:

> *At present*, however, all self-organization scenarios fail in explaining the generation of sufficient information content to qualify a structure as a life form . . . an adequate self-organization scenario *may* never be discovered. The information generation in living matter is not likely to flow from the law of physics or chemistry alone.

Perhaps someone will discover an unconventional algorithm or unconventional law that could generate biological information. But such a discovery would not be dispositive of the question of Where did this algorithm or law come from and why is there something rather than nothing? Who or what wrote the algorithm or law?[10]

In *A New Kind of Science*, Stephen Wolfram assumes that the laws of nature are derived from a simple computer program or algorithm. But this moves our question just one step back to ask Who or what produced the program or algorithm? Why does it exist? Who is the programmer?

Moreover, Wolfram's view of complexity differs from Chaitin's. Chaitin does not consider *pi* complex under the principles of algorithmic information theory. But Wolfram begs the question by asserting that it is complex if it *looks random*. However, this seems to me to be a rather arbitrary method of defining randomness and complexity.[11]

We are still at the place of Hawking's question: Why is there a physical universe? What breathes the fire into the algorithm to generate a world of information? We are still left with the question of existence and why the physical world is rational, intelligible, and governed by contingent laws.[12]

As noted above, it is a basic error in logic to think that Darwin's theory of evolution explains why there is something rather than nothing and why that something is rational, intelligible, and inherently mathematical. Even if Darwin is correct, his theory does not explain the existence of the universe or the existence of rational, intelligible laws. Where did the physical framework underlying his theory come from? Leibniz's basic question is not addressed by Darwin's theory. Where did contingent laws come from? How does Darwin's theory address the more basic foundational question: Why is there something rather than nothing? These are the more significant foundational questions. Einstein held that the most incomprehensible thing about the universe is that it is comprehensible. I want to know why it is comprehensible and why is there such a thing as existence. Darwin was completely perplexed by the question of the origin of life (first living organism). His theory does not address why anything exists and why it is intelligible.[13]

I will now conclude this Appendix A by giving a summary of the relevant principles of algorithmic information theory as they apply to the instructions (information) in all living matter:

1. Information is defined as instructions or a message in considering a definition for the term *information* in the DNA of all living matter. This information is nonmaterial in the following sense. When I type these letters, the information contained in this message is encoded in matter in my computer and on my computer screen. It is compressed and, if I wanted to email this message, I could send it on to you by use of a signal. Assuming I did so, when you print out the message on a laser printer, it would be encoded in ink and paper. The message would not be derived from the ink or paper. They are only the means of encoding the message in matter; they are not themselves the message and the message did not arise from them.
2. Were you to then show the printed email to a friend, the information contained in the message would use photons to illuminate the matter (ink and paper) and allow your friend to absorb

the information that would then be encoded in the matter (physical cells) in his or her brain. The information would not be derived from anything physical. Physical entities, such as ink, paper, electricity, and neurons would simply serve to encode the information, but they are not the source of the information. Physical entities merely carry the information. The information is independent of the substances used to encode it.

3. The same analysis applies to the information in the DNA molecule. It is independent of the bases of sugars and phosphates that comprise the molecule. Information is independent from the chemicals of matter encoding the information. The information I am sending in my email is not generated by the matter and energy used to convey the message. One must distinguish between the medium and the message.
4. In Chaitin's information theory, one must understand that randomness means something that cannot be compressed or reduced. Chaitin's randomness means a sequence that cannot be compressed into a shorter algorithm that could generate the sequence. This randomness is correlated with complexity. A sequence that is incompressible to a shorter algorithm is a random sequence. Chaitin argues that randomness is at the heart of pure mathematics and is the underlying reason behind Gödel's incompleteness theorem and Turing's incompatibility theory. There are real limits to mathematical reasoning and to any formal reasoning. For purposes of this Appendix, my main point is that although we cannot prove that a given sequence is random, the laws of physics and chemistry are limited by the algorithmic information content in their formulas.
5. I am not saying that the information in DNA is *inconsistent* with the laws of physics but that the laws of physics do not have sufficient information content to *generate* the almost random sequence of symbols necessary to convey the amount of information necessary for the instructions in the smallest living cell. Unlike the elements in the physical, chemical world, the communication system in the genetic information system is essentially a data recording and processing system.
6. Algorithmic information theory holds that the length of a sequence (in bits) in the shortest algorithm that generates the sequence is the

entropy of the sequence. Randomness and entropy are correlated. The entropy of the compressed sequence (the algorithm's sequence) measures the amount of randomness. Yockey was the first person to relate the Kolmogorov-Chaitin definition of complexity to protein sequences in molecular biology. The complexity of a sequence is a measurement of the quantity of information stored in the sequence. This relates to the length of the semantic sequence, in bits, required to describe the shortest algorithm that specifies the semantic sequence. If one can compress a very long sequence into a much shorter sequence, the long sequence is not random and not complex.

7. This means that the amount of randomness in *pi* is the shortest algorithm that calculates the *pi* sequence. The shorter the algorithm the more *orderly* the sequence.
8. Randomness is correlated with complexity. The more random a sequence is, the greater is its complexity (information content).
9. *Order* should be distinguished from *highly* organized. Semantic novel information (such as DNA) is highly organized, which is the opposite of highly ordered.
10. *It is true that we cannot prove* a certain sequence to be random. As Yockey noted, when we attempt such a proof, we run into the liar's paradox. (A Cretan says, "All Cretans always lie." Is this statement true?) We can't prove that no shorter program exists that could generate what appears to be a totally random sequence. (We know that *pi* is not random, but it appears that way at first glance.)
11. When a sequence is highly organized, we need a long algorithm to describe it so that it has a high entropy and high complexity (entropy is correlated to the shortest algorithm needed to compute a sequence is its complexity).
12. Genetic noise is corrected by repair processes in DNA by a proofreading task of translation in the DNA-RNA methodology, which is consistent with the laws of physics. Amazingly, it is a digital system.
13. As noted, there is no trace in physics or chemistry of the control of chemical reactions by a sequence of any sort or of a code between sequences.
14. Gödel demonstrated that the axioms of number theory are insufficient to prove certain theorems that are known to be true.

Chaitin found a form of Gödel's theorem in algorithmic information theory, which when applied to the genetic logic system, shows that that system cannot function unless it is generated by something with sufficient information to perform the tasks of metabolism and reproduction. This is a large amount of information, far greater than the amount of the information content in the laws of physics. Chaitin has programmed the laws of physics and found the information content (in his definition of complexity) to be very insufficient. Because this is a form of Gödel's incompleteness theorem, it may not be subject to a god-of-the-gaps criticism.

15. The sequence hypothesis set forth above means that the sequence is *consistent with but independent of* the laws of physics and chemistry. The complex sequences are not contrary to the laws of physics, but they cannot be generated by the laws of physics.

THE LIMITS OF MATHEMATICS AND THE LIMITS OF REASON

Why Everyone Will Always Live by Faith Rather than Certainty

In the 1920s, German mathematician David Hilbert proposed a formalist foundation of mathematics. The purpose of Hilbert's program was to formalize all mathematics and determine proofs for the consistency of mathematics. Hilbert attempted to reduce mathematics to an axiomatic, formal system containing no contradictions and capable of demonstrating truth or falsity by valid, logical mathematical inferences from the axioms. Hilbert tried to represent mathematical statements with the language of formal axiomatics, using the symbols of propositional and predicate calculus. Hilbert's concept of formalized mathematics permitted any proof to be expressed as a series of inferences from mathematical axioms.

In 1931, however, Austrian mathematician Kurt Gödel, using Hilbert's expressions of formal axiomatics, demonstrated that for any consistent mathematical system there exists within the system a well-formed statement that is not provable under the rules of the system. Gödel's incompleteness theorem is in part due to his analysis of Bertrand Russell's writings. British philosopher Bertrand Russell attempted to resolve the liar's paradox by rejecting all statements that produce vicious circularity as meaningless and neither true or false.

Kurt Gödel took Russell's monumental *Principia Mathematica* and designated a number for each one of Russell's symbols and then produced mathematical formulations of Russell's concepts. Gödel intended to prove that Russell's system was free from logical contradictions. However, Gödel discovered that to prove Russell's system consistent, he had to be able to demonstrate that any formula is or is not provable within the system. Instead of confirming Russell, Gödel developed his incompleteness theorem and demonstrated the impossibility of proving all true statements within a formal, logical system.

Gödel used his designated numbering system to demonstrate that in any consistent deductive system a valid statement exists that is not provable by the rules of the system. In a mathematical system there are mathematical statements that are true but cannot be proven by the logical proofs of the mathematical system. Similarly, there are statements that are false but not provable. Gödel demonstrated that in any deductive system there is a sentence that asserts, "This sentence is not provable." Gödel was again faced with the contradictions in the liar's paradox.

Gödel's incompleteness theorem requires us to take the paradox seriously. The incompleteness theorem is actually a variation on the liar's paradox contained in the statement by Epimenides, a Cretan, who asserts, "All Cretans are always liars." If one assumes that Epimenides is telling the truth, then he is lying. But he cannot be lying because we have assumed that he is telling the truth. Similarly, if Socrates asserts, "What Plato says is a lie," and if Plato responds, "What Socrates says is true," we are faced with another logical paradox. If what Plato says is a lie, then Socrates's assertion is true. But if Socrates's assertion is true, then Plato's response is a lie and Socrates's assertion must be false.

Gödel's theorem demonstrates that mathematics is incomplete because the system leaves unanswered the truth or falsity of certain mathematical propositions that are the logical results of valid mathematical inferences. This theorem shook mathematics and all formal theories that include the arithmetic of natural numbers. If consistency could not be demonstrated within a mathematical system, at any moment a contradiction could arise and shake the system down to its foundations. There is clearly a limit on the ability of human reasoning to know that logical thought processes will lead to truth.

Although mathematics works remarkably well in describing the physical world and in application to the many technical products we use every day, our observation, logical thought processes, and mathematical analysis face real limits. Adding further significance to the limits of reason demonstrated by Gödel (and Alan Turing), Gregory Chaitin's work in algorithmic information theory demonstrates that many things are not subject to proofs. Chaitin's work has a long, distinguished lineage; as Hubert Yockey notes, Socrates's problem of doubling the square may be solved, but the solution to the doubling of a cube is unknowable. This does not mean that no cube exists that is not double the size of another cube, but that the principles of number theory cannot decide the solution to the problem of doubling a cube.

The laws of physics and our understanding of quantum particles limit our ability to speculate as we approach the singularity of time zero of the Big Bang. At Planck time or time zero the theories of physics fail completely. Quantum physics and other classical theories of physics no longer suffice to describe the state of the universe. At Planck time the universe is smaller than its quantum wavelength and is consequently hidden in the impenetrable clouds of quantum uncertainty. In this uncertainty we simply cannot know the geometry of reality or the positions of any reality. Einstein's theory of gravitation also breaks down. The identification of the force or forces that brought the universe into being appears to be unknowable. This does not mean that we should not look for a solution, but the shroud of quantum uncertainty seems to prevent our ever lifting the veil to know what actually happened at "pre" Planck time.

There are real limits to any formal reasoning system attempting something in the nature of a mathematical proof. Science and faith share a common belief that what we see as normal reality is not actual reality; the observable has something more fundamental hidden behind it. Attempts to structure systems that open up all of that reality face real obstacles. This may be part of the reason a *compelling* proof of God's existence or nonexistence may not be possible. Certainty in this world may not only be unknowable (to use Chaitin's term) but is also unavailable. This does not mean that an argument cannot be rational and plausible, but perhaps it cannot compel one to choose in a certain direction.

The result of these deeply embedded undecidable fundamentals in mathematics and all formal reasoning systems is that everyone has to make Pascal's wager or Kierkegaard's leap of faith. There are no exemptions. Because abstention is a vote, agnosticism is not a real option. Everyone lives and dies with a faith, whether the faith is theistic or naturalistic. This is the way our reality appears to be structured, and everyone ultimately makes a choice, whether that choice is passive or active.

THE EVIDENCE FROM CONTEMPORARY PHYSICS SUPPORTS THE CONCEPTS OF PERSONAL RESPONSIBILITY AND FREE WILL

Henry Stapp is a highly regarded Berkeley theoretical physicist who studied under Nobel Laureates Emilio Segre and Owen Chamberlain. He worked with Wolfgang Pauli and developed his ideas from von Neumann's work on the mathematical foundations of quantum theory. He has centered a substantial portion of his work on the quantum measurement problem and the influence of conscious thought. In his recent book, *Mindful Universe,* he writes:

"It is often claimed that science stands mute on questions of values: that science can help us to achieve what we value once our priorities are fixed, but can play no role in fixing these weightings. That claim is certainly incorrect. Science plays a key role in these matters. For what we value depends on what we believe, and what we believe is strongly influenced by science.

"A striking example of this influence is the impact of science upon the system of values promulgated by the church during the Middle Ages. That structure rested on a credo about the nature of the universe, its creator, and man's connection to that creator. Science, by casting doubt upon that belief, undermined the system of values erected upon it. Moreover, it put forth a credo of its own. In that 'scientific' vision we human beings were converted from sparks of divine creative power, endowed with free will, to mechanical automata—to cogs in a giant machine that grinds inexorably along a preordained path in the grip of a blind causal process.

"This material picture of human beings erodes not only the religious roots of moral values but the entire notion of personal responsibility. Each of us is asserted to be a mechanical extension of what existed prior to his or her birth. Over that earlier situation one has no control. Hence for what emerges, preordained, from that prior state one can bear no responsibility.

"This conception of man undermines the foundation of rational moral philosophy, and science is doubly culpable. It not only erodes the foundations of earlier value systems, but also acts to strip man of any vision of himself and his place in the universe that could be the rational basis for an elevated set of values.

"During the twentieth century this morally corrosive mechanical conception of nature was found to be profoundly incorrect. It failed not just in its fine details, but at its fundamental core. A vastly different conceptual framework was erected by the atomic physicists Werner Heisenberg, Niels Bohr, Wolfgang Pauli and their colleagues. Those scientists were forced to a wholesale revision of the entire subject matter of physical theory by the peculiar character of the new mathematical rules, which were invariably validated by reliable empirical data.

"The earlier 'classical' physics had emerged from the study of the observed motions of the planets and large terrestrial objects, and the entire physical universe was, correspondingly, conceived to be made, essentially, out of miniaturized versions of these large visible objects. . . . These laws were independent of whether or not anyone was observing the physical universe: they took no special cognizance of any acts of observation performed by human beings, or of any knowledge acquired from such observations, or of the conscious thoughts of human beings. All such things were believed, during the reign of classical physics, to be completely determined, insofar as they had any physical consequences, by the physically described properties and laws that acted wholly mechanically at the microscopic scale. But the baffling features of new kinds of data acquired during the twentieth century caused the physicists who were studying these phenomena, and trying to ascertain the laws that governed them, to turn the whole scientific enterprise upside down.

"Perhaps I should say that they turned right side up what had been upside down. For the word 'science' comes from the Latin word 'scire', 'to know', and what the founders of the new theory claimed, basically is that the proper subject matter of science is not what may or may not be 'out there', unobserved and unknown to human beings. It is rather what we human beings can know, and can do in order to know more. Thus they formulated their new theory, called quantum mechanics, or quantum theory, around the knowledge-acquiring actions of human beings, and the knowledge we acquire by performing these actions, rather than around a conjectured causally sufficient mechanical world. The focus of the theory was shifted from one that basically ignored our knowledge to one that is about our knowledge, and about the effects of the actions that we take to acquire more knowledge upon what we are able to know.

"This modified conception differs from the old one in many fascinating ways that continue to absorb the interest of physicists. However, it is the revised understanding of the nature of human beings, and of the causal role of human consciousness in the unfolding of reality, that is, I believe, the most exciting thing about the new physics, and probably, in the final analysis, also the most important contribution of science to the well-being of our species. . . . (A)ccording to the new conception, the *physically described world* is built not out of bits of matter, as matter was understood in the nineteenth century, but out of objective *tendencies*—potentialities—for certain discrete, whole *actual events* to occur. Each such event has both a psychologically described aspect, which is essentially an increment in knowledge, and also a physically described aspect, which is an action that *abruptly changes* the mathematically described set of potentialities to one that is concordant with the increase in knowledge. This coordination of the aspects of the theory that are described in physical/mathematical terms with aspects that are described in psychological terms is what makes the theory practically useful. Some empirical predictions have been verified to the incredible accuracy of one part in a hundred million."[1]

NOTES

PREFACE

1. Thomas Aquinas, *Summa Theologiae* I, q. 2, a. 1, ad. 1. Quoted in Plantinga (2000), p. 170.

2. Romans 1:20.

3. John Calvin, quoted in Plantinga (2000), p. 172.

4. Allen (1985), pp. 3–4.

5. See discussion on the limits of mathematics and the limits of formal reasoning in Appendix B.

6. Adler (1992), p. 267.

7. Quoted in Magnin writing in Staune (ed.) (2006), p. 138.

CHAPTER 1

1. University of Washington astrobiologists Peter D. Ward and Donald Brownlee present a thought-provoking argument that, although the widely held belief is that complex life in the universe is widespread, advanced life may be very rare. The precarious fine-tuning surrounding the earth's existence is unlikely to be repeated even given billions and billions of stars. See Ward and Brownlee (2000).

2. Graph from Barrow (2002), p. 115.

3. Cambridge University physicist and theologian Sir John Polkinghorne notes the inexorable bleak future of the universe: "That universe itself, on the largest possible scale on which we observe it, is balanced between the competing effects of the initial big bang (blowing matter apart) and the pull of gravity (drawing matter together). Our knowledge is not sufficiently accurate to enable us to be sure which tendency will ultimately win, but either way the observable universe is condemned to eventual futility. If expansion predominates, the galaxies will continue to move apart forever, at the same time condensing

and decaying within themselves into ever-cooling low-grade radiation. If contraction predominates, the universe will eventually collapse upon itself into the fiery melting pot of the big crunch." Polkinghorne and Welker (2001), p. 51.

4. See Keith Ward's discussion on the question of value in finite existence in Ward (1998), p. 24.

5. Frankl stressed that meaning had to transcend the self and reach fulfillment outside of one's self: "By declaring that man is responsible *and* must actualize the potential meaning of his life, I wish to stress that the true meaning of life is to be discovered in the world rather than within man or his own psyche, as though it were a closed system. I have termed this constitutive characteristic 'the self-transcendence of human existence.' It denotes the fact that being human always points, and is directed, to something, or someone, other than oneself—be it meaning to fulfill or another human being to encounter. The more one forgets oneself—by giving oneself to a cause to serve or another person to love—the more human he is and the more he actualizes himself. What is called self-actualization is not an attainable aim at all, for the simple reason that the more one would strive for it, the more he would miss it. In other words, self-actualization is possible only as a side effect of self-transcendence: 'Thus far we have shown that the meaning of life always changes, but that it never ceases to be. According to logo-therapy, we can discover this meaning in life in three different ways: (1) by creating a work or doing a deed; (2) by experiencing something or encountering someone; and (3) by the attitude we take toward unavoidable suffering.'" Frankl (1959), p. 115.

6. Frankl (1959), p. 151.

7. Frankl (2000), pp. 152–53.

8. Frankl (1959), p. 153.

9. Weinberg (1977), p. 149.

10. Shelley quoted in Perrine (1956), p. 93.

11. William Shakespeare, *Macbeth*, Act V, Scene V.

12. Polkinghorne (1994), p. 18.

13. Verification implies the existence of truth. I am convinced that truth exists and join John Lennox in encouraging readers with a postmodern view to continue reading: "My mention of truth leads me to fear that some people of postmodernist persuasion may be tempted not to read any further, unless of course they are curious to read (and maybe even attempt to deconstruct) a text written by someone who actually believes in truth. For my part I confess to finding it curious that those who claim that there is no such thing as truth expect me to believe that what they are saying is true! Perhaps I misunderstand them, but they seem to exempt themselves from their general rubric that there is no such thing as truth when they are either speaking to me or writing their books. They turn out to believe in truth after all. In any case, scientists have a clear stake in truth. Why, otherwise, would they bother to do science?" Lennox (2007), p. 13.

CHAPTER 2

1. Gödel's incompleteness theorem, algorithmic information theory, and the Heisenberg uncertainity principle are three areas of mathematics and science that confront us with uncer-

tainty, the unknowable, and the undecidable. There are real limits to human reason (see Appendix B). Dinesh D'Souza has noted the limits of reason in his recent writings and emphasized the need for faith. I want to join him in that emphasis, but I also concur with Jacques Maritain, John Polkinghorne, and several thinkers who stress the unity of truth in all areas of knowledge and the validity of empirical, metaphysical, and mystical ways of knowing. D'Souza and I use different approaches but arrive at a similar destination. As will become apparent, I do not share his enthusiasm concerning Immanuel Kant's theory of knowledge.

2. Harvard psychiatrist Dr. Armand M. Nicholi Jr., in his brilliant book, *The Question of God*, notes that none of us can tolerate the idea that our worldview may be founded on an invalid presupposition or premise. The fear of having a false premise may cause us to distract ourselves with constant diversions to avoid examining our lives. Yet there is no escape from the requirement of some worldview that allows us to function in the world. Nicholi emphasizes the importance of our worldview in its effect on how we interpret evidence.

3. Paul Davies, "Taking Science on Faith," *New York Times*, November 24, 2007.

4. The lack of certainty in Sagan's and Weinberg's statements is well illustrated by a story told by Dr. Viktor Frankl in *Man's Search for Ultimate Meaning*. In that story, Frankl asks the question whether an ape, which was being used in the development of a serum and was subjected to repeated punctures of his flesh, would have grasped the meaning of his suffering. The unanimous response was that the limited intelligence of the ape precluded him from entering into the human world, i.e., the world where the meaning of his suffering could be comprehended. Frankl then asks whether man could not be at the end point of cosmic development so that there could still be another dimension or a world beyond the human world where the ultimate meaning of human suffering could be understood. Frankl notes that in another dimension outside the reach of contemporary science, ultimate meaning may exist: "I just referred to 'another dimension,' at the same time indicating that it would not be accessible to reason or intellect. By the same token, it necessarily would elude any strictly scientific approach. Small wonder that ultimate meaning is missing in the world as described by science. However, does this imply that the world is *void* of ultimate meaning? I think it only shows that science is *blind* to ultimate meaning. Ultimate meaning is scotomized by science. However, this state of affairs does in no way entitle a scientist to deny that ultimate meaning possibly does exist. It is perfectly legitimate that the scientist as such restricts himself to a certain 'cross section' he cuts through reality, and it may well happen that within this cross section no meaning whatsoever can be found. But he should remain aware that also other cross sections are conceivable." Frankl (2000), pp. 144–45.

5. Allport (1950), p. 54.

6. Allport (1950), p. 53.

7. Private letter from Richard Smalley to Dr. James Bultman.

8. Buckley (2004), p. x.

9. Dante Alighieri, quoted in Mack (ed.) (1956), p. 600.

10. Buckley (2004), p. xvi. No one prays to a god who is only an inference at the end of a syllogism.

11. Developments in philosophical thought and in contemporary science strengthen Adler's argument. I will discuss these developments throughout the text.

12. Ward (1998), pp. 18, 52.

13. This approach is in keeping with Michael Buckley's more recent writing: "Perhaps above all we must realize that one cannot excise, cannot bracket the religious, in order to

come to the existence of God, that one must bring to experience and reflection the manifold of the religious itself in order to justify the assertions of religion. One must include all of the components that constitute religion in its fullness, as, for example, one finds outlined in the great treatise of Baron von Hugel: the intuitional, historical, and traditional. None of these can be finally omitted without being false to the authenticity of the religious." Buckley (2004), p. 138.

14. In the seventeenth century, John Locke began an empiricist approach in epistemology in *An Essay Concerning Human Understanding* (1690). It is not technically correct to state that his empiricism was limited to sense experience, because he included in his definition of experience our processes of perception and reason. For our purposes the term *empiricism* is adequate to describe Kant's synthetic attempt.

15. Kant influenced the development of the Idealist philosophies in the nineteenth century. However, in the twentieth century, idealism was replaced by logical positivism (also influenced by Kant's theory of knowledge in his emphasis on human understanding resulting from sensory experience). Logical positivism was in turn replaced by logical analysis, which required an empirical verification for any statement to be considered meaningful. The verification principle, however, could not be verified empirically nor could history be the subject of empirical verification or falsification. Many statements regarded as meaningful cannot be empirically verified (e.g., moral statements and personal action statements). An adequate discussion of the logical positivist influence from the Vienna Circle forward to the early and late Wittgenstein would require a separate book, and, as mentioned above, one that also discussed postmodern philosophy in more detail with an emphasis on the later Wittgenstein's thought on private language games. My main point for the moment is to indicate Kant's influence on many varieties of nineteenth-, twentieth-, and twenty-first-century thought.

16. Kant attempted to show our inability to know anything apart from the world of our sensory experience. For Kant, reason is not able to address the question of the existence of God, because by definition God is outside of our sense experience. However, Kant argued that we can know God's existence through our experience of morality and the notion of duty. In his *Critique of Practical Reason* Kant bases an argument for the existence of God, freedom, and immortality on the basis of unconditional or categorical moral obligations. For human beings to have freedom of choice, Kant argues that they must be morally obliged. For Kant, immortality and the existence of God are not postulates derived from knowledge but from duty.

17. Kant's denial that one could know anything about God from sensory experience was fairly questioned by Hegel in his analysis of history as a continuum manifesting ultimate reality. According to Hegel, reality is a continuum in which something's identity includes its relations to other things, and not separate or discrete particulars. Hegel developed (or overdeveloped) an elaborate system to demonstrate the power of reason to know the reality of the continuity of history. Hegel's elaborate system provoked Kierkegaard to write extensively concerning Hegel's lack of understanding of the meaning of an existing human being. Kierkegaard emphasized the subjectivity of knowledge and the freedom of choice a human has in ethics and in religious faith. An infinite God cannot be placed within a system or box by a finite mind. God is "Wholly Other" and not an object to be placed in a class or category. As Wholly Other, God transcends all categories of thought, including Kant's categories of the mind. British philosopher John Cottingham describes the limits of empirical

and positivistic reasoning concerning a transcendent reality: "When we reflect further on the kinds of philosophical project found in Hume or Kant, or the early Wittgenstein, it becomes clear that they do not, and indeed *could not* with any plausibility propose to eliminate the very possibility of a domain of reality lying beyond the phenomenal world. It would be outrageous arrogance to suppose that the limits of our puny human scientific or even conceptual resources must necessarily determine the actual limits of reality." Cottingham (2005), p. 120.

18. Kenny (2006), p. 163.

19. Polkinghorne (1996), pp. 98–100.

20. This refers to God as a spiritual being. Christians held that Jesus was God and man. A valid postresurrection experience in the classical sense would be an empirical experience. I will put this qualification aside for now but address the issue in a subsequent book.

21. Adler (1980), pp. 67–68.

22. Evans (1998), pp. 72–75.

23. Polkinghorne (1998), p. 17.

24. Evans (1998), p. 98.

25. Tillich (1957), p. 7.

26. Keith Ward, former head of theology at Oxford University, holds the view that the reason people decide whether or not to believe in God also applies to whether or not one decides to accept the evidence for the claims of the Christian or any other faith: "The real reason people believe or disbelieve in God is not to do with science, but with highly personal factors that predispose people to be either sympathetic or antagonistic to the experiential and moral claims of religion. If one has had experiences in religious contexts which have been positive and life-enhancing, which have helped one to overcome hatred and greed and achieve a more integrated and committed life, one will be well disposed to the claims of religion. If one has suffered from censorious, petty-minded or intolerant religious believers, one will naturally be much less sympathetic. It may be that one has simply not had any experiences that seem to be of a transcendent or spiritual reality. Or perhaps personal tragedies have made one skeptical about there being any moral order in the universe at all. There are many different reasons for being religious or non-religious, but usually personal experience, not abstract speculation, is the decisive factor." Ward (2002), p. 18. C. S. Lewis and Hurd Baruch believe that the basic determinant concerning nonbelief is pride. The point of all these thinkers is that no one approaches the question of God from an impartial, neutral perspective.

27. See discussion in chapter 7, "Richard Dawkins commits the elementary logical fallacy of circular reasoning in his principal argument for the nonexistence of God," on Mortimer Adler's statement that, like Gödel's incompleteness theorem in mathematics, a negative existential proposition cannot be proved.

28. Stephen T. Davis, writing in Craig (ed.) (2002), p. 88.

29. In philosophy the distinction between God's being and any other being is sometimes symbolized by referring to God as having a "necessary" existence and all other beings having a "contingent" or dependent existence. Diogenes Allen of Princeton Theological Seminary described the distinction between necessary and contingent existence as follows: "The difference between Creator and creature is sometimes expressed in terms of the distinction between necessary and contingent beings. . . . Things which are contingent begin and end; a necessary being is everlasting. Particular beings, such as leaves and trees which start and

end in the created universe may be contrasted to matter and energy which according to our sciences, are conserved in all transformations. But the contrast between existing things in the universe, such as leaves and trees on the one hand, and matter and energy on the other, is not as fundamental as that between God and the universe. Matter and energy, like leaves and trees, are contingent. Even though they are conserved in all transformations of various things within the universe, they and indeed the entire universe *began*, and they and it may end, should God so will. Only God is everlasting, and is so by divine nature. Matter and energy depend on God for their creation and continued existence." Allen (1985), p. 9.

30. In his *Summa Theologiae*, Thomas Aquinas described Five Ways to demonstrate God's existence. For our purposes the Third Way is the most relevant. Aquinas states the Third Way as follows: "The third way is taken from possibility and necessity and runs thus. We find in nature things that are possible to be and not possible to be, since they are found to be generated and corrupted. But it is impossible for these always to exist, for that which can not-be at some time is not. Therefore, if everything can not-be, then at one time there was nothing in existence. Now if this were true then even now there would be nothing in existence, because that which does not exist begins to exist only through something already existing. Therefore if at one time nothing was in existence, it would have been impossible for anything to have begun to exist; and thus now nothing would be in existence—which is absurd. Therefore, not all beings are merely possible, but there must exist something the existence of which is necessary. But every necessary thing has its necessity caused by another, or not. Now it is impossible to go on to infinity in necessary things which have their necessity caused by another, as has already been proved in regard to efficient causes. Therefore, we cannot but admit the existence of some being having of itself its own necessity, and not receiving it from another, but rather causing in others their necessity. This all men speak of as God." Thomas Aquinas, *Summa Theologiae* q. 3. art. 3.

His argument may be described as an argument from contingency. Aquinas notes a distinction between contingent or possible beings. Contingent beings are not necessary beings, because their existence is only a possible existence; they do not have to exist and they may cease to exist. Necessary beings must always exist. If only possible (contingent) beings exist in an infinite time, then nothing would exist now (a questionable conclusion). But we know that something exists now. Consequently, some being must be a necessary being. Necessary beings must have their existence in themselves or in another. An infinite regress of necessary beings that have their necessity caused by another is impossible. Therefore, a necessary being that has its necessity in itself must exist. This necessary being is God. This is the essence of Aquinas's argument from contingency. I would not call it a cosmological argument, because he is not using the concept of the whole universe (cosmos), but rather the concept of a contingent being.

31. Stephen Barr, professor of physics at the University of Delaware, in his excellent book, *Modern Physics and Ancient Faith*, discusses the distinction between contingent and necessary: "An example of a contingent truth is that there is a sycamore tree in my front yard. This is true, but it did not have to be true; it just happens to be true. One may, therefore, legitimately ask how it came to be true, what caused the sycamore tree to be there. On the other hand, that 317 is a prime number is a necessary truth. It cannot be otherwise. It makes no sense to ask how it came to be that way, or what caused it to be that way, at least not in the same sense that these questions can be asked about the sycamore's presence in my front yard." Barr (2003), p. 263.

32. As noted, some physicists attempt to describe a quantum fluctuation as a coming to be *ex nihil*, but the idea of a universe beginning out of nothing in a quantum fluctuation violates the equation of Heisenberg's principle, the conditions of quantum fields, and the definition of *nihil*. Overman (1997), pp. 154–59.

33. Adler (1980), pp. 124–25.

34. Aquinas's argument from the contingency of the components of the universe is not a truly cosmological argument. A truly cosmological argument is concerned with an explanation for the existence of the universe (cosmos) in all its totality.

35. Physicist Stephen Barr notes the absurdity involved if the existence of the universe itself were considered to be necessary rather than contingent: "The main problem with this idea is that it is patently absurd. The existence of the particular universe in which we live is plainly *not* a necessity. In this particular universe there is a sycamore tree in my front yard. It might just as well have been an apple tree. To say that this universe, in all its particularity, with all of its details, had necessarily to exist is not only absurd, it is also profoundly unscientific in spirit. It would mean that everything about the world could be deduced by pure thought without taking the trouble to do any experiments or make any observations. If the world with all its contents were necessarily as it is, then Columbus did not have to sail the ocean blue—he might have been able to deduce the existence of America and even to have mapped all its mountains and charted all its waterways without leaving his armchair." Barr (2003), pp. 25–26.

36. To be valid the argument that the universe is contingent because it is only a possible universe does not require evidence of the actual existence of other universes. For the argument to be valid it only requires the *logical possibility* of other universes, not the *actual* existence of other universes. Here modern cosmology serves to enhance the validity of the argument that the universe is contingent because it could have been otherwise. It is not necessary to have evidence of multiple universes, only the logical possibility of their existence.

37. If the universe were contingent and perished, unlike the various parts of the universe or components of the universe, such as you and me, the universe would not be transformed into something else. The ceasing to be of the universe would be replaced by sheer or absolute nothingness. Adler termed this characteristic to be a radical (as opposed to a superficial) contingency. If the universe ceased to be, it would be annihilated. Moreover, the arguments we are considering concerning the radical contingency of the universe are not based on a fallacy of composition whereby one argues that because the components of the universe are all contingent, the universe must be contingent. Rather, we are noting that the universe has only a possible existence, which carries with it the potential for nonexistence. This fact alone makes the cosmos radically contingent.

38. As Conway writes: "If one assumes that a contingent universe has always existed, one still needs to explain why the universe exists: 'Even were the physical universe eternal, and so, in consequence, there was never a time at which it did not exist, its being eternal would not necessarily obviate its need for a cause at every moment of existence. This is so, if, as seems to be the case, its existence is contingent. No matter how long the world might have existed, even if from eternity, if its existence is only contingent, . . . Provided that the existence of the universe is contingent, there is as much need of an explanation of its existence at each and every moment of its existence, as there is to account for its coming into existence at some moment. Therefore, even if the universe has always existed, its existence at each moment of it still stands in need of causal explanation.'" Conway (2000), p. 109.

39. Keith Ward notes: "To say that the existence of this universe is necessary is to say that no other universe could possibly exist. But how could one know that, without knowing absolutely everything? Even the most confident cosmologists might suspect that there is something they do not know. So it does not look as though the necessity of this universe can be established . . . The physical cosmos does not seem to be necessary. We can seemingly think of many alternatives to it. There might, for instance, be an inverse cube law instead of an inverse square law, and then things would be very different, but they might still exist. We can see how mathematics can be necessary, but it is a highly dubious assertion that there is only one consistent set of equations which could govern possible physical realities. We cannot bridge the gap between mathematical necessity and physical contingency. How could a temporal and apparently contingent universe come into being by quasi-mathematical necessity?" Ward (1996), pp. 23–24.

40. This argument is also consistent with Leibniz's cosmological argument, which differed from Aquinas's argument from contingency. Leibniz differed from Aquinas in removing some of the Aristotelian themes and relying on the principle of sufficient reason that requires an explanation for the existence of the universe. As noted above, Aquinas did not focus on a sufficient reason for the universe's existence but emphasized the impossibility of an infinite causal regress.

41. In a previous book I addressed the speculation of a quantum fluctuation from a quantum vacuum and showed how that scenario is not feasible. Moreover, all of the known physical laws break down at Planck time. Overman (1997), pp. 152–59.

42. Reichenbach (Fall 2006), p. 17.

43. Wheeler (1999), p. 301.

CHAPTER 3

1. Hume (1993), p. 90.

2. Hume (1993), p. 91.

3. Hume (1993), p. 91.

4. Reichenbach (1972), pp. 116–17.

5. Conway comments on Haldane's insight: "This objection of Hume's has force only if he is correct that the existence of something could be necessary in and of itself, only if the thought of that thing's non-existence were to involve some internal contradiction. This, however, is open to doubt. To suppose that, unlike the physical universe, God exists necessarily in and of Himself is not to suppose that the notion of God's non-existence contains, or, by itself, entails, a formal contradiction. Rather, it is only to suppose that, in the words of John Haldane whose view we follow here, God 'exists eternally, . . . does not owe [His] being to anything else and . . . cannot not exist.' Clearly, it is possible for us to conceive that no such Being exists, without any contradiction being involved in our conception. Our being able to do this does not show that it is not possible that there could be a Being who satisfies this description. It is only a Being who answers this latter description that the Cosmological Argument is designed to establish the existence of. It is not intended to establish it *to be intrinsically necessary* that such a Being exists." Conway (2000), p. 110 (emphasis added).

6. Diogenes Allen's insight agreed with Conway's and Haldane's insights: "In recent years, however, it has been pointed out that the sense of necessary Hume is using is of the *logical* necessary. Christianity speaks of God as a necessary being in the sense of one who has no beginning and no end because God is not dependent on anything in order to exist. Nothing could cause God to begin or to end. To say that God has no beginning or end because God does not depend on anything to exist does not show that God actually does exist. It does mean, however, that if God exists, that existence is a necessary existence. This understanding of necessary being does make sense. It is not incoherent." Allen (1985), pp. 199–200.

7. Conway (2000), p. 114.

8. Conway emphasizes: "However, it does not follow this that there is no internal incoherence in our notion of the non-existence of a thing with such a status when such a notion is combined with the notion of the contingency of the physical universe and the necessity for there to be something capable of accounting for the existence of the physical world. . . . (T)he notion of the non-existence of a necessary being *will* involve an internal incoherence when it is combined with the notion of the existence of a contingently existing physical existence which stands in need of an explanation in terms of something that is not itself contingent." Conway (2000), pp. 114–15.

9. This is not to say that Hume's and Kant's writings did not result in some very worthwhile philosophical developments. Kierkegaard, for example, is indebted to Kant for several aspects of his writings. See Green (1992). Kant's attempt to find a middle way deserves substantial respect. His emphasis on subjectivity is not misplaced. We all see reality from distinct perspectives and our own peculiar experiences. We act from a first-person sense of being.

CHAPTER 4

1. Quoted in Overman (1997), p. 159.

2. Polkinghorne (1998), p. 72.

3. Similarly, in noting that in science order comes from greater order Barr writes: ". . . in every case where science explains order, it does so, in the final analysis, by appealing to a greater, more impressive, and more comprehensive underlying orderliness . . . when the scientist has done his job there is not less order to explain but more. The universe looks far more orderly to us now than it did to the ancients who appealed to that order as proof of God's existence. . . . As one goes deeper and deeper into the workings of the physical world, to more and more fundamental levels of the laws of nature, one encounters not less structure and symmetry but even more. The deeper one goes the more orderly nature looks, the more subtle and intricate its designs. . . . We can be sure that whatever new and deeper theory comes along, it will reveal to us more profound principles of order and greater and more inclusive patterns. . . . Science has given us new eyes that allow us to see down to the deeper roots of the world's structure, and there *all* we see is order and symmetry of pristine mathematical purity." Barr (2003), pp. 79, 81, 87.

4. Torrance (1989), p. 28.

5. One example of the physicists' search for TOE is a new, unified simple theory of everything that unifies gravity without resorting to string theory. Mathematicians mapped a theoretical structure termed Lie group E8. Lie (pronounced "Lee") refers to the Norwegian

mathematician Sophus Lee who invented Lie groups. E8 is the most complex of these groups and its proof requires about 60 times the data of the Human Genome Project. We will have to see if E8 geometry can advance a coherent, grand, unified theory.

6. Paul Davies, "Taking Science on Faith," *New York Times*, November 24, 2007.

CHAPTER 5

1. Craig and Smith (1993).
2. Barrow and Tipler (1986).
3. Barr (2003), pp. 58–59.
4. Borde et al. (2003).
5. Vilenkin (2006), pp. 175–76 (emphasis added). Vilenkin's example in his book may not be as simple as he indicates. My modification, thanks to the insights of Dr. Robert Kaita, a Principal Research Physicist at Princeton University's Plasma Physics Laboratory, emphasizes what different observers measure to understand where contradictions can arise with the theory of relativity. The actual conclusion in the BGV proof set forth in the April 2003 *Physical Review Letters* paper is that "if H[the ratio of the speed of recession of a galaxy to its distance from the observer]>0 along any null or noncomoving timelike geodesic, then the geodesic is necessarily past-incomplete." As the BGV paper states: ". . . we have shown under reasonable assumptions that almost all causal geodesics, when extended to the past of an arbitrary point, reach the boundary of the inflating region of spacetime in a finite proper time (finite affine length, in the null case). . . . unless the averaged expansion condition can somehow be avoided for all past-directed geodesic, inflation alone is not sufficient to provide a complete description of the Universe, and some new physics is necessary in order to determine the correct conditions at the boundary. This is the chief result of our Letter."
6. Penrose (1989), p. 344.
7. See Craig (1994, 2002).
8. This argument is not analogous to Zeno's paradox of motion for Achilles. As Craig has noted, Zeno's paradox represents an attempt to transverse a potential and unequal infinity of intervals. This argument considers a past infinity of actual and equal intervals. Zeno's unequal intervals sum to a finite distance, but this argument addresses an infinite number of equals and actual intervals. See W. L. Craig et al. (2003) p. 475.
9. Quoted in Flew (2007), p. 140. Antony Flew now agrees with Swinburne's statement: "The whole infinite series will have no explanation at all, for there will be no causes of members of the series lying outside the series." Ibid. Now that the errors in Hume's criticism of the cosmological argument are exposed, one can appreciate the power in noting the philosophical significance of the Big Bang cosmology. Swinburne's argument that we can explain states of affairs only in terms of other states of affairs is also relevant, because laws by themselves cannot explain these states: "We need states of affairs as well as laws to explain things," he writes. "And if we do not have them for the beginning of the universe, because there are no earlier states, then we cannot explain the beginning of the universe." Quoted in Ibid., p. 141.
10. Ward (1996), p. 40.

11. Ward (1966), pp. 39–40. M. A. Corey's analysis is consistent with Ward's position as he presents a theist's perspective on a quantum fluctuation as the basis of cosmogenesis: "This view (non-theistic cosmogenesis) is fallacious, however, because sudden quantum appearances don't really take place out of 'nothing.' A larger quantum field is first required before this can happen, but a quantum field can hardly be described as being 'nothing.' Rather, it is a thing of unsearchable order and complexity, whose origin we can't even begin to explain. Thus, trying to account for the appearance of the universe as a sudden quantum fluctuation doesn't do away with the need for a Creator at all; it simply moves the whole problem backwards one step to the unknown origin of the quantum field itself." Corey (1993), p. 43.

CHAPTER 6

1. Polkinghorne (1998), p. 73.
2. Antony Flew does not believe that the laws of nature are social or cultural constructs. He rejects the idea that the laws of physics are imposed by the human mind upon the universe. They truly exist and the task of the scientist is to discover them, not create them. Flew asks: Where do the laws of physics come from? Why are they the particular laws they are? Why are they fine-tuned for the emergence of conscious life? Flew concurs with Oxford philosopher John Foster, author of *The Divine Lawmaker: Lectures on Induction, Laws of Nature, and the Existence of God*, that the "only serious option" for the source of these laws is the divine Mind. Flew (2000), pp. 109–10. Davies (1992), p. 151.
3. Penrose (1994), p. 415.
4. Paul Davies joins Roger Penrose in marveling at the matching of abstract mathematics with the hidden subatomic world. As he wrote about what Eugene Wigner described as the "unreasonable effectiveness" of mathematics in physical science: "No feature of this uncanny 'tuning' of the human mind to the workings of nature is more striking than mathematics. Mathematics is the product of the higher human intellect, yet it finds ready application to the most basic processes of nature, such as subatomic particle physics. The fact that 'mathematics works' when applied to the physical world—and works so stunningly well—demands explanation, for it is not clear we have any absolute right to expect that the world should be well described by our mathematics. . . . If mathematical ability has evolved by accident rather than in response to environmental pressures, then it is a truly astonishing coincidence that mathematics finds such ready application to the physical universe. If, on the other hand, mathematical ability does have some obscure survival value and has evolved by natural selection, we are still faced with the mystery of why the laws of nature are mathematical. After all, surviving 'in the jungle' does not require knowledge of the *laws* of nature, only of their manifestations." Quoted in Overman (1997), p. 145.
5. John Polkinghorne comments on Dirac's search for beautiful equations and the relationship of the inherent mathematical nature of the universe to beauty: ". . . it is *mathematics* which gives us the key to unlock the secrets of nature." Paul Dirac spent his life in the search for beautiful equations. "That is a concept not all will find immediately accessible, but among those of us who speak the language of mathematics, mathematical beauty is

a recognizable quality. . . . Time and again we have found that it is equations with that indispensable character of mathematical beauty which describe the nature of the physical world. If you stop to think about it, that is a very significant thing to have discovered. After all, mathematics arises from the free rational exploration of the human mind. Yet it seems that our minds are so finely tuned to the structure of the universe that they are capable of penetrating its deepest secrets." Quoted in Overman (1997), p. 149. Physicist Heinz Pagels wrote: "All profound human creatures are beautiful and physical theories are no exception. An ugly theory has a kind of conceptual clumsiness which it is impossible to hold in the mind for too long. That is the basis for the appeal to aesthetics in the construction of physical theory. When physicists really understand the internal logic of the cosmos it will be beautiful—our attraction to the beautiful, what is coherent and simple, is at the heart of the human capability of rationally comprehending the material world." Pagels (1983), p. 305.

6. Penrose (1989), pp. 421–22.

7. Penrose (1994), p. 411f.

8. Dubay (1999), pp. 55, 66.

9. Quoted in Dubay (1999), p. 57.

10. Richard Swinburne is also impressed with the beauty derived from an orderly world: "But beyond that an orderly world is a beautiful world. Beauty consists in patterns of order. Total chaos is ugly. The movements of the stars in accord with regular laws is a beautiful dance. The medievals thought of the planets as carried by spheres through the sky, and their regular movements producing the 'music of the spheres' whose beauty humans casually ignored, although it was one of the most beautiful things there is. God has reason to make an orderly world, because beauty is a good thing—in my view whether or not anyone ever observes it, but certainly if only one person ever observes it. The argument to God from the world and its regularity is, I believe, a codification by philosophers of a natural and rational reaction to an orderly world deeply embedded in the human consciousness. Humans see the comprehensibility of the world as evidence of a comprehending creator." Swinburne (1996), p. 54.

11. Barr (2003), p. 130.

12. Barr (2003), p. 130.

13. As Stephen Barr notes: "Even if the cosmological constant had the much smaller value of 10^{-80}, the universe would have doubled in size every thousandth of a second or so, which would be so fast that your body would be ripped apart by the expansion. If the universe was to have sufficiently gradual expansion over billions of years to allow life to evolve, then the cosmological constant had to be less than or about 10^{-120}. In order for life to be possible, then, it appears that the cosmological constant, whether it is positive or negative, must be extremely close to zero—in fact, it must be zero to at least 120 decimal places. This is one of the most precise fine-tunings in all of physics." Barr (2003), p. 130.

14. Penrose (1989), p. 344. There are many other examples of anthropic coincidences that have been elaborated upon in many writings in recent years, beginning with the work of astrophysicist Brandon Carter in the 1970s. I discuss several in my book, *A Case Against Accident and Self-Organization*. I recommend a reading of chapter 15 of Stephen Barr's fine work, *Modern Physics and Ancient Faith*, in which he gives very clear explanations of not only the strength of the strong nuclear force and the triple alpha process but also clearly demonstrates the fine-tuning in the stability of the proton, the strength of the electromagnetic force, the vacuum expectation of the Higgs field that determines the masses of most

of the fundamental particles, the cosmological constant, the flatness of space, the number of space dimensions, the quantum nature of the world, the existence of electromagnetism, and the existence of matter.

15. Barr (2003), p. 75.

16. Physicist Barr sees some humor in the requirement that materialists postulate a series of unobservable infinities in order to allow for a nontheistic perspective on life in this universe: ". . . it is interesting that in order to explain the origin of life from inanimate matter in a way that does not invoke divine intervention it may be necessary to postulate an unobservable infinity of planets. . . . We shall see . . . other cases where the materialist, in order to avoid drawing unpalatable conclusions from scientific discoveries, has to postulate unobservable infinities of things. How ironic that, having renounced belief in God because God is not material or observable by sense or instrument, the atheist may be driven to postulate not one but an infinitude of unobservables in the material world itself!" Barr (2003), p. 75.

17. Flew (2007), pp. 119–20. Paul Davies agrees: "The multiverse theory is increasingly popular, but it doesn't so much explain the laws of physics as dodge the whole issue. There has to be a physical mechanism to make all those universes and bestow bylaws on them. This process will require its own laws, or meta-laws. Where do they come from? The problem has simply been shifted up a level from the laws of the universe to the meta-laws of the multiverse." "Taking Science on Faith," November 24, 2007, *New York Times*.

18. The very nature of the questions raised by this intelligibility are outside the abilities of science to answer: "Those imbued with a thirst for understanding will not find that science alone will quench it. Not only is there the teeming chaotic fertile world of personal experience, which the cold clear lunar landscape of science, populated by metastable replicating systems but with no people in it, so signally fails to describe. (Who thinks of himself as a collection of quarks, gluons and electrons?) There is also the founding faith that science depends upon, the *data* which themselves call irresistibly for deeper explanation. That the world is intelligible is surely a non-trivial fact about it and the basic laws and circumstance of the universe exhibit a delicate balance which seems necessary if its processes are to evolve such complex and interesting systems as you and me. It is surely inevitable to inquire if these facts are capable of more profound comprehension than simply the statement that they are the case. If that further understanding is to be had it will be beyond the power of science to provide it. . . . We are so familiar with the fact that we can understand the world that most of the time we take it for granted. It is what makes science possible. Yet it could have been otherwise. The universe might have been a disorderly chaos rather than an orderly cosmos. Or it might have had a rationality which was inaccessible to us." Polkinghorne (1988), p. 20.

19. Allen (1985), p. 167.

20. Allen (1985), pp. 167–68.

21. Allen (1985), p. 201.

CHAPTER 7

1. Adler (1990), pp. 36–39.
2. Adler (1990), p. 39.
3. Plantinga (2007).

4. Quoted in Overman (1997), p. 60.
5. Dawkins (1986), pp. 11–14.
6. Plantinga (2007).
7. Plantinga (2007).
8. Plantinga (2007).

CHAPTER 8

1. For a discussion of the application of algorithmic information theory to the source of the instructions contained in the DNA of all living matter, see Appendix A. I have not included this discussion in the main text because it is not part of my central argument.
2. Barr (2003), pp. 230–31.
3. Barr (2003), p. 233.
4. Barr (2003), p. 238.
5. Barr (2003), p. 240.
6. Polkinghorne (1998), pp. 54–55.
7. Hodgson (1991), p. 342.
8. Polkinghorne (1996), pp. 70–72.
9. Polkinghorne (1996), p. 60.
10. Stapp (2003), p. 270.
11. Stapp (2003), pp. 237–38.
12. Stapp (2007), p. 5.
13. Stapp (2007), pp. 6–9.
14. Stapp (2003), pp. 271–72 (emphasis added).
15. Quoted in Morris (1994), p. 49.
16. Morris (1994), p. 50.

CHAPTER 9

1. Brünner (1936), p. 5.
2. Evans (1998), p. 128.
3. Evans (1998), p. 128.
4. Quoted in Stackhouse (1998), p. 71.
5. The assumption that an omnipotent God can do everything does not mean that he can do things that are logical contradictions. As C. S. Lewis wrote in the *Problem of Pain*: "His Omnipotence means power to do all that is intrinsically possible, not to do the intrinsically impossible. You may attribute miracles to Him, but not nonsense. This is no limit to His power. If you choose to say, 'God can give creatures free will and at the same time withhold free will from it', you have not succeeded in saying *anything* about God: meaningless combinations of words do not suddenly acquire meaning simply because we prefix to them the two other words 'God can.' It remains true that all *things* are possible with God: the intrinsic impossibilities are not things but nonentities. It is no more possible for God than for the weakest of His creatures to carry out both of two mutually exclusive alternatives; not be-

cause His power meets an obstacle, but because nonsense remains nonsense even when we talk it about God." Lewis (1940), p. 18.

6. Hick (1989), pp. 178–79.

7. John Stackhouse describes the limits of human knowledge: "No human being in any situation has perfectly certain knowledge. Human knowledge is like human beings: finite and fallen. First, our knowledge is finite: we normally do not know all of the information relevant to an intellectual problem; even if we did, we could not know for sure that we had acquired all such information (maybe some of it lurks just out of sight in a location we haven't thought to investigate); we sometimes do not infallibly interpret the data (sometimes we compute the measurements incorrectly or hit the wrong keys on the calculator); and even if we normally do, we could not know for sure that we had infallibly interpreted the evidence this time. . . . Second, human beings are fallen as well as finite. Christians believe that the Fall affected our ability to think, as well as our ability and inclination to make moral choices. Whether we believe in a 'Fall' or not, however, most of us would agree that our morality affects our cognition. We tend to see what we want to see and to believe what we want to believe. Even scientists do this: after all, if you've spent most of your adult life believing that X is the case, and your own research program is built on the belief that X is the case, and your career success depends on continuing to show that X is the case, then you clearly have a compelling interest to continue to find that X is the case." Stackhouse (1998), p. 158.

8. Stephen Wykstra, in an essay on avoiding the evils of "appearance," emphasizes the limits of human understanding: "We must note here, first, that the outweighing good at issue is of a special sort: one purposed by the Creator of all that is, whose vision and wisdom are therefore somewhat greater than ours. How much greater? A modest proposal might be that the Creator's wisdom is to ours, roughly as an adult human's is to a one-month old infant's. (You may adjust the ages and species to fit your own estimate of how close our knowledge is to omniscience.) If such goods as this exist, it might not be unlikely that we should discern some of them: even a one-month old infant can perhaps discern, in its inarticulate way, some of the purposes of his mother in her dealings with him. But if outweighing goods of the sort at issue exist in connection with instances of suffering, that we should discern most of them seems about as likely as that a one-month old should discern most of his parents' purposes for those pains they allow to suffer—which is to say, it is not likely at all. So for any selected instance of intense suffering, there is good reason to think that if there is an outweighing good of the sort at issue connected to it, we would not have epistemic access to this . . ." Wykstra writing in Adams (1990), pp. 155–56.

9. Wykstra uses the example of searching for a table in a cluttered large room where the table might well be hid from view and raises the question whether our inability to see the table allows us to conclude with any certainty that the table is not in the room: "Searching for a table, you look through a doorway. The room is very large—say, the size of a Concorde hangar—and it is filled with bulldozers, dead elephants, Toyotas, and other vision-obstructing objects. Surveying this clutter from the doorway, and seeing no table, should you say: 'It does not appear that there is a table in the room'?" Ibid., p. 151.

10. Evans (1998), p. 133.

11. Evans (1998), p. 134.

12. Stackhouse (1998), p. 69.

13. Stackhouse (1998), p. 67 (emphasis added).

14. Moltmann (1995), p. 233.

15. Moltmann (1995), p. 234.

16. Quoted in Stackhouse (1998), p. 115.

17. Perhaps the problem of evil that includes the problem of suffering can only be understood by contemplating the suffering of the Incarnate God. In this suffering we see One: "(who) forgives humanity our sin of ingratitude, who 'takes it' without reprisal, who drinks to the last drop our poisonous betrayal. It is an utter mystery even to the best Christian minds how all of the sin of all humanity could be funneled into that single episode of Jesus's suffering and death. Perhaps, though, we can see at least that God has endured the very worst we could deal out. God has faced the most degrading humiliation, the most heartrending rejection, the most complete dishonor possible, and received it with unquenched love for us all. This is the true sacrifice of forgiveness." Stackhouse (1998), p. 118.

CHAPTER 10

1. Quoted in Baillie (1939), p. 158.

2. Baillie (1939).

3. Baillie (1939), p. 162.

4. Polanyi (1958), p. 282.

5. Newton also wrote the well-known hymn, "Amazing Grace."

6. Evans (1998), p. 105.

7. Evans (1998), p. 153.

8. Evans (1998), p. 121. Evans notes Kierkegaard's emphasis on a direct encounter with God in human form. In this encounter with the God-Man, one is enabled to recognize one's selfish condition through a recognition of the divine unconditional love: "It (faith) is the result of some kind of direct encounter with the God who has taken human form. It is through becoming acquainted with the God who has entered human history that people are transformed and acquire the ability to believe . . . the characteristics of reason that make faith difficult are the egoism and pride of the reasoner. So it is reasonable to surmise that the transformation of the self that amounts to 'receiving the condition' will be a transformation in which the self humbly recognizes its own limits and also begins to care about something other than itself. I think that we can see how an encounter with God in human form could do both of those things. Such an encounter would be humbling because it is by coming to know God's love and compassion that I recognize how selfish and unloving I am. And yet an experience of being loved by God in a deep and profound way might also be the trigger to overcoming that selfishness. Insofar as any purely human analogy can be given, no human experience seems to be more powerful in transforming an individual for good than the experience of being loved deeply." Evans (1998), p. 143.

9. "If one asks what such different thinkers as Heidegger and Jaspers, Marcel and Sartre, Berdyaev and Kierkegaard have in common and which allows them to be grouped together as existentialists (however much some may object to the label) the answer is not precisely that they have discovered that the God of the demonstrations is dead. What they have in common is not a view about God at all; it is on this subject that they differ most widely. What they hold in common and what acts as a central reference for their thought is the *perception* of man as experientially incomplete in himself. This existential mode of self-pres-

ence peculiar to man is variously described as being-to-the-world, being-unto-death, being-condemned-to-freedom, etc. The way in which this existential openness of man perceived by all of the existentialists *is interpreted* accounts for the far-reaching differences in their discussions about the reality of God." Pax (1995), p. 93.

10. Buber (1958), p. 60.

11. As Buber wrote: "The form that confronts me I cannot experience nor describe; I can only actualize it. And yet I see it, radiant in the splendor of the confrontation, far more clearly than all the clarity of the experienced world. Not as a thing among the 'internal' things, not as a figment of the 'imagination,' but as what is present. Tested for its objectivity, the form is not 'there' at all; but what can equal its presence? And it is an actual relation: it acts on me as I act on it." Buber (1958), p. 61.

12. Buber (1958), pp. 164–65.

13. Following Otto's work, Caroline Franks Davis published her research on religious experience at Brasenose College, Oxford, *The Evidential Force of Religious Experience* (Oxford University Press). Commenting on the meaning of the experience of the *numinous*, she notes that a *numinous* experience could exhibit one, all, or a combination of the following features: "The 'feeling of the numinous' consists of 'creature-consciousness', that is, the feeling that mortal flesh is somehow despicable in the face of eternal majesty, and 'mysterium tremendum', which comprises (i) awe, dread, or terror before the numen, (ii) the sense of being completely overpowered in the presence of such majesty, (iii) an experience of intense, almost unbearable energy or urgency, (iv) the sense that the numen is 'wholly other', and (v) a fascination with or attraction to the numen, and rapture upon contact with it. . . . The awe involved in numinous experiences is no ordinary fear. It is the dread before the uncanny which makes our hair stand on end, terror before such grandeur that we feel compelled to kneel, incomprehension before such mystery that we are struck dumb. 'Let all mortal flesh keep silence, and with fear and trembling stand', says the ancient Greek hymn; and the feeling is echoed in countless individual experiences." Davis (1989), pp. 48–49, 50.

14. As Baillie wrote: "The fundamental heresy of it lies in its dissociation of the ultimate springs of our moral consciousness from all that is religious. Such a dissociation seems to me to be as fatal to a true *understanding* of the essence of morality as of the essence of religion. For while, on the one hand, morality loses its essential character if we take away from it that truly 'numinous' attitude of reverence which (in his doctrine of *Achtung*) it was the great merit of Kant to describe as its only true core, no less does religion, on the other hand, lose its essential character if it be reduced to a mere sense of eeriness in the presence of a mysterious something which may not yet have come to be regarded as having any rightful or righteous claim upon our obedience. . . . Whatever opinions we may hold 'with the top of our minds' about the existence of God, there is *something* which every one of us recognizes as holy, and before this holy thing we are all ready to bow in reverence. . . . What is holy to us somehow resides in what we know we ought to be. Something is being asked of us, expected of us, and it is at the source of that expectation that holiness lies." Baillie (1939), pp. 242–43.

15. Otto (1958), pp. 168–69 (parentheses added).

16. Pax (1995), p. 74.

17. Marcel (1982), p. 180.

18. Pax (1995), p. 80.

CHAPTER 11

1. Reprinted from *Christian Classics in Modern English*, pp. 212–15. Copyright 1991 by David Winter. Used by permission of WaterBrook Press, Colorado Springs, CO. All rights reserved.

2. Lewis (1940), pp. 69–70.

3. The Memorial is taken from *Greater Shorter Works of Pascal*, trans. Emile Caillet and John C. Blankenagel (1948); also quoted in Kerr (1983).

4. Houston (1989), pp. 14–15.

5. Tolstoy; Kentish (1988), pp. 13–14.

6. Excerpt from *A Confession and Other Religious Writings* by Leo Tolstoy, trans. with an intro. by Jane Kentish (Penguin Classics, 1987), pp. 53–65. Copyright Jane Kentish, 1987. Reprinted with permission (1988).

7. Allen (1997), p. 54.

8. Excerpted from *The Brothers Karamazov* by Fyodor Dostoevsky, trans. Richard Pevear and Larissa Volokhonsky. Copyright 1990 by Richard Pevear and Larissa Volokhonsky. Reprinted by permission of North Point Press, a division of Farrar, Straus, and Giroux, LLC. (Farrar, Straus and Giroux, 1990), pp. 313, 315.

9. As Gordon writes: "As well as being a description of his (Dostoevsky in exile) degradation, *The House of the Dead* is a metaphor of human existence similar to the one used earlier by Pascal: namely, we are all cast into the death cell, and we experience daily our own death in the death of the other. This may be regarded as the basis of Christian existentialism. Descartes' famous dictim, *Cogito, Ergo sum* (I think, therefore I am), presumes that reason precedes existence. This is the fallacious premise which closed the Fabian intellect of Ivan Karamazov to the primacy of existence. But sin is not a failure of conditioning or an unwholesome idea. It is a major fact of the human condition." Gordon (1988), pp. 15–16.

10. Malcolm Muggeridge often cited Augustine's *City of God* in making this argument, contrasting it with the "City of Man," which is finite, perishable, and imperfect. Christianity is not a political proposition but a relationship with a triune God. Justice flows through the pages of Scripture so there is a guide, but the gospel is about the person of Jesus, not about doctrine or politics. This does not mean that Christians should not be politically involved, but it does mean that the New Testament that Dostoevsky came to love is not a political document and does not give a road map for a political utopia.

11. In *Notes from the Underground* Dostoevsky writes concerning the power to choose as the most precious thing for humankind. Reason may be compatible with this choice, but free will is more important because it preserves our integrity as persons.

12. See James Morse McLachlan, *The Desire to Be God: Freedom and the Other in Sartre and Berdyaev*.

13. For Berdyaev a human being can only reach his potential by developing his spiritual nature into the dominant element of his existence. He held that only in the existential encounter between the human and the divine can there be an intuitive apprehension of the divine. Berdyaev would not reduce God to an object and believed that a person's knowledge of God must be intuitive and subjective. God is not another object like the components of the universe, which one can objectively examine. God can never be considered as an object, for God is always a subject.

14. Berdyaev (1957), p. 7.

15. Quoted in Spinka (1962), pp. 196–97.

16. Dostoevsky (1990), pp. 313, 315, 318, 319.

17. From *The Road to Damascus* by John A. O'Brien, copyright 1945 by John A. O'Brien. Used by permission of Doubleday, a division of Random House, Inc. (1955), pp. 205–6.

18. Quoted in Barlow (1985), pp. 105–6.

19. Muggeridge (1978), p. 14.

20. From *Waiting for God* by Simone Weil, translated by Emma Craufurd, copyright 1951, renewed copyright 1979 by G. P. Putnam's Sons. Used by permission of G. P. Putnam's Sons, a division of Penguin Group (USA) Inc., p. 62.

21. Weil (1951), pp. 68–69.

22. Weil (1951), pp. 71–72.

23. Allen (1997), p. 60.

24. Allen (1997), p. 60.

25. Allen (1997), p. 62.

26. Weil (1951), p. 74.

27. Clark (ed.) (1993), p. 24.

28. Taken from "Philosophers Who Believe" edited by Kelly James Clark, pp. 36–37. Copyright 1993 by Kelly James Clark. Used with permission of InterVarsity Press, P.O. Box 1400, Downers Grove, IL 60515. Ivpress.com (ed.).

29. Quoted in Clark (ed.) (1993), pp. 36–37.

30. Quoted in Clark (ed.) (1993), p. 38.

31. Quoted in Clark (ed.) (1993), pp. 39–40.

32. Quoted in Clark (ed.) (1993), p. 44.

33. Reprinted with the permission of Scribner, an imprint of Simon & Schuster Adult Publishing Group, from *A Second Look in the Rearview Mirror* by Mortimer J. Adler, p. 209. Copyright by Mortimer J. Adler (1992). All rights reserved.

34. Adler (1992), p. 272.

35. Adler (1992), p. 278.

36. Adler (1992), pp. 276–78, 283.

CHAPTER 12

1. William Wordsworth, "Lines Composed a Few Miles Above Tintern Abbey," quoted in Woods (1958), p. 122.

2. Willoughby G. Walling II quoted Reinhold Niebuhr as saying, "More powerful than 10,000 sermons is the community out of which one moves." Yet, Paul Tillich also told Walling of his need for daily meditation in solitude. Community and solitude strengthen each other, but they are contrasting approaches to the spiritual dimension.

CHAPTER 13

1. Quoted in Magnin writing in Staune (ed.) (2006), p. 138.

2. Allen (1989), p. 60f.

3. Quoted in Reichenbach (Fall 2006), p. 8.

4. Quoted in Reichenbach (Fall 2006), pp. 68–70. Recent discoveries in cosmology and astrophysics also confirm that the concept of the universe as a concrete entity is coherent. Asking why the universe exists with the particular components it has is a legitimate question. Reichenbach (Fall 2006), p. 6.

5. Antony Flew notes that Oxford professor Brian Leftkow holds that the theory of special relativity is consistent with the idea of a Supreme Being outside space and time: "If God is timeless, then everything he does, he does so to speak, all at once, in a single act. He couldn't do one thing first and then another later on. But that one act might have effects at different times." Quoted in Flew (2007), pp. 151–52. Richard Ingersoll pointed out this same relationship in the early 1970s.

6. Flew (2007), pp. 88–89. In his investigation three domains of scientific inquiry were most relevant for Flew. (1) How did the laws of nature come to be? (2) How did life as a phenomenon originate from nonlife? and (3) How did the universe, by which he meant all that is physical, come into existence?

7. I question the rationale of a neutral position on the question of God's existence. I am not certain that agnosticism is a valid option. Perhaps not to choose theism is to choose atheism. In Kierkegaard's words, there may be an *either/or* requirement. If one attempts to take an agnostic position and states I don't know, one may not be removed from the obligation to choose. The atheist makes a leap of faith that God does not exist. The agnostic also makes a leap of faith in refusing to make a leap of faith in either direction. There may be no path to remove the requirement of choice from one's life. In that sense we all have some responsibility for our own worldview.

APPENDIX A

1. Chaitin (2006), pp. 79–81.

2. Overman and Yockey (2001).

3. See *Information Theory and Molecular Biology*, Cambridge University Press (1992). Yockey was one of J. Robert Oppenheimer's top physics students at Berkeley and went with him on the Manhattan Project. He is not only the author of the leading text in the field of information theory and biology but is also an adventurous member of the New York Explorer's Club.

4. A codon is a group of three bases—A, T, C, or G—and codes for a single amino acid. (The amino acids are strung together to make proteins.) A start codon is made up of the letters ATG, which codes for the amino acid methionine. When the machinery of the cells sees that first ATG, it knows to start making the protein there. The code is always read in groups of three, so the start codon also gives the cell's machinery its so-called reading frame. Each set of three letters thereafter corresponds to a single amino acid.

5. Reprinted with the permission of Scribner, an imprint of Simon & Schuster Adult Publishing Group, from *The Great Gatsby* by F. Scott Fitzgerald, p. 189. Copyright 1925 by Charles Scribner's Sons. Copyright renewed 1953 by Francis Scott Fitzgerald Lanahan.

6. Davies (1999), pp. 254–56.

7. Lennox (2007), pp. 151–52.

8. When I was engaged in my Templeton work at Oxford in the late 1990s, I asked an Oxford Don with a doctorate in physics and biology why most biologists had not considered

the implications of algorithmic information theory. His response was that they were not familiar with it. I am not certain that Chaitin's mathematics is thoroughly discussed among biologists today. This will change unless someone decisively disproves Chaitin and Kolmogorov's theories. In his new book, *Information Theory, Evolution, and the Origin of Life*, Yockey uses the material from our Princeton article and gives a very good explanation on how one measures the information content in the genetic message. See Yockey (2005), pp. 27–32.

9. I am not making an argument that the immaterial nature of information is spiritual even though Chaitin has written: "Consciousness does not seem to be material, and information is certainly immaterial, so perhaps consciousness, and perhaps even the soul, is sculpted in information, not matter." Chaitin (1999), p. 106.

10. Hawking understands we are still only left with an equation or formula.

11. See Chaitin (1999), pp. 107–9.

12. The laws are contingent because they could have been otherwise.

13. Natural selection can only function after a self-replicating organism (one cell or otherwise) exists. Experiments to create life out of nonlife are not an answer to the question of the origin of life. The scientist who is involved in the experiment and his computer bring rational powers not present in the materials of the early earth.

APPENDIX C

1. Excerpted from *Mindful Universe*, Henry Stapp (Springer-Verlag, Berlin, 2007), pp. 5–6.

SELECTED BIBLIOGRAPHY

BOOKS

Ackroyd, P. (1984), *T.S. Eliot: A Life*, Simon & Schuster.
Adams, M. (1990), *The Problem of Evil*, Oxford University Press.
Adler, M. J. (1980), *How to Think About God*, Macmillan Publishing Company.
— (1990), *Truth in Religion: The Plurality of Religions and the Unity of Truth*, Collier Books/ Macmillan Publishing Company.
— (1992), *A Second Look in the Rearview Mirror*, Macmillan Publishing Company.
Alighieri, D. (Sayers, D. L., trans.) (1949), *The Divine Comedy (Cantica I)*, Penguin Books.
Allen, D. (1985), *Philosophy for Understanding Theology*, John Knox Press.
— (1989), *Christian Belief in a Postmodern World*, Westminster/John Knox Press.
— (1997), *Spiritual Theology*, Cowley Publications.
Allport, G. W. (1950), *The Individual and His Religion*, Macmillan Publishing Company.
Anderson, J. N. D. (1974), *A Lawyer Among the Theologians*, Wm. B. Eerdmans Publishing Company.
Augustine, *Saint Augustine Confessions* (Chadwick, H., trans.), Oxford University Press.
Baillie, J. (1939), *Our Knowledge of God*, Charles Scribner's Sons.
Barlow, Geoffrey (ed.) (1985), *Vintage Muggeridge*, Wm. B. Eerdmans Publishing Company.
Barr, S. (2003), *Modern Physics and Ancient Faith*, University of Notre Dame Press.
Barrow, J. D. (2002), *The Constants of Nature*, Pantheon Books.
—, Tipler, F. (1986), *The Anthropic Cosmological Principle*, Oxford Clarendon Press.
Bauckham, R. (1998), *God Crucified*, Wm. B. Eerdmans Publishing Company.
Begbie, J. S. (2000), *Theology, Music and Time*, Cambridge University Press.
— (ed.) (2002), *Sounding the Depths*, SCM Press.
Berdyaev, N. (1957), *Dostoevsky*, Meridian Books.
— (1960), *The Destiny of Man*, Harper & Row.
Bretall, R. (ed.) (1946), *A Kierkegaard Anthology*, Princeton University Press.
Brünner, E. (1936), *Our Faith*, Charles Scribner's Sons.

Buber, M. (1958), *I and Thou,* Charles Scribner's Sons.
Buckley, M. J. (2004), *Denying and Disclosing God: The Ambiguous Progress of Modern Atheism,* Yale University Press.
Chaitin, G. J. (1987), *Algorithmic Information Theory*, Cambridge University Press.
—— (1998), *The Limits of Mathematics*, Springer-Verlag.
—— (1999), *The Unknowable*, Springer-Verlag.
Clark, K. J. (ed.) (1993), *Philosophers Who Believe,* InterVarsity Press.
Collins, F. S. (2006), *The Language of God*, Free Press.
Conway, D. (2000), *The Rediscovery of Wisdom*, St. Martin's Press.
Corey, M. A. (1993) *God and the New Cosmology*, Roman & Littlefield Publishers, Inc.
—— (2001), *The God Hypothesis,* Rowman & Littlefield Publishers, Inc.
Cottingham, J. (2005), *The Spiritual Dimension*, Cambridge University Press.
Craig, W. L. (1994), *Reasonable Faith*, Crossway Books.
—— (2002), *Philosophy of Religion*, Rutgers University Press.
Craig, W. L. and Moreland, J. P. (2003), *Philosophical Foundations for a Christian Worldview,* InterVarsity Press.
Craig, W. L. and Smith, Q. (1993), *Theism, Atheism, and Big Bang Cosmology*, Oxford University Press.
Dauer, F. W. (1989), *Critical Thinking: An Introduction to Reasoning,* Oxford University Press.
Davies, P. (1992), *The Mind of God*, Simon & Schuster.
—— (1999), *The Fifth Miracle: The Search for the Origin and Meaning of Life,* Simon & Schuster.
Davies, P. C. W. and Brown, J. R. (1986), *The Ghost in the Atom*, Cambridge University Press.
Davis, C. F. (1989), *The Evidential Force of Religious Experience,* Oxford University Press.
Davis, S. T. (1997), *God, Reason & Theistic Proofs*, Edinburgh University Press.
Dawkins, R. (1986), *The Blind Watchmaker*, W. W. Norton & Company.
—— (2006), *The God Delusion*, Houghton Mifflin Company.
Dostoevsky, F. (Pevear, R. and Volokhonsky, L., trans.) *The Brothers Karamazov* (1990), Farrar, Straus and Giroux.
Dubay, T. (1999), *The Evidential Power of Beauty,* Ignatius Press.
Edmonds, D. and Eidinow, J. (2001), *Wittgenstein's Poker,* HarperCollins.
Einstein, A. (1956), *Out of My Later Years,* Citadel Press.
Ellul, J. (1977), *Hope in Time of Abandonment,* The Seabury Press.
Evans, C. S. (1982), *Philosophy of Religion: Thinking About Faith,* InterVarsity Press.
—— (1986), *Why Believe? Reason and Mystery as Pointers to God,* Wm. B. Eerdmans Publishing Company/InterVarsity Press.
—— (1998), *Faith Beyond Reason,* Wm. B. Eerdmans Publishing Company.
Ferré, F. (1961), *Language, Logic & God,* University of Chicago Press.
Fitzgerald, F. S. (1925), *The Great Gatsby,* Charles Scribner's Sons, Simon & Schuster.
Flew, A. (1998), *How to Think Straight: An Introduction to Critical Reasoning,* Prometheus Books.
—— (2007), *There Is a God: How the World's Most Notorious Atheist Changed His Mind,* HarperOne.
Frankl, V. E. (1959), *Man's Search for Meaning,* Simon & Schuster.
—— (2000), *Man's Search for Ultimate Meaning,* Basic Books.
Gingerich, O. (2006), *God's Universe,* Harvard University Press.
Gordon, E. et al. (1988), *The Gospel in Dostoyevsky*, Orbis Books.

Green, R. M. (1992), *Kierkegaard and Kant: The Hidden Debt*, State University of New York Press.
Greene, B. (1999), *The Elegant Universe*, W. W. Norton & Company.
Hanson, A. T. and Hanson, R. (1981), *Reasonable Belief*, Oxford University Press.
Hick, J. (1989), *Philosophy of Religion*, Prentice Hall.
Hodgson, D. (1991), *The Mind Matters*, Oxford University Press.
Houston, J. M. (ed.) (1989), *The Mind on Fire*, Hodder and Stoughton.
—— (2006), *Joyful Exiles*, InterVarsity Press.
Hume, D. (1993), *Principal Writings on Religion Including Dialogues Concerning Natural Religion and The Natural History of Religion*, Oxford University Press.
Jaki, S. (1978), *The Road of Science and the Ways to God*, University of Chicago Press.
Kaufman, G. D. (1993), *In Face of Mystery*, Harvard University Press.
Kenny, A. (1979), *The God of the Philosophers*, Oxford University Press.
—— (1994), *The Oxford Illustrated History of Western Philosophy*, Oxford University Press.
—— (2006), *The Rise of Modern Philosophy*, Oxford University Press.
Kerr, H. T. and Mulder, J. M. (eds.) (1983), *Conversions*, Wm. B. Eerdmans Publishing Company.
Kierkegaard, S. (Steere, D. V., trans.) (1938), *Purity of Heart Is to Will One Thing*, Harper & Row.
—— (Hong, H.; Hong, E., trans.) (1962), *Works of Love*, Harper & Row.
Lennox, J. (2007), *God's Undertaker: Has Science Buried God?* Lion Hudson, PLC.
Levinas, E. (Bergo, B., trans.) (1986), *Of God Who Comes to Mind*, Stanford University Press.
Lewis, C. S. (1940), *The Problem of Pain*, HarperCollins.
Mack, M. (ed.) (1956), *World Masterpieces, V. 2.1 and 2*, W. W. Norton & Company.
Marcel, G. (1960), *The Mystery of Being*, Henry Regnery Company.
—— (1982), *Creative Fidelity*, The Crossroad Publishing Company.
Marion, J. L. (1991), *God without Being*, University of Chicago Press.
Maritain, J. (1941), *Ransoming the Time*, Charles Scribner's Sons.
—— (1954), *Approaches to God*, Macmillan Publishing Company.
—— (1999), *Degrees of Knowledge*, University of Notre Dame Press.
McGrath, A. (2005), *Dawkins' God*, Blackwell Publishers, Ltd.
McLachlan, J. M. (1992), *The Desire to Be God*, Peter Lang Publishing, Inc.
Menninger, K. (1973), *Whatever Became of Sin?* Hawthorn Books, Inc.
Moltmann, J. (1992), *History and the Triune God*, The Crossroad Publishing Company.
—— (1995), *The Crucified God*, Fortress Press.
Mongrain, K. (2002), *The Systematic Thought of Hans Urs von Balthasar*, The Crossroad Publishing Company.
Morris, T. V. (ed.) (1994), *God and the Philosophers*, Oxford University Press.
Muggeridge, M. (1976), *A Third Testament*, The Plough Publishing House/Little, Brown and Company, Inc.
—— (1978), *A Twentieth Century Testimony*, Thomas Nelson Publishers.
Munitz, M. K. (1986), *Cosmic Understanding*, Princeton University Press.
Nicholi, A. (2002), *The Question of God*, Free Press.
O'Brien, J. A. (1945), *The Road to Damascus*, Image Books division of Doubleday & Co., Inc.
Otto, R. (1958), *The Idea of the Holy*, Oxford University Press
Overman, D. L. (1997), *A Case Against Accident and Self-Organization*, Rowman & Littlefield Publishers, Inc.

Pagels, H. R. (1983), *The Cosmic Code*, Bantam Books.
Pannenberg, W. (1976), *Theology and the Philosophy of Science*, Darton, Longman & Todd.
Pax, C. (1995), *An Existential Approach to God: A Study of Gabriel Marcel*, Kluwer Academic.
Penrose, R. (1989), *The Emperor's New Mind*, Oxford University Press.
— (1994), *Shadows of the Mind*, Oxford University Press.
— (1997), *The Large, the Small and the Human Mind*, Cambridge University Press.
Perrine, L. (1956), *Sound and Sense*, Harcourt Brace.
Peterson, M. (ed.) (1992), *The Problem of Evil*, University of Notre Dame Press.
Polanyi, M. (1958), *Personal Knowledge*, University of Chicago Press.
Polkinghorne, J. C. (1986), *One World: The Interaction of Science and Theology*, Princeton University Press.
— (1988), *Science and Creation: The Search for Understanding*, Shambhala Publications, Inc.
— (1994), *The Faith of a Physicist*, Princeton University Press.
— (1996), *Beyond Science*, Cambridge University Press.
— (1996), *Quarks, Chaos & Christianity*, The Crossroad Publishing Company.
— (1998), *Belief in God in an Age of Science*, Yale University Press.
— (1998), *Science & Theology*, SPCK/Fortress Press.
— (2000), *Faith, Science & Understanding*, Yale University Press.
—,Welker, M. (2001), *Faith in the Living God*, SPCK.
— (2002), *The God of Hope and the End of the World*, Yale University Press.
— (2003), *Living with Hope*, Westminster/John Knox Press.
— (2004), *Science and the Trinity*, Yale University Press.
— (2005), *Exploring Reality: The Intertwining of Science and Religion*, Yale University Press.
— ,Welker, M. (eds.) (*2000*), *The End of the World and the Ends of God*, Trinity Press International.
Reichenbach, H. B. (1972), *The Cosmological Argument: A Reassessment*, Charles C. Thomas Publisher.
Schaefer, H. F. (2003), *Science and Christianity: Conflict or Coherence?* The Apollos Trust.
Schumm, B. A. (2004), *Deep Down Things: The Breathtaking Beauty of Particle Physics*, Johns Hopkins University Press.
Schwartz, J. M.; Begley, S. (2002), *The Mind and the Brain: Neuroplasticity and the Power of Mental Force*, HarperCollins.
Searle, J. R. (1997), *The Mystery of Consciousness*, NYREV, Inc.
Spinka, M. (1962), *Christian Thought from Erasmus to Berdyaev*, Prentice Hall, Inc.
Stackhouse, J. G. (1998), *Can God Be Trusted?* Oxford University Press.
— (2001), *No Other Gods Before Me?* Baker Academic/Regent College Publishing.
Stannard, R. (ed.) (2000), *God for the 21st Century*, Templeton Foundation Press.
Stapp, H. P. (2003), *Mind, Matter and Quantum Mechanics*, Springer.
— (2007) *Mindful Universite*, Springer.
Staune, J. (ed.) (2006), *Science and the Search for Meaning: Perspectives from International Scientists*, Templeton Foundation Press.
Swinburne, R. G. A. (1979), *The Existence of God*, Oxford University Press.
Tillich, P. (1957), *Systematic Theology*, Vol. II, University of Chicago Press.
Tolstoy, L. N. (Garnett, C., trans.) (1984), *The Kingdom of God Is Within You*, University of Nebraska Press.
—, Kentish, J. (1988), *A Confession and Other Religious Writings*, Penguin Books.

Torrance, T. F. (1989), *The Christian Frame of Mind*, Helmers & Howard Publishing.
Tournier, P. (1958), *Guilt & Grace*, Harper & Row.
Turner, D. (2004), *Faith, Reason and the Existence of God*, Cambridge University Press.
Van Inwagen, P. (2006), *The Problem of Evil*, Oxford University Press.
Varghese, R. A. (2003), *The Wonder of the World*, Tyr Publishing.
Vilenkin, A. (2006), *Many Worlds in One*, Hill and Wang, a division of Farrar, Straus and Giroux.
Von Baeyer, H. C. (2004), *Information*, Harvard University Press.
Ward, K. (1996), *God, Chance & Necessity*, One World Publications.
— (1998), *God, Faith & the New Millenium*, One World Publications.
— (2002), *God: A Guide for the Perplexed*, One World Publications.
— (2004), *The Case for Religion*, One World Publications.
— (2006), *Pascal's Fire: Scientific Faith and Religious Understanding*, One World Publications.
Ward, P. and Brownlee, D. (2000), *Rare Earth*, Copernicus.
Weil, S. (1951), *Waiting for God*, Harper & Row.
Weinberg, S. (1977), *The First Three Minutes*, Basic Books.
Wheeler, J. (1999), *Geons, Black Holes & Quantum Foam*, W. W. Norton & Company.
Wiener, L. (ed.) (1904), *The Complete Works of Count Tolstoy*, D. Estes and Co.
Wiker, B. and Witt, J. (2006), *A Meaningful World: How the Arts and Sciences Reveal the Genius of Nature*, InterVarsity Press.
Winter, David. (1991), *Christian Classics in Modern English*, WaterBrook Press.
Wood, A. W. (2001), *Basic Writings of Kant,* The Modern Library.
Woods, G. B. et al. (1958), *The Literature of England, Vol. II*, Scott Foresman and Company.
Yockey, H. (1992), *Information Theory and Molecular Biology*, Cambridge University Press.
— (2005), *Information Theory, Evolution, and the Origin of Life*, Cambridge University Press.

ARTICLES AND ESSAYS

Borde, A., Guth, A. H., and Vilenkin, A., "Inflationary Spacetimes Are Incomplete in Past Directions," *Physical Review Letters*, vol. 90 (2003), p. 151301.
Chaitin, G., "The Limits of Reason," *Scientific American*, vol. 294, Issue 3 (March 2006), pp. 74–81.
Cramer, J., "Adler's Cosmological Argument for the Existence of God," *Science in Christian Perspective* (March 1985), The American Scientific Affiliation, www.asa3.org/ASA/PSCF/1995/PSCF3-95Cramer.html.
Davies, P., "Taking Science on Faith," *New York Times* (November 24, 2007).
Overman, D. and Yockey, H., "Information, Algorithms and the Unknowable Nature of Life's Origin," *The Princeton Theological Review*, VIII, Vol. 4 (2001).
Plantinga, A., "The Dawkins Confusion," *Books & Culture* (March/April 2007).
Reichenbach, B., "Cosmological Argument," *Stanford Encyclopedia of Philosophy* (Fall 2006), Edward N. Zalta (ed.), http://www.plato.stanford.edu/entries/cosmological-argument/.

INDEX

ABOUT THE AUTHOR

For several decades Dean L. Overman was a senior partner of Winston & Strawn, a large international law firm. At age thirty-four he was appointed the partner-in-charge of the firm's Washington office, practicing corporate law on behalf of multinational clients in a broad spectrum of legal areas. He is presently co-chair of the Advisory Board of First Trust Portfolios, L.P., an asset management firm, and a Visiting Senior Research Fellow at The Van Raalte Institute.

While practicing in the area of international law, he taught a secured financing course as a member of the faculty of the University of Virginia Law School and also served as a Visiting Scholar at Harvard University. He was a White House Fellow and served as Special Assistant to Vice President Nelson Rockefeller and as Associate Director of the White House Domestic Council for President Ford. He was also an investor/entrepreneur developing office parks and a shopping center. He is the co-author of several law books, the author of many law review articles on banking, commercial, corporate, tax and securities laws, the co-author of a book concerning quantitative financial valuation (now in its eighth edition), the author of a book on effective writing, and the author of *A Case Against Accident and Self Organization*, for which he was selected as a Templeton Scholar at Oxford University for seminars in religion and science.

He received his Juris Doctor from the University of California at Berkeley (Boalt Hall) and did graduate work at the University of Chicago and Princeton Theological Seminary. He is a member of the Triple Nine Society and the International Society for Philosophical Enquiry.